ISRAEL AT SE

IN WEIZMANN'S IMAGE

HOWARD EPSTEIN

ISRAEL AT SEVENTY-FIVE: IN WEIZMANN'S IMAGE

BY

HOWARD DAVID EPSTEIN

Cover photo from 1973 Bank of Israel 50-lira note
Under Licence

This book is a work of non-fiction based on the personal experiences, knowledge and researches of the author.

ISBN: 9798806133701

FOREWORD

Like many British-born, baby-boomer Jews who were privileged to have a solid Jewish and Zionist education, I thought I knew all there was to know about the establishment of our precious State of Israel.

How wrong I was!

Howard Epstein's thoroughly researched and skilfully constructed volume, dealing with the Zionist enterprise, placing the life of Chaim Weizmann at its fulcrum, has taken my knowledge and understanding of the events of the late 19th and early 20th Century to a newer, deeper and eminently more satisfying level.

Epstein clearly holds his subject in the greatest of awe, makes no apologies for his reverence of him and bemoans what he describes as "injustices done to his legacy". And rightly so.

By casting a light on Weizmann's experiences in both the Jewish and non-Jewish world, the author demonstrates the genius of Weizmann's chemistry as well as his unsurpassed diplomatic skills.

The sometimes fraught and often difficult relationship between Weizmann and the other giant of Zionism in those days, David Ben-Gurion, is dealt with in great detail, with the author pulling no punches, and letting his readers know his own unequivocal opinion fearlessly.

As well as being a book packed full of facts and information, it is a jolly good read - this particular reader consumed its pages greedily, finishing it over one long Shabbat.

I have come to know Howard Epstein personally in recent times. I am honoured to consider such an accomplished author as a friend, and I feel privileged to add my absolute recommendation of his excellent work.

RABBI DR JONATHAN LIEBERMAN – JUNE 2021

ACKNOWLEDGEMENTS

This work owes its origin to a casual after-dinner conversation early in 2017 between friends, all with Anglo-Saxon roots and living in Israel. We were aware that the centenary of the Balfour Declaration would be celebrated before the year was out, and that it had been the achievement of Chaim Weizmann, but none of us was clear on the full story. I decided to investigate — and was amazed, for it soon became plain that Chaim Weizmann was a phenomenon. How was it that none of us knew?

My thanks for what follows go to:

- Steve Kramer, for looking out for my verbal and grammatical glitches;

- Leslie Artman for his extensive library, generously shared, his wide knowledge of relevant matters and his patience in being a responsive and knowledgeable sounding-board over several months;

- Merav Segal and Lior Hecht-Yacoby of the Weizmann Archives in Rechovot for their great generosity towards me and my queries;

- Micaela Ziv, of the illustrious Sieff family of Manchester and London, for providing me with the Sieff material mentioned in this work, which gives an intimate view of their Zionist hero from the family's viewpoint; and

- my long-standing and revered friend, Dr David Weitzman, with my sincere appreciation for his indulgence. For many years, David (no relation of the subject of this work, yet immersed in the same field) was a professor of biochemistry at Bath University in England. His review of, in particular, the scientific references and explanations that I have used has been invaluable. Without his meticulous attention to detail, and corrections, I could not have been confident that I would not lead the reader astray on the technicalities of Dr Chaim Weizmann's scientific work.

I apologise for any remaining inaccuracies, for they are mine.

HOWARD EPSTEIN, ISRAEL - SEPTEMBER 2021

PREFACE

The epicentre of Judaism is Mount Zion[1] in Jerusalem, Israel. Temple Mount, the site of the temples of the Jewish Kings, David and Solomon, is that same Mount Zion. Zionism is essentially the self-identification of the Jewish people with its origins.

Chaim Azriel Weizmann was born in 1874 in Motol, Belarus. Moscow lies some 1,000 kms to the east. Berlin, to the west — in the West — is equidistant, and it was there that, by the age of twenty, Weizmann had established himself, already absorbed by both Zionism and the study of chemistry.

For Weizmann, chemistry was doubly important: it was the field in which he worked as a research scientist and it was something magical that he was able to create between himself and a large number of diverse and essential actors on different continents, and over several generations. With his gravitas and charisma facilitating that chemistry between himself and those others, Weizmann secured exactly what Zionism required at two pivotal moments in Jewish history.

Weizmann may be said to be the world's first 20th century — even 21st century — man. If any aspects of modern life became supremely important last century, and remain so in this, they are science and technology — and networking. Weizmann's skills in interacting with others, fed by his success in the laboratory, led to his four great political coups, each essential to the emergence of the State of Israel. In addition, he pulled off three major educational feats that secured the country's future and ensured its remarkable success.

In the case of the political achievements, only Weizmann could have wrought those outcomes. In the case of the others, only he did. Despite these signature successes, today little is known of

---

[1] In Hebrew: *"Har HaBayit"*, Mount of the House (of God), the closest place to *"HaShechinah"* (the Divine Presence).

him and what he achieved. Why this should have been so is revealed in a tale of rivalry between two political giants: Weizmann, the greater talent, but the older, faded before his nemesis, David Ben-Gurion. Nevertheless, Chaim Weizmann is the one, the only one, of the many who sought, and fought, to re-establish the Jewish people in their ancient land in our time, who should be regarded as the indispensable Zionist.

~~~

The autobiography of Chaim Weizmann, *Trial and Error*, runs to two substantial volumes. In addition, as befits so illustrious a personality, many scholarly writers have enlightened us with lengthy, meticulously detailed and authoritative biographies[2]. Why another?

This work sets out not to catalogue the minutiae (or, as others have[3], the peccadilloes) of a fascinating, dynamic and fruitful life, but to illuminate its several matchless accomplishments: Weizmann's contribution to the conversion of 19th century theoretical Zionism into the dynamic 20th century movement that would re-establish a Jewish homeland in May 1948 in *Eretz Yisrael*, after an absence of two thousand years; his securing (as no others could have done), from political leaders of two distinct generations, four momentous decisions vital to the future of the Jewish people; and, in case all that was not enough, his catalyzing of the establishment of three august institutions of education and science that would give what was to become the State of Israel the character and the tools essential for its endurance and success.

In referring to the bare bones of those epoch-making attainments, this work's objective is confirmed: it makes no pretensions to an overarching review. Rather, it is a précis. Its

---

[2] *"The Founding Father, Chaim Weizmann: Biography 1922-1952"* by Profs. Motti Golani of Tel Aviv University and Jehuda Reinharz of Brandeis University. In Hebrew only.

[3] See above.
~~~

aim is to throw a spotlight on Weizmann's vital, essential, crucial and, yes, indispensable contributions to the birth and life of one of the most remarkable and successful countries of the modern world[4].

The author's hope is that the reader finds this work achieves its purpose.

~~~

[4] In February 2020, Faisal al-Qassem, a Qatari television host called Israel "the most successful project of the 20th and 21st centuries".
~~~

GLOSSARY AND ABBREVIATIONS

Aliyah:	literally, "going up" to *Eretz Yisrael.*
APZ:	American *Po'alei Zion*
Britain:	see under Great Britain.
Cheder:	Jewish religious school.
Chovevei Zion:	also *Chibath Zion*; literally, "Lovers of Zion", in which several Zionist groups formed in response to Russian pogroms of the late 19th century became the forebears and architects of modern Zionism.
DPs:	"displaced" persons held in camps in Europe after WWII for Jews who had survived the Holocaust.
Eretz Yisrael:	literally, "the Land of Israel." Note: The terms *Eretz Yisrael,* the Holy Land and Palestine are used interchangeably to suit the context. The first two terms have the same meaning while the third usually means the British Mandated territory from 1917 to 1948 (and the province of southern Syria under the Ottoman Empire) and not the state that the Palestinian people wish to create on the West Bank of the Jordan River, occupied by the Hashemite Kingdom of Jordan between 1948 and 1967.
Galut:	the Diaspora, the dispersion of Jews who live outside their ancestral homeland *Eretz Yisrael* (ie as opposed to the *Yishuv*).
Great Britain:	England, Scotland and Wales, used interchangeably with "the UK" (which includes also Northern Ireland).
Haskalah:	literally, "wisdom"; an intellectual movement; the Jewish Enlightenment.
Heim:	literally, "home"; the traditional areas of Jewish settlement in Russia and the Pale of Settlement.
Heimische:	of and pertaining to the *heim* as romanticised memories of traditional Jewish liturgy or cooking.
Kehillah(/ot):	Jewish community(ies) or synagogue congregation(s).

Kibbutz(im):	collective farm(s).
Maskilim:	members of or adherents to *Haskalah.*
Moshav/(im):	semi-privatised version of *kibbutz(im).*
MP:	Member of Parliament (UK).
Pale of Settlement: *Pale*:	the territories of Estonia, Latvia, Lithuania, Poland, Belarus, Moldova and Ukraine to which Tsarina Catherine the Great banished most of the Jews of Russia.
Po'alei Zion:	"Workers of Zion" movement.
Shtetel/shtetlach:	small town(s), mostly or entirely Jewish, in the *heim.*
Torah:	the Bible - usually the Five Books of Moses.
UK:	the United Kingdom of Great Britain and Northern Ireland - used interchangeably with Britain and Great Britain;
USPTO:	United States Patent and Trademark Office.
UN:	The United Nations Organisation.
Yeshiva:	Jewish seminary
Yiddish:	the language of the *heim*, an amalgam of German, Hebrew and Aramaic.
Yiddishe:	Jewish, as pertaining to the *heim.*
Yishuv:	those Jews who had remained or settled in *Eretz Yisrael* (as opposed to the *Galut).*
Zionism:	the movement that strove to re-establish Jewish autonomy in *Eretz Yisrael.*
ZF:	the Zionist Federation of the United Kingdom and Ireland;
ZO:	the Zionist Organisation founded by Theodor Herzl in 1897 as the driving force of Zionism (not to become the World Zionist Organisation until 1960).

CONTENTS

PART I – THE DIPLOMATIC ACHIEVEMENTS

1. OUT OF MOTOL 13
2. GERMANY 23
3. THEODOR HERZL 35
4. WEIZMANN IN THE AGE OF HERZLIAN ZIONISM 53
5. STEADY PROGRESS 75
6. WEIZMANN IN *ERETZ YISRAEL* 85
7. THE QUIET YEARS 91
8. THE APPROACH OF WAR AND THE SHELL CRISIS 97
9. WHAT MANNER OF REWARD? 113
10. THE DECLARATION DECLARED 123
11. A CHRISTMAS PRESENT FOR THE BRITISH 135
12. THE ZIONIST COMMISSION 141
13. DECLARATION - AND INDISPENSABILITY - CONFIRMED 158
14. FROM EUPHORIA TO ANGUISH 166
15. THE RUBBER CRISIS 176
16. IN THE GIFT OF TRUMAN I - THE NEGEV 184
17. IN THE GIFT OF TRUMAN II - PARTITION AND RECOGNITION 200

PART II – THE EDUCATIONAL ACHIEVEMENTS

18. EVERYTHING THE MIND OF MAN EMBRACES 219

PART III – THE ZIONIST TITANS

19. REPUTATIONS IN CONFLICT 241
20. WHAT MANNER OF MAN? 261
21. EPILOGUE 273

APPENDIX 1 - PRE-HERZLIAN ZIONISM 275
APPENDIX 2 - WAR CABINET MINUTES, 31 OCTOBER 1917 286
APPENDIX 3 - LETTER C TO V WEIZMANN, 26 MAY 1918 288
APPENDIX 4 - DEPRIVATION OF PALESTINIAN STATEHOOD 294
APPENDIX 5 - BEN-GURION ON CHAIM WEIZMANN 292
BIBLIOGRAPHY 298
INDEX 298

1

OUT OF MOTOL

MOTOL

Motol, Belarus, is today a remote village of some 4,000 inhabitants in the darkest backwater of Europe, suffering its sole remaining autocratic government. Belarus — small, poor and landlocked — is a quasi-client state of the Federation of Russia. Its people, well-educated in the painstaking Russian tradition, desperate to capitalise on their talents in the wider world forbidden to them, are constrained, living in forlorn hope of escaping and blossoming. In these respects, there have been few changes since Chaim Weizmann was born there on 27 November 1874.

Belarus or, as it was known until 1990, Byelorussia, was at the time that interests us, the late 19th century, part of the so-called Pale of Settlement. In (pre-Soviet) Imperial Russia, the Pale[5], on the western extremity of that vast country that stretches over seven time zones, was supposedly the area in which Jews were allowed permanent residence, in freedom — although their freedoms were heavily circumscribed, their permanence was always threatened and many Jews lived all over Russia.

For several generations, the Pale included what we recognise today as Estonia, Latvia, Lithuania, Poland, Belarus, Moldova and Ukraine, aggregating an area around twice the size of France or Texas. Hidden away from the great centre of Yiddish culture in the city of Vilna (in the Baltic sector), from the grandeur of Kiev (the capital of the Ukrainian sector) and even from the worldliness of close-by Minsk (Byelorussia's capital) were thousands of villages in which the majority, or in some cases the

[5] An unsatisfactory explanation (although a better one has not been found) is that "pale" means a type of fence and the Jews were, in the Pale, fenced in.

totality, of the populations were Jews.

Anti-Semitism in the Pale was as rife as it was brutal, and the history of the late 19th century (no less than in the eons that preceded it) is full of examples of bestiality to the Jews, committed by the indigenous non-Jewish populace. Pogroms against and expulsions of Jews were unexceptional and had begun to stimulate emigration to the USA and to *Filastin*, as it was then known by its Ottoman Empire rulers — or Palestine, by the time the British drove them out in 1917.

Most of the Jews in the Pale were poor, some (devoted to learning) by choice, others just scraping out an existence in subsistence farming. Yet the comparative affluence of others suggested the reason for the establishment of the Pale in the first place: Muscovite merchants, resentful of keen local competition from Jewish businessmen, persuaded Tsarina Catherine the Great in 1791 to banish them — to send them to the Pale — so that they became less local, and commercially less threatening.

Natural talent tends to win through, and mercantile inclinations and experience from Moscow, after displacement and resettlement, soon took root. Some of the exiles therefore became business people and some of them were successful, too.

Forests abound in Russia, no less in Belarus, and the demand for wood in pre-industrialised Russia was great. There were opportunities for those who knew how to turn a tree into planks for housing, benches, flooring, tables, chairs, beds and wagons, and into logs for heating and cooking. First, however, trees needed felling and then to be transported to factories and workshops. One engaged in that work was Oizer (or Ezer) Weizmann.

THE FAMILY WEIZMANN

Oizer Weizmann, of Motol, was a successful timber merchant,

whose work was exceptionally demanding[6]. The forests being mired in the wetlands of the Pripet Marshes, the trees could be felled, and taken to the river for transportation, only in the depths of the Russian winter when a firm platform was provided by the ground having frozen solid.

Life was not only tough, it was uncertain, too. The Jews, despite their Russian presence having lasted innumerable generations[7], were effectively stateless, and all who were sentient knew that their daily survival would from time to time be punctuated by some fresh outrage, killing, wounding or uprooting them. For the Jews of Eastern Europe and Russia — the overwhelming majority of world Jewry at that time — life was lived as precariously as the fabled fiddler on the roof[8], depicted in the painting *The Fiddler* by the Jewish-Russian-French artist, Marc Chagall.

Weizmann writes about Motol:

> "*We were strangers to their* [the non-Jewish villagers'] *ways of thought, to each other's dreams, religions, festivals, even languages. There were times when the non-Jewish world was practically excluded from our consciousness, as on the Sabbath and, still more, on the spring and autumn festivals.... We were separated from the peasants by a whole inner world of memories and experiences.... My father was not yet a Zionist, but the house was steeped in rich Jewish tradition, and Palestine was at the centre of the ritual... the Return was in the air, a vague, deep-rooted Messianism, a*

---

[6] *Trial and Error: The Autobiography of Chaim Weizmann* (Schocken Books, 1966)

[7] Jews first settled in Russia in the 7th century CE.

[8] *Fiddler on the Roof* is a musical show, and movie, set in the Pale of Settlement in 1905, based on the novel, *Tevye and his Daughters*, by the great Yiddish playwright, Sholem Aleichem.

hope which would not die."[9]

Reb Oizer, and his wife, Rachel (Czermerinsky), had greater riches than the trees could provide. They had fifteen children (three of whom died in infancy) and they sent no less than nine of the surviving dozen to university. From where had this parental ambition for the education of their children sprung?

Books and newspapers from the cities rarely penetrated the afforested villages. This was long before radio or television. Such entertainment as was available, for relief from life's drudgery, was simple and seasonal. Recreation centred mostly on the *Kehillah* and arose out of Jewish events: the festivals, a circumcision, a barmitzvah or a wedding — each was treated as an occasion for song and dance and, being amongst Jews, polemics. This last was fed by new movements of thought.

THE JEWISH ENLIGHTENMENT

After the early 18th century Enlightenment and the European revolutions of 1848-9, several progressive libertarian movements had later taken root, amongst firstly the bourgeoisie and the intellectuals of France and Germany, and then the Jews of Europe and Russia.

Several emergent leaders competed for attention. Some sought to promote Jewish nationality; others advocated complete assimilation. One, Leon Pinsker (1821-1891), physician, Zionist pioneer, activist and the founder and leader of the *Chovevei Zion*, theorised that the Jews were the ghosts of a murdered nation, haunting Gentiles and causing unease, fear and hatred everywhere. The nomadic ghosts would not be laid, he urged, until they achieved a land of their own, whether in *Eretz Yisrael*

[9] *Trial and Error* (ibid)

or elsewhere[10]. Another, Moshe Leib Lilienblum[11] (1843-1910), scholar and author, took a more focussed approach and insisted that the Jews were attached, by their history and very existence, to the Holy Land, so that it could only be on their own soil that they could achieve true independence. This dichotomy of ambition divided Zionism until May 1948.

Between the 1770s and 1880s, another movement emerged: *Haskalah* (Education)[12]. Its adherents, the *Maskilim*, saw themselves as the European Jewish Enlightenment, promoting education as the route by which Jews would blend into modern society. The *Maskilim* established schools and published works of cultural importance. Somehow, these lofty, and secular, aspirations reached the backwoods of the Pale and influenced Oizer Weizmann to introduce his substantial family to the ideas of *Haskalah*. From that, it was short step for Oizer and Rachel to promote the idea of higher education to the children.

THE *CHEDER*

Educated in a Motol *cheder* — not in Russian, but in Yiddish — Weizmann gives us, perhaps guilelessly, a glimpse of what was to follow. He wrote of an (unnamed) *cheder* teacher:

> *"He was a man of the 'enlightened' type; that is, he had been touched by the spirit of the modernising 'Haskalah' (or Enlightenment) which was then abroad in the larger centres of Russian Jewry. Very surreptitiously he managed to smuggle into intervals in our sacred studies some attempts at instruction in secular knowledge. Thus, I remember how he brought into class, furtively and gleefully, a Hebrew*

---

[10] The *"Lovers of Zion"* movement, owed its origins to Pinsker's awareness of strong popular movements amongst Russian Jews, focussed on Palestine as the territory in which a self-determined autonomous Jewish culture could prosper, and preceded the modern Zionist movement of Herzl.

[11] See: http://www.yivoencyclopedia.org/article.aspx/Lilienblum_Mosheh_Leib

[12] See: http://www.yivoencyclopedia.org/article.aspx/haskalah

textbook on natural science and chemistry, the first book of its kind to come into those parts. How this treasure fell into his hands I do not know, but without ever having seen a chemical laboratory, and with the complete ignorance of natural science which was characteristic of the Russian ghetto Jew, unable therefore to understand one scientific paragraph of the book, he gloated over it and displayed it to his favourite pupils. He would even lend it to one or another of us to read in the evenings. And sometimes — a proceeding not without risk, for discovery would have entailed immediate dismissal from his post — he would have us read with him some pages which seemed to him to be of special interest. We read aloud, of course, and in the Talmudic chant hallowed by tradition, so that anyone passing by the school would never suspect but that we were engaged in the sacred pursuits proper to a Hebrew school."[13]

Whether that early introduction to science and chemistry sparked some anticipatory interest can only be a matter of conjecture (as Weizmann does not admit to it). Further exposure was to follow in Pinsk some 50 kms from Motol, where Chaim, out of *cheder* and out of Motol, went to school.

PINSK

Since long before the eleven-year-old Chaim Weizmann arrived in Pinsk in 1885, it was as Jewish a city as any in Eastern Europe. Jewish domination by the last quarter of the 19th century may be seen in one statistic alone: some 75 percent of the population were Jewish. As a result, it had become the archetypal Jewish centre — it was, religiously, politically, culturally and socially, representative of East European Jewish towns, since there was probably no Jewish activity current at the time that was not available in Pinsk.

While the Hebrew, Yiddish, Jewish and Zionist publications that

---

[13] *Trial and Error* (ibid)

permeated the forests into Motol were hungrily seized upon there because of their rarity, in Pinsk there was an abundance of such periodicals and books. The writings of Peretz Smolenskin[14], Leon Pinsker, Achad Ha'am and other Zionist thinkers and writers were studied, and the Yiddish works of Mendele (Mocher Sforim) and Sholom Aleichem were avidly consumed[15].

The ideas of these luminaries thoroughly infused the Pale and, while it is true that the bulk of world Jewry was concentrated in that area by the end of the 19th century, thanks to Russian Imperial decree, it seems reasonable to conclude that what was also concentrated there were minds, ambitions and spirit focussed on Zion for, of the fifty Zionist activists[16] referred to in the following pages (apart from Weizmann himself) thirty-four were products of the Pale.

The ironic assassination in 1881 of reforming Tsar Alexander II[17] ignited anti-Jewish legislation, an uninhibited

---

[14] See: http://www.yivoencyclopedia.org/article.aspx/Smolenskin_Perets

[15] *Chaim Weizmann: A Biography By Several Hands*, edited by Meyer W Weisgal and Joel Carmichael (Weidenfeld and Nicolson, 1962)

[16] Leon Pinsker, Moshe Leib Lilienblum, Peretz Smolenskin, Achad Ha'am, Schmarya Levin, Leo Motzkin, Nachman Syrkin, Victor Jacobson, *Arthur Hantke, Heinrich Lowe,* Zelig Soskin, *Willi Bambus,* Leo Motzkin, Rabbi Menachem Mendel, the Vilna Gaon, Rabbi Zvi Hirsch Kalischer, *Rabbi Judah Alkalai, Moses Hess,* Judah Leib Pinsker, Naftali Herz Imber, Kalonimus Wolf Wissotzky, *Nathan Birnbaum,* Eliezer Ben-Yehuda, *Dr Moses Gaster,* David Ben-Gurion, Shloyme Rappoport, *Berthold Feivel, Martin Buber,* Joseph Massel, *Charles Dreyfus,* Harry Sacher, *Max Nordau,* David Wolffsohn, Arthur Ruppin, Joshua Chankin, *Herbert Samuel,* Ze'ev Jabotinsky, Simon Marks, Israel Sieff, Nachum Sokolow, *Joseph Cowen, Herbert Bentwich, Aaron Aaronsohn, David Eder, Joseph Trumpeldor,* Dr Menachem Ussishkin, Nahman Bialik, Yitzchak Ben-Zvi, Abba Eban and Meyer Weisgal. (The 16 shown in italics did not originate in the Pale.)

[17] .... although the perpetrators were from the revolutionary "People's Will" group. The assassination of the Tsar who had taken upon himself the

rage against the Jews, spiralling anti-Semitism and widespread pogroms. Some 25,000 of those anxious to avoid the penury, mutilation and death that were the camp followers of the pogroms emigrated to Palestine in the First *Aliyah*. (A second such mass movement during 1890-1891, also part of the First *Aliyah*, resulted from the expulsion of Jews from Moscow and further anti-Jewish legislation.) For those who survived the pogroms yet remained, there was always the unwelcome attention of the Tsarist police, and the fear of the next pogrom.

Understandably, given this backdrop, Jewish students of the time were driven by strong Jewish-nationalist feelings. The new political thinking, that barely penetrated the forests surrounding Motol, flourished in Pinsk. The city was abuzz with the activities of the *Haskalah*, *Chovevei Zion*, *Po'alei Zion* and other movements. Nor were they inaccessible to mere boys such as the pre-barmitzvah Chaim Weizmann, since each had its youth group. One as aware of current events and the potential of Zionism as the young Chaim easily found opportunities to join these movements, and he himself became greatly influenced by Zionist ideas in their various forms.

At this time, too, Chaim first became aware of *Achad Ha'Am* (literally: "One of the People," the pseudonym of Asher Ginzburg), whose pamphlet "*Truth From Palestine*" he read at the impressionable age of seventeen, regarding it as "*a classic of Zionist history and literature*".[18] The admiration that sprang from the youth for the work of the philosopher eighteen years his senior, was neither misplaced nor transient: their lives were to become ever more closely enmeshed in the future.

Chaim's main purpose in Pinsk was to attend high school. There, he quickly came to the attention of the science teacher,

---

emancipation of Russia's serfs in 1861 — thus earning the sobriquet "Alexander the Liberator" — triggered across Russia a major suppression of civil liberties, anti-Semitic legislation and anti-Jewish pogroms.

[18] *Trial and Error* (ibid)

Kormienko. Recognising a boy with unusual qualities, Kormienko took him under his wing and influenced him to specialise in chemistry. In later years, Weizmann described this teacher as "*a man of exceptional gifts and ... of exceptional devotion to his vocation.*" ... "*Very possibly,*" wrote Weizmann, "*I owe to him whatever I have been able to achieve in the way of science.*"[19]

In November 1887, Chaim celebrated his barmitzvah in Pinsk. As a product of the *cheder*, he was well-schooled in Jewish learning and traditions; but, not being closely attached to orthodoxy, he was intent on a secular life. Even as he became, according to Jewish tradition, a man, he had already built up a following amongst his contemporaries, being described by them as "*combining luminous intelligence and uncommon capacity for thorough and continuous work, with a strength of character, vitality, gaiety and a biting wit which gave him an easy ascendancy over his milieu*".[20]

After a further five years of conscientious study, Chaim matriculated, reportedly excelling across the board. At eighteen, he left school, turned away from Russia to the West, and started his university education in Germany.

CODA: Barely out of Motol, in Pinsk in 1885, stimulated perhaps by the death in that year of the distinguished Italian-Anglo-Jewish financier and banker, activist, philanthropist — and Zionist — Sir Moses Montefiore, the eleven year old Chaim, wrote:

> *"the kings and nations of the world are plainly set upon the ruin of the Jewish nation; the Jews must not let themselves*

---

[19] *Trial and Error* (ibid)

[20] *Chaim Weizmann: A Biography By Several Hands* (ibid) by Sir Isaiah Berlin (1909-1997). Jewish-Russian-British social and political theorist, philosopher, historian of ideas, Berlin was a founder and the first President of Wolfson College, Oxford University.

> *be destroyed; England alone may help them to return and rise again in their ancient land of Palestine."*[21]

His words are remarkable in several respects for they illuminate the mortal threat to the Jews, that the era of Jewish self-determination had arrived, that *Eretz Yisrael* should be their inevitable destination and that the starting point of their journey to their salvation may be England.

We shall see that, not only do Weizmann's words amount to a prophesy but also, remarkably, the boy-author would be, within thirty years, the architect and facilitator of what he foretold — in England.

~~~

[21] *Chaim Weizmann: A Biography By Several Hands* (ibid) by Sir Isaiah Berlin.
~~~

2

GERMANY

DARMSTADT

In 1892, Chaim Weizmann enrolled at the Polytechnic Institute of Darmstadt, Germany, to study chemistry. The ensuing two months were to prove unhappy for him.

The Weizmann family was not so wealthy that it had (after feeding and clothing many children) the means to indulge Chaim's education. He was not to be deterred, however, and undertook to provide, after his daily studies, private Russian language lessons at a Jewish school in Pfungstadt, some 10 kms from Darmstadt. The commuting back and forth by train, and the extra hours of work, weakened the lone 18-year-old youth's health.

Chaim now went through a period of exhaustion. The cause, however, was not only the extra-curricular work and travel: it arose mainly from his encounter with an attitude of mind, that at the college in Darmstadt. For the first time, he came across Jews who described themselves as "Germans of the Mosaic persuasion." If that expression, a self-deceptive product of German assimilation, was not shocking enough for the previously-sheltered young man from the *heim*, he then had to contend with another novel experience: those same Jews insouciantly dismissed German anti-Semitism (which was as rife — though without the pogroms — as the Russian variety) as transient and inconsequential. Thus they sought to rationalise away the intellectual persecution all around them.

The young Weizmann, struggling to comprehend what was to him a wholly new phenomenon, soon appreciated that he was quite unable to communicate his own views to his German contemporaries and, before long, abandoned all hope of opening their eyes to what he saw as their deluded patriotism and hypocrisy. This first confrontation with assimilation and assimilationists was shocking, but it would prove to be a worthwhile preparation for what lay ahead.

A further matter of discomfort to Weizmann was the absence of *yiddishkeit* amongst his Darmstadt school-friends, something entirely different from the *heimische* atmosphere of Motol and Pinsk. The German approach to Judaism and Jewish life seemed to him cold, unnecessarily "modernised" and errant, if not entirely lost. He wrote:

> *"'In Russia at least we...had a culture of our own, and a high one. We had standing in our own eyes. We did not dream that our Jewish being was something to be sloughed off furtively.' He despised the philosophy of assimilation as demeaning, degrading, humiliating, and he often confessed, sadly, that he felt more at home in the company of Gentiles than assimilated Jews. Despite his western education and his political sophistication, he remained, until the end, ein Russischer Jüde. Ultimately, this was the source of his strength both with his own people and with his Gentile friends."*[22] (See, out of interest, panel 1.)

1

GEORGE ELIOT'S *DANIEL DERONDA*

In *Daniel Deronda* (see further at Appendix 1), the novel which biographer Norman Rose asserts Weizmann kept by his bedside[23], British authoress, George Eliot, in an open expression of the English Protestant empathy for the Jews of the time, puts into the mouth of her character, Joseph Kalonymos, the following words: *"the learning of all Germany is fed and fattened by Jewish brains — though they keep not always their Jewish hearts."*

Weizmann was in Darmstadt to study, and again he impressed

---

[22] *Chaim Weizmann: A Biography*, Norman Rose (Weidenfeld and Nicolson 1987)

[23] *Chaim Weizmann: A Biography*, Norman Rose (ibid)

his fellow-students and teachers alike with his intelligence and industriousness. So exceptional a student was he that, within months, he was moved to the more prestigious Technical University of Berlin in order to study the embryonic niche of biochemistry. The culture-shock of Darmstadt proved a mild introduction to the assimilationist atmosphere of the German capital.

BERLIN

The city of Berlin that Chaim Weizmann reached in 1893 (aged 19) was the beneficiary of several historical trends: the German Enlightenment; a German predilection for, not to say addiction to, science; and the unification in 1871 by master statesman, Count Otto von Bismarck, of many princedoms and statelets into a German behemoth[24]. All these had combined to propel Berlin towards its belated emergence as one of the great capitals of Europe, representing all contemporary trends of thought and endeavour.

In 1850, the population of Berlin had been a mere 412,000; by 1890, it exceeded one million. Expansion was visible everywhere. To make way for the trappings of a major metropolis, and so as to be able to expand their workshops and factories on the outskirts of the city, the great industrial concerns moved out of the centre. Neighbouring towns, such as Charlottenburg, Lichtenberg, Schöneberg and Spandau, became part of a then unofficial Greater Berlin. Meanwhile, in the centre, Berlin was beginning to live up to its new rôle as the capital of the German Empire, with broad boulevards and magnificent public buildings.

New museums were being built and existing ones enlarged. The music scene, benefiting from the legacies of German composers such as Beethoven, Brahms, Bruch, Mendelssohn, Wagner and

[24] Comparative populations in 1900 – UK and France, each: ~ 40 million; Germany: ~ 52 million.

many others, was flourishing. The theatre, with the state sponsored Opernhaus and Schauspielhaus, and several private theatres, was thriving. In short, Berlin was a city of culture long before anyone had thought formally to bestow such a title on a European city.

While Paris (with more than twice the population) was the *fin-de-siècle* city of gaiety, style and culture, *sans pareil*, Berlin took itself more seriously as the beneficiary of the 18th century German Enlightenment movement, with its tradition of acceptance of all-comers, based not on background or wealth but on character alone — although complete tolerance of the Jew was not a noticeable feature.

Under the Enlightenment, freedom of belief and expression were welcome for the diversity they brought and, being German, the projection in Berlin of scientific endeavour in the interests of human progress sat comfortably alongside intellectual and cultural life. The German capital, home to such intellectuals as writers Fontane, Storm, Eichendorff and Keller, and philosophers Hegel, Schelling and von Hartmann, was quickly becoming a powerhouse, rivalling or even surpassing Paris.

Jewish Berlin was no less enriched by past intellectual giants, nor was it less dynamic and feverish. If Jews made Pinsk the archetypical Russian Jewish city, in Berlin a similar if more European rôle was played by the Jews. Representing only five percent of Berlin's population, the Jews were asymmetrically prominent, particularly in the centre, in business, the professions and the arts; and every trend of Jewish thought and Zionist activity was not merely available but, rather, flourishing throughout the city. There was a rich history, too.

THE BERLIN ZIONISTS

In 1743, Moses Mendelssohn (1729-1786) an impoverished, young, orthodox Jew from Dessau, Saxony, entered Berlin through the gate reserved for cattle and Jews. Despite this unpromising start, through sheer force of intellect and personality, as a popular philosopher and a man of letters, he exemplified the opportunities for Jews in terms of integration with and acceptance by non-Jews. He was to make an impact upon the intellectual and cultural development of Berlin society as a whole.

The ambition for many German Jews had become — a basic theme of *Haskalah* — emergence from the ghetto and assimilation amongst the Gentiles. The leading light in this context became Moses Mendelssohn himself.

Haskalah, of which Weizmann had, thanks to his father, become keenly aware as a child in Motol, was a multi-faceted phenomenon, expressed in cultural, intellectual and political pursuits. Its influence ebbed and flowed over time, and across vast territories, as for many years it had no fixed base. Over a century before Weizmann's arrival, however, Mendelssohn caused it to settle in Berlin. After that, it was primarily the Berlin *Haskalah* writers who published the wide-ranging tracts, some in pursuance of the revival of Hebrew as a literary language for secular purposes, that were widely distributed to the *Maskilim* all over Europe and in Russia.

By the time of Weizmann's arrival, there were many examples of *Yiddishe* life in Berlin. As in Pinsk and Darmstadt, so too, but on a much larger scale, in Berlin, there was a plethora of Jewish movements across the spectrum, from *Haskalah*, through the *Allgemeiner Deutscher Arbeiterverein* (General German Workers' Association) of Ferdinand Lassalle, to the eastern/Russian, mainly Zionist, movements flourishing in the city. Significant in this last category was the *Russisch-Jüdischer Wissenschaftlicher Verein* (Russian-Jewish Scientific Society), founded by several Russo-Jewish-Zionist activists in 1889.

Weizmann was not slow to join the Scientific Society, and he held it in awe as *"the cradle of the modern Zionist movement"*.[25]

---

[25] *Trial and Error* (ibid)

Its leading lights, Schmarya Levin, Leo Motzkin, Nachman Syrkin, Victor Jacobson, Arthur Hantke, Heinrich Lowe, Zelig Soskin, Willi Bambus and many others, were destined to become prominent in the developing Zionist movement.

Weizmann's new friends were, and revelled in being, intellectuals, an outlook to which he made no pretentions. He was all too aware that he had come from the backwoods in the East to a sophisticated Western capital city, so initially he was hesitant in their company. More importantly, he was first and foremost a scientist and his world was a highly practical one. While others wrote pamphlets and indulged themselves with academic argument, he was delving into the secrets that science had barely begun to surrender up to man. For others, discourse; for him, experimentation. This practicality would stand him in good stead as the Zionist dream emerged as a real force.

Despite his initial diffidence, realising he was beginning to earn the respect of his peers, Weizmann gradually found his feet, and his place in the Scientific Society. The polemicists, for their part, soon noticed that while Weizmann was different from them, he had a real contribution to make. Within a year, Weizmann achieved elevation with his election to the executive committee of the Scientific Society. Yet, despite increased exposure to those less industrious than he, Weizmann abandoned none of his innate drive, remaining focussed and hard-headed, free from the ungrounded meanderings of his colleagues. They were content with academia; he had work to do. For them, the debating hall; for him the laboratory.

With one of the leading lights in the Scientific Society in particular, Leo Motzkin, Weizmann had a complicated relationship. At first hugely impressed by Motzkin, Weizmann later became disillusioned with him. As Norman Rose writes:

> *"A gifted mathematician and seven years older than Weizmann, Motzkin, by virtue of his seniority and experience, overawed his young companion with the 'sweep*

of his vision'. Motzkin introduced Weizmann to the mature world of Zionism, to the subtleties of its politics, and he himself went on to a commendable career in Jewish and Zionist politics.

Weizmann wrote later: 'He became...a VereinsMeier, a Johnny Joiner, frittering away his days and nights in innumerable little student gatherings, and taking with tremendous seriousness every minor incident in student political life.'

.... Although they collaborated for many years, their early intimacy soon withered. Motzkin progressed from being 'a very odd person' to a 'pathologically vain' one."[26]

Nevertheless, Weizmann and Motzkin were to remain associated for years to come, sometimes collaborating, other times drifting apart. Yet it was Motzkin to whom Weizmann owed the most in terms of his development as a Zionist.

ACHAD HA'AM

Throughout Weizmann's life, one thinker alone had the greatest effect on him: Achad Ha'am; and "*it was Motzkin who helped initiate Weizmann into the Berlin circle of Achad Ha'Am.*"[27]

Weizmann had first become aware of the Zionist philosopher in Pinsk. In Berlin, Achad Ha'Am was recognised as the most profound thinker in, and the most important member (though not the leader) of, the *Chovevei Zion*, and this despite his frequently challenging its principles and even its core beliefs, such as over the colonisation of *Eretz Yisrael*, based on Rothschild-family largesse.

Unconventional though he was, Achad Ha'Am exerted a great

[26] *Chaim Weizmann: A Biography*, Norman Rose (ibid)

[27] *Chaim Weizmann: The Making of a Zionist Leader*, Jehuda Reinharz (Oxford University Press 1985)

influence over the Jewish student body generally and the members of the Scientific Society in particular. Indeed:

> *"The appearance of one of Achad Ha'Am's articles was always an event of prime importance. We read him, and read him again, and discussed him endlessly."*[28]

As for the particular effect that Achad Ha'Am had on Weizmann, the latter wrote:

> *"For him Zionism was the Jewish renaissance in a spiritual-national sense. Its colonisational work, its political programme had meaning only as an organic part of the re-education of the Jewish people. A facade of physical achievement meant little to him; he measured both the organisation in exile and in the colonies in Palestine by their effect on Jewry. His first concern was with quality ... he put the emphasis on perfection. .... As a writer, Achad Ha'Am never put forth less than his best; he was precise and penetrating in his thoughts; he was sparing and exact in his style, which became a model for a whole school."*[29]

One such Achad Ha'Am publication was "*Lo Ze ha-Derekh*" (This Is Not the Way), in which he demanded (in 1889, between the First *Aliyah* and the Second) that no more immigrants be settled in *Eretz Yisrael* until the settlements had a secure legal basis. In particular, he was highly critical of their dependence for their survival on charitable donations from the *Galut*.

Achad Ha'am became the greatest inspiration for Weizmann's development as a Zionist during his Berlin days. Moreover, while Weizmann started out as a disciple of the illustrious philosopher, they were destined, within the span of ten years. to regard each other as equals.

Despite his deep immersion in Zionism, Weizmann was also

---

[28] *Trial and Error* (ibid)

[29] *Trial and Error* (ibid)

both worldly and cultured. His love of music (Beethoven, in particular) and the theatre (Goethe, Shakespeare and Ibsen) were within the student's reach for 50 pfennigs. Whole Sundays were spent away from the twin tracks of biochemistry and Zionism.

Weizmann was in Berlin to continue his pursuit of the mysteries of biochemistry. With his studies and research, on the one hand, and Zionism, on the other, the pattern of his life was set — he indulged each equally, the former feeding into the latter — ultimately to the direct benefit of a Jewish homeland of which, at this stage, even he had only the haziest of notions.

THE MISSIONARY

Like most students, in the vacations Weizmann would return to his family (removed from Motol to Pinsk by 1891). Unlike the typical student, however, vacations for Weizmann did not mean rest or play. In the afforested *shtetlach* around Pinsk were many isolated Jewish communities, to whom were quite unknown — until Weizmann's visits to them — even a conceptual notion of Zion, let alone movements such as the *Chovevei Zion* and the various other organisations that emerged in reaction to the pogroms that had stimulated their neighbours to undertake the First *Aliyah*.

Weizmann took upon himself missionary work in far-flung communities, spreading the Zionist message; but he was acutely aware that, according to the Tsarist authorities, this was unlawful political activity. For appearances sake, it was arranged that the people who learnt from him the several possible paths to secular salvation did so seated as though congregants at prayer in their synagogues.

Starting out in the diminutive *kehilot* of the fens and forests, Weizmann worked his way up through Kalenkovitch, Mozyr and, nostalgically, Motol, graduating later to the cities of Vilna in the Lithuanian north, and Kiev and Kharkov in the Ukrainian south. Now the committed Zionist had become an activist, too. His own recognition of this was plain:

> *"Nine months of the year I spent in the 'free' Western world; but every June I returned to the East, and until the autumn I was the militant Zionist in the land where Zionism was illegal."*[30]

THE CHEMIST

While in Berlin, Weizmann spent six or seven hours a day on his academic pursuits; but we learn little from his autobiography of his time as a student at Charlottenberg Polytechnik. Elsewhere, we read that his college was:

> *"one of the most prestigious in Germany, where, under the directorship of Carl Liebermann, the organic chemistry laboratories were engaged in significant work on coal-tar derivatives. This would certainly be a giant step forward in his scientific grounding, and would bring him into contact with mature and reputable scientists and intriguing paths of research. Under the direct supervision of Alfred Bistrzycki, he was to explore the industrial potential for synthetic dyes, for which there was a growing commercial demand."*[31]

Weizmann developed a taste for research and scientific discovery both as an end in itself and for his own financial reward. He started to register patents and to sell them, tentatively at first and later with confident regularity. Patents would eventually change the poor student's fortunes beyond his dreams.

By 1897, after a year's sabbatical with his family in Pinsk and another year of study, Weizmann was ready to move on. As he wrote later:

> *"In Berlin, I grew out of my boyhood Zionism, out of my adolescence, into something like maturity. When I left Berlin ... the adult pattern of my life was set. Of course, I learned a*

---

[30] *Trial and Error* (ibid)

[31] *Chaim Weizmann: A Biography*, Norman Rose (ibid)

great deal in later years; but no fundamental change took place; my political outlook, my Zionist ideology, my scientific bent, my life's purposes, had crystallised."[32]

The year before Weizmann left Berlin, the Zionist movement underwent a tumultuous change.

~~~

[32] *Trial and Error* (ibid)
~~~

3

THEODOR HERZL

Theodor Herzl (1860-1904) was born in Hungary into a German-speaking, secular and assimilated Jewish family. If the Herzl household had any appreciation of the long saga of Zionism, it is hard to unearth any evidence of it. Herzl's paternal grandfather, Shimon Loeb Herzl, had attended the synagogue in Belgrade, Serbia, of proto-Zionist writer, Rabbi Judah Alkalai, whose sermons might be supposed to have reflected his texts. Rabbi Alkalai's Zionism may have touched Shimon Loeb, who could well have passed it down the family line but, if so, it does not appear to have inspired any inquisitiveness on the part of the young Theodor. Indeed, Zionism seems to have eluded him completely — until the need for a national home for the Jews hit him like a thunderbolt in Paris in 1894. Herzl's awakening to the need for a Jewish homeland was as abrupt as the history of Zionism is protracted, complex and rich.

Both for us today and throughout the last 125 years, Zionist history falls to be divided into two distinct eras: pre-Herzlian Zionism and modern Zionism, for which Theodor Herzl was responsible. It is necessary to review the former to understand what followed in the latter.

EMANCIPATION

After the Enlightenment of the 18th century — with its concepts of rationalism, limitless examination and scientific analysis — came emancipation: essentially the recognition that all men are equal. Although the universal implementation of that ideal is still work-in-progress, we should, so far as the Jews are concerned, recognise these milestones:

1776: the American Declaration of Independence stated: *"We hold these truths to be self-evident, that all men are created equal, that they are endowed by their Creator with certain unalienable Rights, that among these are Life, Liberty and the pursuit of Happiness."* The Jews were not excepted from these ideals.

1789: the French Revolutionary *Declaration of the Rights of Man and of the Citizen* guaranteed freedom of religion and free exercise of worship (provided that it did not contradict public order), and by which France became the first country in Europe to grant Jews equality under the law.

1858: Britain, where serfs and peasants had left the scene long before, and which had a growing middle class, started in this year to grant Jews equal rights.

Jewish national emancipation in the form of independence and a national home, however, remained a remote prospect.

Chaim Weizmann was driven into the arms of Zionism by Russian repression of the Jews. While those in the more sophisticated environment of Europe had sought their escape (perceived or real) from oppression through assimilation, in Russia generally, and the Pale in particular, that route was unavailable. Straddling the two worlds, Weizmann could make an informed East-West comparison. His conclusion was that essentially there was no difference:

> *"In the West it was an open fight, in the East a conspiracy. The West preached liberty, the East practised repression; but East and West alike were the enemies of the Zionist ideology."*[33]

Since the narrative of the persecution of the Jewish people — commonly referred to as anti-Semitism[34] — has been fully dealt with elsewhere, we need not cover that ground. Mention of the term is, however, made to remind the reader that Zionism had its

[33] *Trial and Error* (ibid)

[34] In *Anti-Judaism: The Western Tradition*, David Nirenberg (Norton Press, 2013), Nirenberg shows *"how foundational anti-Judaism is to the history of the West. Questions of how we are Jewish and, more critically, how and why we are not, have been churning within the Western imagination throughout its history."*

provenance in cruelty, subjugation and persecution.

The Enlightenment and post-Enlightenment eras gave birth to early Zionist movements and to the proto-Zionists, both Jewish and Gentile.

Herzl was quite unaware of what preceded him, yet it is worthy of consideration, so, in Appendix 1, the reader will find an examination of pre-Herzlian Zionism, with some fascinating vignettes.

MOSES MONTEFIORE

Sir Moses Chaim Montefiore (1784-1885), a Jewish-Italian-British financier, banker, philanthropist and activist, had an enduring fascination with the Holy Land. No pulpit-thumping, desk-bound or armchair proto-Zionist, he stands out as having made a vast contribution to the life of the *Yishuv*, not least for his many visits, the first as early as 1827. His arrival in the Holy Land would change it significantly for the better but, upon his first encounter with it, he was changed too, for at once he became religiously observant. By the time he was 91, he had returned six times, notwithstanding the gruelling and dangerous nature of travel at that time.

Sir Moses, given his background, connections[35] and wealth, was an able political operator. As the President of the Board of Deputies of British Jews, he corresponded in 1841/2 with Charles Henry Churchill (of whom more in Appendix 1), the British consul in Damascus, over the idea of creating a national home for the Jewish people in Palestine.

In 1855, Sir Moses purchased an orchard on the outskirts of Jaffa and set up a school for teaching agricultural techniques to local Jews. Within five years, he had established the first Jewish

[35] Quite apart from his own connections, his wife's sister married N M Rothschild, the founder of the London branch of the great eponymous bank.

residential settlement outside the ancient city of Jerusalem, offering financial support to families that would take up residence there. Other Jewish neighbourhoods funded by him followed, most iconically *Yemin Moshe*, where he had constructed the eponymous windmill to supply flour at affordable prices to poor Jews that still dominates the suburb facing the Jaffa Gate of the Old City.

Montefiore went on to invest in light industry, education and health services for the Jewish community of *Eretz Yisrael.* He was less successful at acquiring large tracts of land for Jewish cultivation, the Ottoman Empire authorities preventing the sale of land to non-Muslims. Finally and notably, Montefiore instituted a series of five censuses between 1839 and 1875 exposing the life of the *Yishuv*.

THE PROTESTANT PROTO-ZIONISTS

If repression of the Jews had led to Jewish Proto-Zionism, what was the catalyst for the emergence of non-Jewish proto-Zionists — and why was England both the incubator of and the front-runner in these ideas?

Christian advocacy for the re-establishment of the Jews in the Holy Land was first heard in the English-speaking world following the 16th century Protestant Reformation. Particularly amongst the Puritans, it became common practice to look forward to, and offer prayers for, the Jews' return to their ancient homeland. In 1762, Charles Wesley, a leader of the Methodist Protestants, included in his canon of more than 6,000 hymns one with an unmistakeably Zionist theme and libretto:

O that the chosen band
Might now their brethren bring,
And gather'd out of every land
Present to Sion's King;
Of all the ancient race
Not one be left behind,
But each impell'd by secret grace
His way to Canaan find!

By the early 19th century, large parts of the Protestant British consciousness were steeped in support for a Jewish return to the Holy Land (some also seeing it also as a means for the extension of the British Empire), and Philo-Semitism had become fashionable among the classically-educated British elite across a wide range of notables. These then were the Christian proto-Zionists (who are considered in Appendix 1) and we shall soon encounter their heirs.

BEN-YEHUDA

In the Bar Kochba revolt of the Jews against the Roman Empire, between 132 and 136 CE, the population of Judea was devastated by battle, murder and exile. After that, the everyday use of Hebrew withered away and it became, for almost the next two millennia, only the language of Jewish prayer and study. It was largely due to the inspiration and dedication of one man that Hebrew was resuscitated in modern times.

Eliezer Ben-Yehuda (1858-1922, born Perlman in Byelorussia) stands out as having made a unique contribution not merely to Zionism but also to the Israeli way of life; indeed, he may be said to have given back to the Jewish people their very spirit.

Ben-Yehuda had an early grounding in Hebrew, learning it in *cheder* from the age of three, the better to study the *Torah*. By the time of his barmitzvah, he was well-acquainted with the *Talmud*. Later, in *yeshiva*, his interests and horizons were broadened when he learned of the Enlightenment. Ben-Yehuda went to Paris to study French and German. Reading Smolenskin's Hebrew language newspaper *HaShahar*, he became acquainted with the strands of Zionism then current.

Either despite or because of his worldliness, Ben-Yehuda concluded (as had others, but merely academically) that, to define a people that aspired to independence, a common language, spoken throughout society and for all its activities was needed. He considered Hebrew and *Eretz Yisrael* to be the sole contenders, writing: *"The Hebrew language can live only if we revive the nation and return it to the fatherland."*

When Ben-Yehuda joined the *Yishuv* in 1881, its people spoke Russian and Yiddish. Hebrew was their language of prayer and its vocabulary was essentially that of the Old Testament.

At around the time of Ben-Yehuda's *Aliyah*, Jews from Yemen started to undertake theirs. Before the days of modern communications, locked away in their Arabian Peninsula fastness, unaffected by any of the tides of civilisation or competing cultures, they spoke the authentic Hebrew of the ancients[36]. It was their form of pronunciation, rather than the Ashkenazi usage, that Ben-Yehuda adopted for Modern Hebrew.

Ben-Yehuda promoted Hebrew through three programmes: *"Hebrew in the Home"*, *"Hebrew in the School"* and *"Words, Words, Words"*. Working tirelessly, touring work-places, *kibbutzim* and schools, he cajoled teachers and enlisted their support, until eventually every child learned Hebrew from the earliest years. Then it became the only language available in infant and higher schools.[37] It was Ben-Yehuda, too, who compiled the first dictionary of Modern Hebrew.

The establishment of Committee for the Hebrew Language (*Va'ad HaLaschon*) was the achievement of Ben-Yehuda, its first president. The organisation continues to this day (as the Academy of the Hebrew Language) updating and refining the modern language of Hebrew or, as it is known, Modern Hebrew.

Ben-Yehuda's achievement with Hebrew — its return to everyday usage — appears to be unique in history, there being

[36] The origins of the Jews in Yemen are lost to scientific definition but most accounts place them there long before the Bar Kochba revolt.

[37] Other than those sponsored by French or German institutions, until the War of the Languages, dealt with under the Haifa Technion story in chapter 18.

no other readily-identifiable example of an ancient, sacred language, used for almost two millennia for prayer alone, being transformed into a modern-day, every-day, national language, spoken, written and read by an entire population. Today, over eight million Israelis use Hebrew as their first language — their mother tongue — in every pursuit, profession and discipline. This colossal social achievement has been summed up thus: *"Before Ben-Yehuda ... Jews could speak Hebrew; after him they did"*[38].

The final stimulus that Hebrew needed for its acceptance into the general life of the *Yishuv*, and later Israel, was the official status it was accorded in the 1922 constitution of the British Mandate for Palestine.[39] In addition, it is necessary to acknowledge the essential contribution of Chaim Weizmann in the emerging academic life of the *Yishuv* of the 20th century (considered in chapter 18) and the support for spoken Hebrew provided by Baron Edmond de Rothschild — both a pre- and a post-Herzlian Zionist.

BARON EDMOND DE ROTHSCHILD

Baron Edmond de Rothschild (1845-1934), born into the Parisian branch of the great banking dynasty, was inspired by his parents' extensive involvement in many philanthropic activities within the French Jewish community. His own benevolence consisted of direct aid to the growing *Yishuv* to assist the people of the First *Aliyah*, upon their arrival. Believing in the right of the Jewish people to live in *Eretz Yisrael*, he

---

[38] Sir Cecil Roth, British Jewish historian Reader in Post-Biblical Jewish Studies from 1939 to 1964, Oxford University.

[39] Article 22 of the Palestine Mandate: *English, Arabic and Hebrew shall be the official languages of Palestine. Any statement or inscription in Arabic on stamps or money in Palestine shall be repeated in Hebrew and any statement or inscription in Hebrew shall be repeated in Arabic* - as has been the position too since the establishment of the State of Israel in 1948 (though English was then dropped as an official language).

became the prime example of a practical Zionist; yet his work, being charitable in concept, offended Achad Ha'am and, for a time, Weizmann too.

In the early 1880s, the *Chovevei Zion* began to establish *moshavim* in *Eretz Yisrael*. They were soon weighed down with serious financial problems, as their work was transformed by the First *Aliyah* from the purely political to the essentially practical — that of settling thousands of Jews fleeing Russian persecution into the Promised Land. Baron Edmond stepped in and funded all the overheads of the newly established *moshavim* of Rishon LeZion, Zikhron Ya'akov and Rosh Pinah.[40]

Visiting Zikhron Ya'akov in 1893, the Baron declared to the local farmers: *"I did not support you and take you under my wing due to your poverty, but due to your passion to work and live in the Holy Land, and to live in accordance with the spirit of the Torah"*, showing himself to be an inspirer of men in addition to his gifts of philanthropy and practicality.

Baron Edmond (more successfully with the Ottomans than Sir Moses Montefiore had been a generation earlier) acquired several tracts of land in *Eretz Yisrael*, introducing European farming experts to assist with the development of the agricultural communities.

Convinced that the Jews of *Eretz Yisrael* would thrive and ultimately achieve independence, the Baron invested broadly and deeply in the *Yishuv's* basic infrastructure, such as power stations, the draining of malarial swamps, the creation of clinics caring for malaria victims, establishing wineries at Zikhron Ya'akov and Rishon LeZion (both still operating today) and

[40] It should be noted that these villages were quite distinct from the socialist-inspired Kibbutzim, and are today, in the case of the first two, well-established cities in the centre of Israel with populations in the hundreds of thousands and, as to Rosh Pinah, a delightful town and artist centre in the North.

setting up factories for the packaging or processing of agricultural produce, as a natural extension of the farming communities he sponsored.

Baron Edmond continued to make vast contributions to the life of the *Yishuv* long after Herzl's death in 1904.

AT LAST - THEODOR HERZL

The young Herzl, a devotee of all things German, was exposed to and grew to love poetry and the humanities, which led him into first playwriting and then journalism. In all of this, he was steeped in German culture, through which, as he believed, man would aspire to a higher sense of morality. He hoped that he and all Hungarian Jews could free themselves from their "shameful Jewish characteristics" caused (he imagined) by their history of subjugation and poverty. Then they would be released to become genuine German *Kulturvolk*.

THE JEWISH QUESTION

In the Vienna of the late 19th century, the burning issue was the so-called Jewish Question. It had started out, in the German Enlightenment, as a debate on what should be the standing in Gentile society of Jews in relationship to non-Jews; but eventually it came to mean: how could German life and culture be rendered *Jüdenrein*[41] (Jew-free)? For Jews who had tried to ignore their origins and become completely assimilated Germans — with the mind-set that confronted Weizmann in Darmstadt and Berlin — this was deeply troubling.

In 1881, Herzl became a law student at the University of Vienna and joined the students' union, Albia. In the same year, Eugen Dühring wrote: *"Die Judenfrage als Frage der Racenschaedlichkeit"* ("The Jewish Question as a Question of Racism"), one of many virulently anti-Semitic tracts by this

---

[41] ie "purified" of the taint of Jews and Jewishness, as would be expressed by Nazism.

disgraced former professor at Berlin University. It was reading this that stimulated Herzl's serious concern with the Jewish Question, yet there is no evidence that any interest in Zionism had yet been aroused within him.

Like any young man enamoured with German culture, Herzl fully participated in the life of Albia, even to the point of bearing facial scarring from his opponents' duelling swords. This outward sign of complete immersion in German culture, however, was not to save him from the reality of anti-Semitic hostility. Albia was increasingly infested with German nationalist adherents raising the Jewish Question.

In March 1883, at a student meeting involving Albia, a deeply anti-Semitic speech caused Herzl to resign his membership and refuse calls to reconsider.

Herzl personally suffered other anti-Semitic incidents, as when, in Mainz, Germany, in 1888, upon leaving a bar, he heard raucous jeering and the racist call: "HEP, HEP!" (see panel 2). Nevertheless, he appears still to have had no knowledge or appreciation of Zionism, its history, proponents and activists.

2

THE HEP-HEP RIOTS

The so-called "HEP-HEP Riots" were pogroms in Bavaria around 1819. Many Jews were killed and much Jewish property was destroyed. HEP is believed to be an acronym based on the Latin expression: *"Hierosolyma Est Perdita"* ("Jerusalem is lost").

PARIS

After university, Herzl fully immersed himself in writing, and became a professional journalist. Steady progress in his career led to his being offered, in October 1891, the post of Paris correspondent of the highly respected Viennese newspaper, *Neue Freie Presse*. Herzl accepted with alacrity but, if he thought that living at a distance from Vienna would spare him from expressions of hatred of the Jews, he was to be cruelly disappointed. While French Jews were well-entrenched in French society, there was a concomitant strong anti-Jewish bias in France.

Initially, Herzl could not have regretted his decision to move to Paris for he soon found himself welcomed as a writer at the city's literary soirées. He met Marçel Proust, Anatole France and Émile Zola. He was also welcomed (doubtlessly confusingly to us) as a frequent guest at the home of Alphonse Daudet, who made no secret of his intellectual anti-Semitism; and Daudet introduced Herzl to Edouard Drumont, the author of *La France Juive* (Jewish France), a widely-read, virulently anti-Semitic pamphlet. Drumont was also the editor of *La Libre Parôle* (Free Speech), a notoriously defamatory anti-Semitic newspaper.

Initially, Herzl turned a blind eye to all this, like many Austrian and German Jews (as Chaim Weizmann had observed) who wished to be assimilated to vanishing point — perceptually rather than physically, of course. Herzl regarded anti-Semitism as something that would blow over. In 1894, however, he wrote, *"Das Neue Ghetto"* ("The New Ghetto"), a play in which he explored the Jewish Problem, and its associated paradoxes of continued attempted assimilation and parallel repression. Herzl offered no solutions — rather he hoped his work would provoke a debate that might produce some. At last, Herzl was beginning to question his long-held belief that the oppression would pass. He was now vulnerable to events and, within months, Herzl experienced a Damascene Conversion as vivid as any in modern times.

ALFRED DREYFUS

As Chaim Weizmann was settling into life in Berlin in 1894, France was still smarting from the siege and occupation of Paris by the German army in 1870/1. Enemy spies were a constant preoccupation and the French Army's counter-intelligence section learned of the passing of information about French military equipment to the Germans by a highly-placed spy. Suspicion fell on the General Staff.

Captain Alfred Dreyfus, an assimilated Jew and a fast-rising 35 year old French Army General Staff officer, was arrested and charged with treason. Herzl, as the Paris correspondent of his Viennese newspaper, went to cover those parts of the court martial that were not held in secret session.

In January 1895, Dreyfus was summarily tried, convicted and sentenced to be stripped of his rank and to life imprisonment on Devil's Island in the remote South American colony of French Guiana. In a ceremony in the courtyard of the *École Militaire* in the centre of Paris, Dreyfus was publicly humiliated before silent ranks of soldiers and less decorous crowds of Parisians that had been assembled to add to the degradation. As his insignia of rank were stripped from his uniform and his sword broken in two, Dreyfus declared: *"I swear that I am innocent. I remain worthy of serving in the Army. Long live France! Long live the Army!"*, while the crowd shouted *"À mort, à mort les Juifs!"* (death, death to the Jews!). Herzl, too, was in the crowd, although silent.

The events became the *cause célèbre* of the day, and were soon seen as scandalous, thanks in no small measure to the writings of Émile Zola, who removed himself to the more tolerant environment of London. The Dreyfus Affair split Paris and France, and would have repercussions for the next half century. (See panel 3.)

3

THE POST-DREYFUS-AFFAIR AFFAIR

The most extravagant manifestation of French anti-Semitism was yet to come. What is not so well-known as the events that engulfed Dreyfus are those that occurred after his belated release.

The most damning evidence before the kangaroo court that doomed Dreyfus in 1894 to Devil's Island had been a document presented by Lieutenant-Colonel Hubert-Joseph Henry. It was later discovered to be a forgery, comprised of two separate documents fused together, thereupon dubbed *"faux Henry"*. Henry, once challenged, confessed and in 1898 was sentenced to military prison. On the first night of his imprisonment, Henry was left alone in his cell with a bottle of rum and an open shaving razor. He was later found lifeless, with half the rum consumed, an incomplete letter to his wife before him and his throat slit. Suicide was declared as the cause.

La Gazette de France praised Henry for sacrificing his life *pour la Patrie* (for the Homeland). A fund was declared for Henry's widow and over 130,000 francs collected. According to Professor Ruth Harris, Senior Research Fellow, All Souls', Oxford University:

> *"Accompanying* [the] *donations are notes... vicious anti-Semitic fantasies and all about how we are going to murder these Jews and defend the cause of Christian solidarity with the wife and the child. ... Henry is seen as a martyr .. Charles Maurras of Action Française said: the blades* [with which Henry cut his throat] *are the new relics of the nation. ... Henry is seen as a saint. His deception is a patriotic forgery. ... Henry becomes elevated from someone who is a forger to a new hero...."*.[42]

In other words, according to the French people, it was the Jews, at a remove of several stages, who killed Henry, with a blade rendered into a religious icon.

There were other repercussions, too. On 13 January 1898, Émile Zola had published in the newspaper, *L'Aurore,* an open letter, "*J'accuse ...!*" ("I accuse...!"), addressed to the French president. Zola accused the French government of anti-Semitism and the unlawful imprisonment of Dreyfus, referring to the absence of proper evidence and the errors of the court. Zola was prosecuted for libel and found guilty. The famous writer fled to England, returning home 18 months later when the charges were dropped.

In 1905, the Church and the State of France were separated. Newly-established state secularism led to the closure of most of

[42] *BBC Radio 4 - In Our Time,* 8 October 2009.

> the church schools of France, to the disgust and deep resentment of many. Some say that the enthusiasm with which the French collaborated with the Germans in deporting the Jews of Paris to Auschwitz in 1942 was pay-back for all this.

Uncertain at first of the truth of the scandal of the apparently-treacherous Dreyfus, Herzl began to ruminate about the possibility that the Jewish soldier was innocent and had been framed; that the trial did not represent merely a miscarriage of justice but rather the general desire of the supposedly-enlightened French Republic to abase the Jews; and what this meant for the assimilationists' theory that, given time, anti-Semitism would wither and fade.

In 1897, having returned to Vienna, Herzl's equilibrium and former optimism about what he had perceived as the impermanence of anti-Semitism was dealt a severe blow. Dr Karl Lüger, a Jew-baiting demagogue, became Mayor of Vienna, and anti-Semitic activity in Austria was raised to new heights. Confronted by this, Herzl was finally shocked into the realisation that assimilation was no remedy for anti-Semitism; nor could there be any future for the Jews without a land of their own.

Thus it was that, following a great deal of introspection, Herzl arrived alone, without any grounding in the history of Zionism, at the recognition that the solution to the Jewish Question was for the Jews to achieve national independence in their own land. In case there were room for doubt, Herzl wrote, in an 1899 article for the North American Review: *"It was the Dreyfus trial that made me a Zionist"*.[43]

TOP-DOWN ZIONISM

To achieve his objective of a national home for the Jews, Herzl embarked on an exhausting programme of approaches to

[43] *Theodor Herzl: Founder of Political Zionism*, Israel Cohen (Thomas Yoseloff, London, 1959)

wealthy Jews who, he thought, might be sufficiently philanthropic to contribute to a fund for the acquisition of territory, its location being a matter of unimportance to Herzl.

In May 1895, Herzl wrote to Baron Maurice de Hirsch seeking a meeting to discuss the Jewish Question. They met in Paris, only for Hirsch to reject Herzl's plan as unworkable. The following July, Herzl approached the Chief Rabbi of Vienna, Dr Moritz Güdemann, but again in vain. The next month he wrote to none other than Count Otto von Bismarck (who had unified Germany, but by then had been out of office for five years). No reply was received. Next, he sought, via Rabbi Güdemann, to engage Albert Rothschild (from the Austrian branch of the banking dynasty) in conversation, confiding in the Rabbi he that he had prepared a long draft document. Güdemann was intrigued and wanted to hear Herzl's proposal.

The following month, Herzl spent two hours reading his plan aloud to Rabbi Güdemann. The rabbi's response was that he thought that Herzl was a latter-day Moses, that he should abandon seeking an audience with Rothschild but develop his plan in the form of a novel (which may sound somewhat patronising to the reader).

At last, in the fervently anti-Semitic atmosphere of Karl Lüger's *fin-de-siècle* Vienna, Herzl began to learn something of the Zionism that had preceded him. He was advised to contact Chief Rabbi Zadok Kahn of France, described as "*an enthusiastic Zionist*"[44], and Leon Pinsker, the author of *Auto-Emancipation*, a pamphlet on the resettlement of the Jews in a land of their own. (At this time, Herzl's own pamphlet was in course of publication.) Herzl returned to Paris to meet Rabbi Kahn but the encounter proved almost fruitless. Herzl was about to discover what the eleven-year-old Weizmann had written in Pinsk — that the road to Jewish deliverance may start in England — for Rabbi Kahn gave Herzl a letter of introduction to author, Israel

[44] *Theodor Herzl: Founder of Political Zionism* (ibid)

Zangwill, in London.

In November 1895, Herzl went to the British capital to meet not just Zangwill but also Chief Rabbi Dr Hermann Adler, Sir Samuel Montagu MP and, in some further exposure to traditional Zionism, Colonel Albert Edward Goldsmid, who headed the British branch of *Chovevei Zion*. The meetings were inconsequential, but before Herzl left London he met Asher Myers, the editor of the weekly newspaper, the Jewish Chronicle. The writer mentioned to the newspaper man the pamphlet he was writing on Zionism. *"There was .... a sequel of vital significance. Myers, as an enterprising editor, asked Herzl to send him a résumé of his forthcoming pamphlet, for publication in the Jewish Chronicle."*[45]

"A Solution of the Jewish Question", the first published polemic on political Zionism, appeared as a special supplement to the Jewish Chronicle on 17 January 1896. Herzl's blueprint was rendered available to Anglo-Jewry. News of the publication filtered back to Vienna, where at first it was badly received.

DER JÜDENSTAAT

Herzl, back home in Vienna, refined his work and, in 1896, published *"Der Jüdenstaat: Versuch einer Modernen Loesung der Judenfrage"* ("The Condition of the Jews[46]: An Attempt at a Modern Solution of the Jewish Question"). While it is plain from a reading of his historic pamphlet that Herzl had at last imbibed some of the history of traditional Zionism, still he appeared to know nothing of the work of Ben-Yehuda and insufficient about the *Yishuv*, nor did he have any fixed idea as to where the required territory should be.

In July 1896, meeting but failing to persuade even Baron Edmond de Rothschild to fund the Jewish state, Herzl decided

[45] *Theodor Herzl: Founder of Political Zionism* (ibid)

[46] Commonly and inaccurately referred to as *The Jewish State*

he would have to create a mass movement for Zionism. *Der Jüdenstaat* was about to bring Herzl celebrity and Zionism a new lease of life.

~~~
~~~

4

WEIZMANN IN THE AGE OF HERZLIAN ZIONISM

Had Herzl thoroughly acquainted himself with not only the history but also the contemporary state of Zionism, he would have found that, by the time he was ready to publish *Der Jüdenstaat*, the traditional Zionist movements had all but reached a dead end. The leading Russian Zionist movement, the Odessa Committee[47], was in a languid condition and the *Chovevei Zion* were running out of steam. Russian Jews (unbeknown to them) were between the First *Aliyah* and the Second, and without immediate pressure to expand their activities. In *Eretz Yisrael*, the *Yishuv* had been thrown a lifeline by the generosity of Baron Edmond de Rothschild; but, according to Achad Ha'am who had visited *Eretz Yisrael* in 1891 and 1893, that beneficence had created an indolent *Yishuv*, always awaiting the next hand-out from a source that could not be infinite.

Chaim Weizmann was only too conscious of the general torpor and, ever the follower of Achad Ha'am, he was also aware that all was not well in the *Yishuv*. It was at this nadir that, by great good fortune, Herzlian Zionism was born. As Weizmann wrote:

> *"I was in my second year in Berlin when, in 1896, Theodor Herzl published his tract, now a classic of Zionism, Der Jüdenstaat — The Jewish state. It was an utterance which came like a bolt from the blue. We had never heard the name Herzl before ... Herzl made no allusion in his little book to his predecessors in the field, to Moses Hess and Leon Pinsker and Nathan Birnbaum — the last a Viennese like Herzl, and the creator of the very word by which the movement is known: Zionism. Apparently Herzl did not know of the existence of the Chibath* [*Chovevei*] *Zion; he did*

[47] Originally the *"Society for the Support of Jewish Farmers and Artisans in Syria and Palestine"* (the sometime secretary of which was Achad Ha'am), had boasted 4,000 members by 1897. Yet, its membership peaked at only 5,000 in a Russia of more than 5 million Jews.

not mention Palestine; he ignored the Hebrew language.

Yet the effect produced by The Jewish State was profound. Not the ideas, but the personality which stood behind them appealed to us. Here was daring, clarity and energy. The very fact that this Westerner came to us unencumbered by our own preconceptions had its appeal."[48]

THE FIRST ZIONIST CONGRESS

With a view to creating his mass movement, Theodor Herzl convened the epoch-making inaugural Zionist Congress, in Basel, Switzerland, in August 1897. It was assembled as a symbolic parliament for the 200 Jews who wished to pursue an active Zionist agenda. The First Zionist Congress resolved to form the Zionist Organisation[49] ("ZO") and set out a comprehensive programme that would propel Zionism into, and throughout, the 20th century. (See panel 4.)

4

THE BASEL PROGRAMME

Zionism aims at establishing for the Jewish people a publicly and legally assured home in Palestine. For the attainment of this purpose, the Congress considers the following means serviceable:

The promotion of the settlement of Jewish agriculturists, artisans, and tradesmen in Palestine.

The federation of all Jews into local or general groups, according to the laws of the various countries.

The strengthening of the Jewish feeling and consciousness.

Preparatory steps for the attainment of those governmental grants which are necessary to the achievement of the Zionist

---

[48] *Trial and Error* (ibid)

[49] The prefix "World" was added in 1960. Care should be taken to avoid confusion with "ZF", the Zionist Federation (of the United Kingdom and Ireland).

purpose.

The foundation of the Zionist Organisation.

The adoption of HaTikvah as its anthem.

The absorption of most of the previous Chovevei Zion societies.

The suggestion for the establishment of a people's bank (the Jewish Colonial Trust).

The election of Herzl as President of the Zionist Organisation and Max Nordau and Dr Moses Gaster as Vice-Presidents.

Herzl confided to his diary:

> *"At Basel I founded the Jewish state. If I said this out loud today I would be greeted by universal laughter. In five years perhaps, and certainly in fifty years, everyone will perceive it"*

which was impressively prophetic, for fifty years and three months later, on 29 November 1947, the United Nations General Assembly adopted the Partition Plan for Palestine and, within another six months, on 14 May 1948, David Ben-Gurion declared the establishment of the Jewish State of Israel in *Eretz Yisrael.*

Weizmann, although the elected Pinsk delegate to the inaugural Congress, had business in Moscow, trying (but failing) to commercialise one of his scientific patents. Delayed travel caused him to miss the Congress and he had some catching up to do. The Second Zionist Congress would take place a year later and by then Herzl would be lionised by the Jewish communities of the West and the East alike. Within that year, *Der Jüdenstaat* revitalised both the Jewish world and Zionism itself.

FRIBOURG

After three years' study in Berlin, and just weeks after the inaugural Congress — and irrespective of his invaluable Berlin-based network of Zionist associates, not least Achad Ha'am — Weizmann, putting his academic career before his Zionist pursuits, moved on for:

> "*In the autumn of 1897 Weizmann followed his favourite instructor from the* [Charlottenberg] *Polytechnik, Karl Anton Augustin Bistrzycki, to the University of Fribourg, Switzerland*[50]*, where the latter had been appointed professor. Since it was Bistrzycki who had guided his early research in Berlin, it was natural for Weizmann to write his dissertation under the guidance of a man whose interests in chemistry were akin to his own.*"[51]

Little is known of Weizmann's life in Fribourg, his home from 1897, except that there were few Jewish students there, and fewer still who were Russian Zionists. Only thirty kilometres away, however, lies Bern, where there were kindred spirits — and romance, for it was there that he met and became engaged to be married to Sophia Getsova, a medical student from Minsk. Sophia's family were close to that of Leo Motzkin.

THE SECOND ZIONIST CONGRESS

In August 1898, the ZO held its Second Zionist Congress, again in Basel, conveniently now for Weizmann. He attended along with some 400 others, double the numbers of the first Congress. Leo Motzkin, recently returned from *Eretz Yisrael*, reported on the condition of the *Yishuv*. The Jewish Colonial Trust, the first Zionist bank, was launched, to be headquartered in London. Weizmann beheld Herzl for the first time in person, and with ambivalence. On the one hand, Weizmann recognised in Herzl:

> "[his] *enduring contribution to Zionism, to have created one central parliamentary authority for Zionism. .... this cardinal achievement must not be forgotten*"

---

[50] And not Freiburg, as referred to in *Trial and Error,* which is in Germany. This and other errors in *Trial and Error* may have arisen because Dr Weizmann dictated the book and his eyesight did not permit him to scrutinise it.

[51] *Chaim Weizmann: The Making of a Zionist Leader,* Jehuda Reinharz (ibid)

yet Weizmann wrote:

> *"though he was impressive, I cannot pretend that I was swept off my feet"*

from which we may conclude that Weizmann allowed himself a certain degree of self-regard. This was not entirely unjustified.

THE REVOLUTIONARIES

Fin-de-siècle Switzerland was (particularly in the cities of Bern and Geneva) a hot-bed of political activity. Weizmann was aware that Lenin, Trotsky and other aspiring revolutionaries, frequently visited Bern, and readily conceded that:

> "[the] *Jewish students were ... overawed-by the intellectual and moral authority of the older revolutionaries … they, however, would not tolerate in the Jewish youth any expression of separate attachment to the Jewish people, or even special awareness of the Jewish problem. My resentment of Lenin .... and the arrogant Trotsky was provoked by the contempt with which they treated any Jew who was moved by the fate of his people and animated by a love of its history and its tradition. They could not understand why a Russian Jew should want to be anything but a Russian."*[52]

(It is tempting to think how differently history might have played out had Zionism not already become so deeply ingrained within Weizmann, as seen in his activism, that he might have been tempted into Lenin's circle — or vice versa.)

Weizmann's activist tendency manifested itself afresh when he co-founded what he claims to have been the first Zionist society in Switzerland, *Ha-Schachar* (The Dawn). The other founders were Shloyme Rappoport (who went on to write, as S Ansky, *"The Dybbuk"*), Abram Lichtenstein (who would later marry one of Weizmann's sisters) and Nachman Syrkin (one of those

[52] *Chaim Weizmann: The Making of a Zionist Leader,* Jehuda Reinharz (ibid)

Weizmann had held in awe when he joined the Scientific Society in Berlin).

Weizmann describes the impact that the launch[53] of *Ha-Schachar* had, thus:

> "*The mere proclamation of our existence created a scandal. ... we called a mass meeting of the Jewish student body for the purpose of increasing our membership.*"[54]

Against much opposition from the revolutionaries (and the assimilationists), Weizmann and his *Ha-Schachar* colleagues, in 1898:

> "*invited down from Berlin two gifted young Zionist speakers, Berthold Feivel and Martin Buber. The meeting, which was held in a Bierhalle, expanded into a sort of congress and lasted three nights and two days! It was before the dawn of the third day, at four o'clock, that the resolution was put to a vote, and we scored a tremendous triumph. A hundred and eighty students enrolled in the Zionist Society — a striking revelation of the true inclinations and convictions of a large part of the Jewish student body.*"[55]

The Bern Rebellion, as Weizmann refers to it, had repercussions throughout Europe as Jewish students took note and were invigorated by it. Perhaps Weizmann could have done more by travelling to speak to them, as he had ministered to the villages in the Pale, but, as always, he felt, as he put it:

> "*the double pull, towards science on the one hand, towards a public life in the Zionist movement on the other.*"[56]

---

[53] This would appear to have been in 1898 or 1899. *Chaim Weizmann: The Making of a Zionist Leader*, Jehuda Reinharz (ibid).

[54] *Trial and Error* (ibid)

[55] *Chaim Weizmann: The Making of a Zionist Leader*, Jehuda Reinharz (ibid)

[56] *Chaim Weizmann: The Making of a Zionist Leader*, Jehuda Reinharz (ibid)

Weizmann also founded the first Zionist student society in Switzerland, the Bern Academic Zionist Society, in 1898, his cultural and educational agenda, plus his stand against orthodox rabbis in the ZO, appealing to many Jewish students.

Weizmann attended the next several Zionist Congresses and found that he was still uncertain about Herzl: granted, Herzl had given fresh vitality to the Zionist movement, but he had provided only the skeleton. To flesh it out was going to take a great deal of polemics and activity — and activism.

Achad Ha'am had no such ambivalence. He was discomfited from the outset by Herzl's policy of seeking to build Zionism from the top down, craving audiences with world leaders, statesmen and diplomats — always hoping for a packet of title deeds that would confer on the ZO some territory for a Jewish homeland. Achad Ha'am saw that as insufficiently practical, preferring a bottom-up approach. Weizmann, however, remained uncertain, for Herzl was, admittedly, capable of mixing with some of the most influential leaders and politicians of the day. In 1898, Herzl met German Kaiser Wilhelm II on his visit to Palestine, at the *Mikveh Yisrael* agricultural college close to Jaffa, and, in 1901, Sultan Abdul Hamid II, ruler of the Ottoman Empire, in Constantinople, although no real estate was conferred by either of them.

DR CHAIM WEIZMANN PHD

Weizmann applied himself to his studies, completing his thesis (on the electrolytic reduction of dyestuffs) and, in January 1899, he was awarded his doctorate *summa cum laude.* He was then able to embark upon an academic career, and the following April took up his first post. At the invitation of Professor Carl Graebe in the Department of Organic Chemistry at Geneva University, Weizmann became a tutor and *privat-docent*[57]. Aged 24, only

[57] The academic title of *privat-docent* (or *privat-dozent* in German) became current around 1860 in Germany, Austria and Switzerland for university

six years after he had left Pinsk, Weizmann had academic standing at a major Swiss university. Speaking Hebrew, Yiddish and Russian as a youngster, he had added German for life in Darmstadt and Berlin. For Geneva he would need to acquire mastery of French, so he set about it and soon became fluent.

While the *privat-docent* appointment did not carry a salary, it conferred the right to tutor students for a fee. Weizmann quickly attracted fifteen scholars, which launched his teaching career. At the same time, the academic and politician had an eye for business too for Weizmann's:

> *"early career as a chemist progressed by leaps and bounds. He was fortunate in that the first years of this century saw a rapid expansion of the chemical industry, fuelled initially by the textile industry's need to find chemical dyes. From the 1880s Germany, with abundant deposits of coal and potash, led the world in chemical innovations, particularly those relating to by-products of coal. By the 1890s, she* [Germany] *had acquired a near monopoly in synthetic dyestuffs, used in the production of artificial fibres, photographic materials, drugs, plastics, new explosives, celluloid, and optical glass. The field was wide open for an ambitious chemist. Weizmann's association with Christian Deichler, begun in Berlin in the early 1890s, prospered. The main thrust of their research was in dyestuffs chemistry. They published papers together and registered joint patents."*[58]

The seeking of patents, and a demanding job he landed at Bayer, the German chemical and pharmaceutical industrial colossus, were important for Weizmann: charging fifty marks per student alone would not have kept him solvent indefinitely.

---

teachers who had not yet achieved appointment to a teaching or research chair.

[58] *Chaim Weizmann: A Biography*, Norman Rose (ibid)

VERA

In November 1900, while still engaged to be married to Bern medical student, Sophia Getsova, Weizmann met 19-year-old Vera Khatzman, also a medical student, at the Zionist Club of the University of Geneva. There followed a complicated period, which culminated in his finally confessing to Sophia, in March 1903, that his attentions had been elsewhere, thus ending the relationship — and souring that of Weizmann with Motzkin, part of the circle of Sophia's family.

Vera represented a challenge for Weizmann. She had been born, on 27 November[59] 1881, into an unusual Russian Jewish family: middle class and assimilated. Vera's father, having served twenty-five years in the Russian army, was not required to live in the Pale. The family Vera was born into lived comfortably in Rostov on the shores of Lake Nero, 200 kms northeast of Moscow.

Vera initially studied music and knew little or nothing of Hebrew, Yiddish, Zionism or, for that matter — apart from the family's observance of Jewish festivals — Judaism. There is, however, no mention of her having had an assimilationist mind-set in the German fashion. She was, therefore, open to persuasion to the views of her suitor, and he duly set about introducing her to all the matters of importance to him. In return, she *"charmed some of the self-devouring intensity out of his personality."*[60] This was a true romance for both of them (she had known that Weizmann was already engaged to Sophia when they met), though she was less demonstrative than he — and she observed that, notwithstanding his attentiveness to her, he continued, even after the betrothal to Sophia had been cancelled, to have an eye for attractive women. Nevertheless, the relationship flourished.

---

[59] Vera and Chaim shared their birthdays.

[60] *Memoirs*, Israel Sieff (Weidenfeld and Nicholson, 1970)

THE DEMOCRATIC FACTION

The Third Zionist Congress, held in Basel in 1899, opened with Herzl's report on his meetings with royalty in Palestine and Constantinople. That he had achieved them at all was impressive, but it was lost on no one that tangible results had not followed. Herzl was plainly preoccupied with political issues while others, Weizmann included, had cultural issues at the top of their agenda. Herzl saw and feared the potential this had for splitting his movement.

In 1900, a group of students, including Martin Buber (the philosopher), Berthold Feivel (the poet), Leo Motzkin and Weizmann, formed a "democratic-progressive" splinter group within the ZO, to which they gave the weighty title of "The Democratic Faction." Its emphasis would be on culture and education, regarded by its promoters as either wanting in, or too much in the hands of the religious section of, the ZO. Being partly a Weizmann-inspired enterprise, practical development in the *Yishuv* formed part of the agenda, the greatly-coveted expression of which was to establish a Jewish university in Jerusalem.

The Fourth Zionist Congress was held in London in 1900, with a view to appealing to the pro-Zionist inclinations of many British establishment figures. Congress debated the plight of Romanian Jewry, many thousands of whom had been forced to emigrate, while those left behind continued to suffer persecution. No practical solution was offered, save that a collection was made amongst the delegates for some recently-arrived Romanian immigrants whose noisy public demonstration outside the Congress somewhat spoiled, it was feared, the desired impression of burgeoning Zionist strength. The religious Zionists demanded that the Zionist movement restrict itself to political matters (contrary to the wishes of Weizmann's Democratic Faction).

Weizmann continued to be animated by the cultural issue. He arranged to meet Herzl personally in October 1901, two months before the Fifth Congress would be held, to put the Democratic Faction case directly to the movement's leader.

> *"Weizmann was keyed up for the confrontation: 'I shall not mince words tomorrow, and I will tell Herzl the unvarnished truth.'"* [61]

Weizmann need not have worried. Herzl had prepared for his meeting with the activist from the ranks so that, when Weizmann, accompanied by Buber, made out his case, Herzl had only words of encouragement.

Weizmann pressed on with his own agenda and, in a circular prepared for the Youth Congress, which would coincide with the Fifth Congress in December, he set out to mobilise Jewish youth for action, thus:

> *"It now falls to the young to do work of the utmost importance — to awaken the masses of the Jewish people, to bring a ray of light into the dim, oppressive atmosphere of the ghetto, to fight against the prejudices and the dark forces which obscure our pure ideal. It falls to the intelligentsia to take the lead in spreading correct and conscious propaganda for our idea, to shoulder the task of information activity on a large and fruitful scale. The duty is laid upon us to draw all the creative classes in the Jewish people to the Zionist flag."*[62]

In fact, Weizmann (at age 27) became the prime mover behind the first Zionist Youth Conference: *"seeing the rôle of the Youth Organisation as a vitalising force within the larger Zionist movement. Weizmann authorised youth to forge a Jewish*

[61] *Chaim Weizmann: A Biography,* Norman Rose (ibid)

[62] *Chaim Weizmann: The Making of a Zionist Leader,* Jehuda Reinharz (ibid)

state."[63] He wrote:

> *"In the depths of the masses an impulse arose, vague, groping. unformulated. for Jewish self-liberation. It was genuinely of the folk: it was saturated with Jewish tradition; and it was connected with the most ancient memories of the land where Jewish life had first expressed itself in freedom. It was, in short, the birth of modern Zionism. Many young Jews, formerly indifferent to Jewish values, now were spurred by the pogroms to take an interest in the fate and fortune of their people."*[64]

At the Fifth Zionist Congress, the Democratic Faction pressed to establish cultural activities within, and to marginalise the religious wing of, the ZO, while Herzl spoke of the Jewish Colonial Trust; but, after five years of diplomatic efforts, even he was ready to concede the failure of his top-down policy.

The Zionist project was becoming mired in disorders of one kind or another, which Weizmann, and doubtless Herzl, found wearying. Nevertheless, the 1901 Congress saw the foundation of the Jewish National Fund[65] for the purpose of raising funds for the purchase of land in *Eretz Yisrael* as the inalienable property of the Jewish people.

Future Zionist Congresses were slated to held every two years so the next, the sixth, would be in August 1903. It would be Herzl's last.

---

[63] *Development of Emerging World Youth*, Yedla C Simhadri (Mittal Publications, 1989)

[64] *The Course of Modern Jewish History*, H M Sachar (Vintage Books, 1990)

[65] Today, the JNF owns over 10% of the land in Israel and has planted over 240 million trees. Israel is a world leader in reversing desertification. The JNF is also responsible for the establishment of over 250 reservoirs in what used to be the water-starved land.

KISHINEV

At the end of March 1903, a few days before Passover, in Kishinev, Moldova, a Gentile child was found dead. The usual calumny in these situations, the blood libel (originating from, at the latest, the 12th century Crusades), that Jews used Gentile blood to make *matzot* (unleavened bread) for Passover, was invoked by the local newspaper, *Bessarabets*. Kishinev's Jews were accused of the ritual murder of the child. A series of vicious anti-Semitic articles in *Bessarabets* followed, accusing the Jews of a litany of crimes.

It soon became plain that the Jews were not responsible for the child's death. Notwithstanding, on 6 and 7 April a major pogrom was unleashed against them. The mob ran amok, killing some 50 Jews, seriously injuring nearly six hundred others and wrecking nearly two thousand Jewish homes and businesses. All this went virtually unrestrained by the Russian authorities — not unexpectedly, given that behind it all were agents of the local branch of the Russian secret service and the guiding hand of the editor of *Bessarabets*, Pavolachi Krushevan. (Within months he was to become the original publisher of the infamous anti-Semitic forgery, "*The Protocols of the Elders of Zion*", the Russian canard, supposedly authored by the Jews, that alleged that the Jews were omnipotent and bent on world domination[66]).

THE UGANDA PROPOSAL

A few weeks after the Kishinev pogroms, Herzl visited London. He was introduced by Israel Zangwill to British Colonial Secretary, Joseph Chamberlain, who shared the general shock at the first infamous pogrom of the 20th century. Chamberlain, a Protestant Zionist, offered Herzl 13,000 km^2 of the Mau Plateau, in the British East African colony of Kenya (but known as "the

[66] in *Warrant For Genocide,* Norman Cohn (Penguin Books, 1970), Oxford don, Cohn, explains that the Protocols appear to have plagiarised *Dialogue aux Enters*, an 1864 critique by French lawyer, Maurice Joly, of Napoleon III and his régime.

Uganda Proposal"), as a refuge from persecution and a homeland for the Jewish people.

Herzl retained the services of law firm, Lloyd George, Roberts & Co, to work on the Uganda Proposal. They prepared a Jewish colonisation scheme for the Zionist Federation of the United Kingdom and Ireland ("ZF") and submitted it to the Foreign Office on Herzl's behalf in July 1903. (Lloyd George, a Baptist with Zionist sympathies, would go on to become the British prime minister in 1917, the year of the Balfour Declaration.)

At the Sixth Zionist Congress in 1903 in Basel, Herzl told the assembly about the Uganda Proposal, sparking heated debate. The African land was proposed as an "ante-chamber to the Holy Land," but there was immediate and vehement opposition to the idea, on the basis that "Uganda" would end up as the sole and ultimate destination of Zionism. The Russian delegates left the gathering noisily, in revulsion at the idea, before it was put to a vote. Their absence cleared the way for the remainder to pass, by a large majority, a resolution to consider the matter further.

The disastrous Sixth Congress laid bare the dichotomy in Zionism. The Politicals were led by Herzl, while Achad Ha'am headed the Practicals. Each had a large following.

Weizmann was initially ambivalent, torn between his continuing shock and fears over Kishinev (not misplaced, given that a second pogrom in Kishinev was to occur within two years, prompting the Second *Aliyah* a year later): on the one hand, Kishinev seemed to demand some (almost any) place of refuge; on the other was Weizmann's abiding love of the concept of Zion itself. Before the conference was over, without too much heart-searching, Weizmann came down clearly against Uganda, appreciating not least that he needed to maintain his credibility with his natural constituency, the Russian Zionists, all of whom were passionately opposed to Uganda.

The lesson of Kishinev was that earliest possible entry into

Palestine, for the largest possible number of Jews to swell the few who were there, was desperately needed.

Meanwhile, in Palestine itself:

> "[in] *1903, 60,000 Jews of Palestine had just held elections for the first national democratic assembly, the grandfather of the present Knesset (Israel's parliament). ... This gathering was special as a first grass-roots attempt to set up the structures of Jewish self-government.*"[67]

LONDON

Worried about the damage that Zangwill might do, Weizmann travelled to London in October 1903, from where he expected to extract in due course a better offer than Uganda. He met first with the Sephardi Chief Rabbi, Dr Moses Gaster, whom he knew to be intensely opposed to Uganda; but Weizmann's primary objective was to meet officials in the Foreign and Colonial Office to gather material to destroy the Uganda Proposal. Weizmann succeeded in this objective with Sir William Evans-Gordon (whom Weizmann had met some years before when Evans-Gordon had toured the Pale[68]), receiving from him some official documents on East Africa. Weizmann also met Sir Harry Johnston, whom Weizmann describes as *"the famous explorer"*, who was of the opinion that *"the practical value of the offer was nil"*.[69]

These meetings gave Weizmann the feeling that he, too, could conduct high-level diplomacy and that a career-move to England might be beneficial. Unfortunately, he ran out of time and had to

[67] http://pard.technion.ac.il/history/

[68] A lengthy and fascinating report by Evans-Gordon of his Russian tour is to be found at: http://www.museumoffamilyhistory.com/20c-evans-gordon.htm

[69] *Trial and Error* (ibid)

cancel a meeting in Manchester with Charles Dreyfus[70], to whom Dr Gaster had spoken about the young biochemist. Dreyfus' company, the Clayton Aniline Works, was engaged in the chemical industry.

MANCHESTER

Nevertheless, Manchester was about to loom large in Weizmann's life. Geneva University was becoming a dead-end for Weizmann. Professor Graebe was due to retire within a couple of years, which would mean the end of the road for his organic chemistry team. Graebe wrote a letter of recommendation for Weizmann to Manchester University. Vera was still studying medicine in Geneva, but Weizmann, suffering from the disappointment of the Sixth Zionist Congress, resolved by the summer of 1904 to move on, even though he and Vera would be forced to live far apart for some time. (The enforced separation would last almost two years.)

At this time, also, Weizmann was offered a post as a science teacher at a Jerusalem college. (There were no universities as yet in Palestine). He made enquiries about the position but was rejected. The employer would have been the *Hilfsverein der Deutschen Jüden*, who were not well-disposed towards Zionists[71]. In any event, Weizmann resolved to go to Manchester.

The head of the organic chemistry laboratory at the University of Manchester, Professor W H Perkin, Jr, had a high reputation as an inspirational researcher and tutor. Perkin had assembled scientific talent from all over the continent of Europe and, in March 1904, Weizmann received a letter from Perkin inviting

---

[70] Born 1848 in Alsace, France, he was a distant relative of the hapless Captain Alfred Dreyfus. See Chapter 3.

[71] See Chapter 18.

him to work with him.[72] Weizmann reported to Dr Gaster: *"Since Perkin is one of the foremost chemists in England, and since a great dye industry exists in Manchester[73], this combination strikes me as very advantageous even though I have to work at first on my own account."*[74]

Weizmann continues:

> *"It so happened that the work I had been doing under Graebe had been on similar lines to that which the father of Professor Perkin, Sir William Henry Perkin, had done nearly half a century before. ... Professor Perkin was rather touched that I should have been working in the same field as his father, and perhaps his kindness to me was due primarily to this quite fortuitous sentimental factor. Whatever the reason, I was very warmly received, as a former pupil of Adolph von Bayer, of Munich. Perkin spoke excellent German."*[75]

Despite the enthusiasm manifest in his letter to Dr Gaster, Weizmann must have felt some of his customary ambivalence, for he also referred to his move to Manchester as being "*reculer pour mieux sauter*" (taking a step back to leap further ahead later). This was to prove prescient, as Manchester was indeed to prove the springboard for all Weizmann's later triumphs. In any event, the move was a good one because:

---

[72] It was by no means pre-ordained that Weizmann would go to England but he had not anything firm offered to him in Europe.

[73] Few are unaware of Manchester's reputation for rain. The inclement climate of the city (and the county of Lancashire) led to the development of what was, for over two hundred years, the world's greatest cotton manufacturing industry. Manchester also became home to many Jewish immigrants who worked with cotton to make the locally sorely-needed raincoat. The dyeing skills were associated with this and the other cotton products of the area.

[74] *Trial and Error* (ibid)

[75] *Trial and Error* (ibid)

"[i]*n academic Manchester, he was in a city which was still the vital centre of the British liberal tradition. Among men accustomed to think internationally, he could find a ready response to the concept of Zionism; and in the light of the far-flung nature of British imperial politics, he himself could see Zionism and Palestine in a new perspective. Secondly, Manchester gave him access to one of the world's great universities, where he moved among, and talked to, men like Sir Arthur Schuster, a philosopher like Prof Samuel Alexander, physicists like Ernest (later Lord) Rutherford, Nils Bohr and other men who many years later were still to be in close contact with Weizmann as active supporters of the Jerusalem University. Thirdly, Manchester gave Weizmann a vital access to one of the world's great newspapers, The Manchester Guardian, whose political interests spanned the globe and whose famous editor, C P Scott, moved as an equal among statesmen.*"[76]

Further, Manchester was the beating heart of British Zionism, with barely an assimilationist Jew to be found. It was the Manchester School of men of rare quality and focus that would provide the necessary dynamism required to win the Balfour Declaration from the British government, a little over a decade after Weizmann established himself amongst them.

THE DEMOCRATIC FACTION

By 1904, the Democratic Faction had ceased to be a force within the ZO, partly because of tensions between Weizmann and Motzkin, but largely because of the great diversion of Kishinev at Passover the previous year. Funds collected for establishing a Jewish university in Jerusalem were applied instead to relief for the victims of the Kishinev pogrom. The University project was ignored or forgotten by successive Zionist conferences — but not by Weizmann.

[76] *Chaim Weizmann: A Biography By Several Hands* (ibid) by T R Fyvel.

DEATH OF HERZL

In July 1904, Weizmann was preparing to leave Switzerland for England. In the midst of his arrangements and much nostalgia (his compatriots from *Ha-Schachar* threw a lavish farewell party for him), news came that on 3 July, exhausted by his exertions and disappointments, and drained by dissensions within the movement he had created, Theodor Herzl died at the age of 44. The whole Zionist movement, supporters and detractors alike, dissolved into profound mourning. Weizmann shared the sense of massive loss equally and, further, anticipated that the mantle of leadership might soon fall on him:

> *"Difficult times await me now. I feel that a heavy burden has fallen on my shoulders...."*[77]

A large group of Zionist colleagues assembled for Weizmann's departure from Geneva railway station on 6 July. The feeling of loss and grief at the mortal departure of Herzl and the physical parting of Weizmann, almost in the same moment, was overwhelming for them.

In Austria, in honour of the departed Herzl:

> *"Deputations from Zionist bodies in almost all the countries of Europe hastened to Vienna to attend the funeral.... It was very simple in character, in accordance with the wishes of the dead leader, the plain coffin being covered with the blue and white Zionist flag which had first been displayed at the First Zionist Congress."*[78]

LONDON

Arriving in London, Weizmann picked up from where he had left off the previous October. He resumed his networking and developed further his diplomatic skills. He made for Dr Gaster and received an introduction to Lord Henry Percy, Under-

[77] *Chaim Weizmann: A Biography,* Norman Rose (ibid)

[78] *Theodor Herzl: Founder of Political Zionism* by Israel Cohen (ibid)

Secretary of State for Foreign Affairs, to sound him out on a legacy issue from the death of Herzl: Uganda. To Weizmann's relief, Percy declared: *"If I were a Jew, I would not give a halfpenny for this proposition."*[79]

While, as Weizmann knew, many English Jews were still favourably disposed to Uganda (as long as, one assumes, they themselves did not have to live there) Weizmann did not as yet hold sway with them. Nevertheless, he was satisfied that the Uganda plan was as good as dead.[80]

Before travelling on to Manchester, Weizmann met with Israel Zangwill (despite their divergent views), Herbert Bentwich (whom Herzl had met), Leopold Kessler and others. Having started to build contacts again in London, Weizmann was ready to begin his new life in Manchester.

CODA - HERZL: While this work is a study of Chaim Weizmann and asserts that he was indispensable to the creation of Israel, it would be churlish to pass over the contribution of Theodor Herzl as though he was just another hero amongst the many responsible for the evolution of Zionism and, ultimately, the creation of the State of Israel. After all, his is the prime memorial stone at Israel's national cemetery, which is itself on the eponymous Mount Herzl in Jerusalem, the capital city of the Jewish State.

It would also be wrong to make comparisons between Herzl and Weizmann. Suffice to repeat: it was Herzl who revivified Zionism, which was fading just before the publication of *Der Jüdenstaat*. Admittedly, under Herzl's leadership it began to flag again by the time of the last Zionist Congress that he attended, that of 1903; but he was dead by the next, in 1905, at the tragically young age of 44. Whether, had he lived longer, he

---

[79] *Trial and Error* (ibid)

[80] As even Herzl had tacitly accepted at an extraordinary Zionist meeting the previous April.

might have swung away from the Politicals, we can never know; and it may be said that his death released the energy of the Practicals to steer the movement thereafter.

One has to end on Herzl, however, with this: whatever we may conjecture about what he might have achieved had he been given longer, his legacy will always be the launching of the Zionist movement into the twentieth century, culminating in the foundation of the State of Israel within his fifty-year prediction.

~~~
~~~

5

STEADY PROGRESS

MANCHESTER

Chaim Weizmann arrived in Manchester on August Bank Holiday 1904 at the age of thirty, during the university's summer vacation. He had one contact, Joseph Massel[81]. An immigrant from Vilna in the Pale, Hebraist, Hebrew language poet and printer, he and Weizmann had met at the Second Zionist Congress six years earlier. Massel welcomed Weizmann off the train from London and took him to some modest accommodation.[82]

Presenting himself at the university, Weizmann found that Professor Perkin had stayed long enough to settle in his latest recruit before leaving for a holiday in Europe. Weizmann was optimistic, and willing to overlook his cramped conditions and solitude. He spent the summer acquiring English by applying himself with his usual enthusiasm and thoroughness, reading Shakespeare, the Bible and the speeches of British politicians. The students returned to their studies by October and found their Russian émigré tutor to be an excellent teacher.

Massel, a Jewish community leader, told Weizmann that he knew Charles Dreyfus (whom Weizmann had been unable to see the previous October) and he brought them together. From Dreyfus, Weizmann imported a happy fusion of the two strands of his life: not only was Dreyfus' company engaged in chemical dying, Weizmann's speciality, but also he was both the chairman of the Manchester Zionist Association and closely involved with

---

[81] Weizmann is said to have described Massel as a "veritable angel" and his Friday evening visits to the Massel household as "the highlights of my life" - *Fifty Years of Zionism*, Oskar Kwasnik Rabinowicz (R. Anscombe, 1952).

[82] As from March 1910, Massel and his son Symon published the periodical; *"The Zionist Banner"*, which later became *"The Zionist"*, edited by Harry Sacher.

the local branch of the British Conservative party, then in government. The prime minister was Arthur Balfour.

Weizmann realised that, as an industrial chemist, he could start making some money again (the cash-flow from his earlier patents having slowed to a trickle). By November 1904, Weizmann had some part-time work from Dreyfus' company, which, conveniently, he was able to carry out in his university laboratory.

The following month, another vacation arrived, and Weizmann applied himself to preparing his first English-language academic lecture, to be delivered in the first month of the new year.

Confronted, in early January 1905, with a crowd of "boisterous" students, the chemist set out to create some chemistry with them:

> *"When I came into the lecture theatre they received me with a friendliness which encouraged me to put my case before them as well as I could. I was a foreigner, I said, and had been in the country only a few months; I was consequently at their mercy. I would do my best, but I would certainly perpetrate many howlers. They could make all the jokes they wanted at my expense after the lecture. The effect of this little introductory appeal was remarkable. They listened to the lecture with the closest attention; when the hour was over, they did not leave the theatre, but stayed on and surrounded me, putting a great many questions to me which showed they had understood the main points of the lecture, and were genuinely interested. So the first ordeal passed triumphantly; the next lecture, a week later, was already routine."*[83]

By this time, Dreyfus had introduced Weizmann to Harry Sacher. A brilliant intellectual and thinker, Sacher was an international lawyer with offices in London, Jerusalem and

---

[83] *Trial and Error* (ibid)

Haifa. Sacher, an active Zionist, was a political analyst writing for *The Manchester Guardian* newspaper, who would open several doors for Weizmann. (Sacher was related by marriage to both Simon Marks and Israel Sieff of emergent retail giant, Marks & Spencer ("M&S"), although, inexplicably, it was not until 1913 that Sacher introduced Weizmann to them.)

THE PATENTS OF CHARLES WEIZMANN

In July 1905, Weizmann was appointed Perkin's assistant and a Demonstrator in the organic chemistry laboratory, tasked to supervise student work. Both appointments brought welcome remuneration.

With his innate ambition, and marriage on the horizon, Weizmann further developed his catalogue of patents. In April 1905, "Charles" Weizmann registered a UK patent: *"Improvements in the Manufacture of Camphene"* (which he sold to Dreyfus' Clayton Aniline Company Limited) and, in October 1906, a similar one in the USPTO. In all, Weizmann registered 235 patents in the 20th century.[84]

THE SEVENTH ZIONIST CONGRESS

The same month, Weizmann was despatched, as the Manchester Zionist Society's delegate, to the Seventh Zionist Congress, once again in Basel. Max Nordau, a writer of considerable note, who had been pushed towards Zionism by repression in the same way as Herzl — and who, like Herzl, had supported the Uganda Proposal — spoke in praise of the former leader, who had died the year after the previous Congress.

Debate resumed on the divisive issue of whether to settle for some place other than Zion itself. A commission of inquiry had been despatched to and returned from East Africa. It reported that the area was unsuitable for the Jewish Homeland. The Uganda Proposal was put to the vote, and formally abandoned.

[84] Source: the Weizmann Archives, Rechovot.

Israel Zangwill led a rowdy departure from Congress of the supporters of the ill-fated Proposal, and went on to form the Jewish Territorial Association. After that, within the Zionist movement itself, the sole focus could be, and was, *Eretz Yisrael*. Weizmann was jubilant.

David Wolffsohn, of whom Weizmann thought little, became Herzl's successor. He would serve as president for the next six years.

In October 1905, in the Ukrainian sector of the Pale of Settlement, a series of pogroms broke out. Hundreds of Jews were killed or injured. This accelerated the Second *Aliyah*, that had begun the previous year, with another 40,000 Jews making for *Eretz Yisrael*. Weizmann was acutely aware of their suffering, flight and, after their arrival, need for security.

In the winter, Vera visited Weizmann in Manchester. The end of her studies was in sight and she was concerned that she should be able to practise medicine in Manchester. It would mean her requalifying but, after an enforced separation of 18 months, Chaim and Vera were determined on their joint course and started to plan their marriage for the following summer.

THE NETWORKING BEGINS

In May 1904, Winston Spencer Churchill had made his maiden speech in Parliament against the Aliens Bill[85] (designed to keep Russian — ie Jewish — immigrants out of Britain). *The*

[85] *The Aliens Bill* of 1904 amounted to ill-disguised anti-Semitic and anti-immigrant electioneering by the Conservative British Government. Churchill opposed it saying: *"A series of pogroms in Tsarist Russia over the previous twenty-five years had brought to England a large and increasing number of Jews, most of them poor, ill-educated and unskilled. To judge by the talk there has been, one would have imagined we were being overrun by the swarming invasion and 'ousted' from our island"* yet *"all the aliens of Great Britain do not amount to a one-hundred-and-fortieth part of the total population."* (Today, the proportion is one in 275.)

Manchester Guardian published a letter from Churchill in opposition to the Bill.[86] Churchill was the Member of Parliament for the Manchester North West constituency, where there was a large Jewish presence. At a public meeting in December 1905 in Churchill's Manchester constituency, at Churchill's invitation, Weizmann spoke to the crowd — in Yiddish — and made a lasting impression on Churchill.

In the following month's general election Weizmann was asked by Churchill's parliamentary agent to canvass votes for Churchill, but Weizmann was reticent about becoming involved in British politics so soon after his arrival on the scene, and declined. Churchill enjoyed the rather more august support, at that time, of Nathan Laski, regarded as the uncrowned king of Manchester Jewry. Shortly after that, Churchill and Weizmann met again over dinner at Laski's home. (Their paths would next cross in 1915, when Churchill was First Lord of the Admiralty and the outcome would be momentous.)

On the eve of the January 1906 British general election, Dreyfus introduced Weizmann to Conservative Prime Minister Arthur Balfour, at the Queens Hotel in Manchester. Reports vary as to whether Balfour wished to know why the Jews had declined the Uganda Proposal or why many British Jews (such as the Rothschilds) were opposed to Zionism. In either case, what has gained common currency is the reportage that Weizmann, to make the case of a Jewish homeland in Palestine, said:

> *"'Mr Balfour, if you were offered Paris instead of London, would you take it?' He looked surprised. 'But London is our own!' I said: 'Jerusalem was our own when London was a marsh.' He leaned back, continued to stare at me, and said two things which I remember vividly. The first was: 'Are there many Jews who think like you?' I answered: 'I believe I speak the mind of millions of Jews whom you will never see and who cannot speak for themselves, but with whom I could*

[86] Which nevertheless was passed into law of *The Aliens Act* 1905.

> *pave the streets of the country I come from.' To this he said: 'If this is so, you will one day be a force.'"*[87]

The next day, Balfour lost both the general election and his own seat, a rare humiliation for a British prime minister. He and Weizmann would not meet again until 1916, the eponymous Declaration being granted the following year, when Balfour was the foreign minister. Neither of them knew that winter's night in 1906 what lay ahead but, according to Balfour:

> *"Conversations I held with Mr Weizmann in January, 1906, convinced me that history could not thus be ignored, and that if a home was to be found for the Jewish people, homeless now for nearly nineteen hundred years, it was vain to seek it anywhere but in Palestine."*[88]

MARRIAGE

Vera graduated in May 1906 and the wedding arrangements proceeded apace. Two religious ceremonies were planned. The first, on 23 August 1906, was celebrated in Zoppot (now Sopot, Poland), on the coast of the Baltic Sea, the most convenient place for the closest Weizmann family members.[89] (The other synagogue ceremony would take place in Manchester.)

What Vera must have made of what followed is not recorded but the events may speak for themselves. The newly-marrieds went from their wedding ceremony to Köln (Cologne) in western Germany, where a Zionist Action Committee meeting was being held. A week of fractious argument followed, in which

---

[87] After The Victorians: The World Our Parents Knew, A N Wilson (Random House, 2006)

[88] Introduction by the Rt. Hon. A. J. Balfour, M P to *The History of Zionism*, Nahum Sokolow (Longmans, 1919)

[89] Weizmann methodically listed by hand 37 cables of congratulations received between 21 and 24 August 1906 from places as diverse as Pinsk, Warsaw, Darmstadt, Charlottenberg, Rostov, Berlin, London and Manchester (Weizmann Archives, Rechovot).

Weizmann and his former Faction colleagues tried unsuccessfully to secure the resignation of ZO President, Wolffsohn.

At the end of the week, the newly-weds at last took their honeymoon — a Rhine river cruise — before travelling on to Manchester, and Weizmann's rented three-room apartment.

MANCHESTER

For a newly-qualified lady doctor from a well-to-do Russian family, this setting must, after Geneva, have seemed bleak. Vera had yet to learn English (her fifth language), was unable to practise as a doctor and would not have enjoyed the Manchester climate: depths-of-winter evenings that (Russian style) start to draw in half-way through the afternoon, and the rain, cold and dreariness that are the ambient hallmarks of Manchester[90].

Life was, however, about to improve for the Weizmanns. They soon rented a house, Vera became pregnant and she struck up friendships with the wives of Weizmann's university faculty colleagues. In particular, Nora Schuster, the wife of professor of applied mathematics, Sir Arthur Schuster, took Vera under her wing and helped her to become proficient in English quite swiftly.

For Weizmann also — in his third year of teaching and research at Manchester University, with several patents to his name, a number of posts in the college, part-time work for Dreyfus and a local network of Zionist friends of some distinction — an upwards trajectory was perceptible.

A son, Benjamin, was born in 1907, and Vera was well on her way to requalifying as a doctor in England. (A second son, Michael, was born in 1916.)

This was the time when Weizmann forged strong connections

[90] The author grew up there!

with influential Manchester Jews: Massel and Dreyfus (Weizmann's co-chair of the Manchester Zionist Society); Nathan Laski (greatly-respected, not only in the Manchester community but also nationally, as a member of the Board of Deputies of British Jews — although no Zionist); and a number of Russian-Jewish émigrés who had settled in Manchester.

SYNTHETIC ZIONISM

With the Territorials out of the ZO, its direction was single-minded: only Zion would do. There was, however, still the dichotomy within the ZO between the Politicals and the Practicals. What did those terms mean?

According to Weizmann, the political Zionists, the Austro-German Zionist organisations and most of the Westerners held that:

> *"Palestine belongs to Turkey. The purchase of land is forbidden by law. We can do nothing now but work for the charter, and use the Great Powers, like England and Germany, to help us obtain the charter"*[91]

while the practical school (largely from the East) took:

> *"... a more organic view of Zionism, and of historical process. In reality the ... 'practical' Zionists ... sought to impress upon the Zionist world the obvious truth that political activity alone is not enough; it must be accompanied by solid, constructive achievement, the actual physical occupation of land in Palestine, which in turn would be accompanied by the moral strengthening of the Jewish consciousness, the revival of the Hebrew language, the spread of the knowledge of Jewish history and the strengthening of the attachment to the permanent values of Judaism."*[92]

---

[91] *Trial and Error* (ibid)

[92] *Trial and Error* (ibid)

It was Weizmann himself who broke the Politicals/Practicals deadlock. At the Eighth Zionist Congress in July 1907 at The Hague, he made "*a most eloquent, influential and seminal plea for the fusion of the 'political' with the 'practical' school of Zionism and expounded 'synthetic' Zionism*"[93], thus:

> "*Our diplomatic work is important, but it will gain in importance by actual performance in Palestine. If we achieve a synthesis of the two schools of Zionism, we may get past the dead point,*"[94]

and stressed that:

> "*a scrap of paper*" would have no value unless it rested, as it were "*on the very soil of Palestine, on a Jewish population rooted in that soil, on institutions established by and for that population.*"[95]

Thus was born "Synthetic Zionism", the merger of Political Zionism and Practical Zionism, the two strands running in parallel and close proximity.

During the Congress, Weizmann was challenged to go and see *Eretz Yisrael* for himself and, as an industrial chemist, to consider the establishment of some manufacturing there. Weizmann wondered whether his knowledge of and work with camphene might be employed in the manufacture of essential oils. Accordingly, instead of returning home to his wife and their six week old son, Weizmann set out for Marseilles and from there by ship for the Holy Land. The time had come for Weizmann to cease regarding the land only from a distance.

---

[93] *Memoirs*, Israel Sieff (ibid)

[94] *Trial and Error* (ibid)

[95] *Trial and Error* (ibid)

6

WEIZMANN IN ERETZ YISRAEL

THE LAND

Famously, and to some[96] infamously, the American writer, Mark Twain visited the Holy Land and recorded his experiences in *"The Innocents Abroad, or The New Pilgrims' Progress"* (1869), an amusing account of Twain's "great pleasure excursion" through Europe and the Holy Land.[97] It appears that he found little that amused him in Palestine, for he wrote:

> *"A desolation is here that not even imagination can grace with the pomp of life and action. We reached Tabor safely. We never saw a human being on the whole route."*
>
> *There is not a solitary village throughout its whole extent — not for thirty miles in either direction. ... One may ride ten miles* [16 km] *hereabouts and not see ten human beings.*
>
> *...these unpeopled deserts, these rusty mounds of barrenness...*
>
> *Palestine ... sits in sackcloth and ashes. Over it broods the spell of a curse that has withered its fields and fettered its energies. Palestine is desolate and unlovely — Palestine is no more of this workday world. It is sacred to poetry and tradition, it is dreamland.*
>
> *There was hardly a tree or a shrub anywhere. Even the olive and the cactus, those fast friends of a worthless soil, had almost deserted the country."*

Chaim Weizmann's first impressions of *Eretz Yisrael* in 1907 were no more complimentary:

> *"A dolorous country it was on the whole, one of the most*

---

[96] Arabs, who resist the narrative that they had done nothing with the land until the Jews arrived.

[97] One of the best-selling travel books of all time.

neglected corners of the miserably neglected Turkish Empire.

I remember Nazareth vividly. We arrived there on a hot afternoon, riding southward, and from the hilltop we looked down on the wide stretch of the Valley of Jezreel, spreading at our feet like a vast carpet framed by the hills of Samaria and Ephraim, with Mount Tabor to the left. It was a superb sight, though the countryside was parched with the late summer heat, and there was hardly a patch of green anywhere for the eye to rest on."

Twain continued:

"We came finally to the noble grove of orange-trees in which the Oriental city of Jaffa lies buried ... Small shreds and patches of it must be very beautiful in the full flush of spring, however, and all the more beautiful by contrast with the far-reaching desolation that surrounds them on every side."

Weizmann neither confirms nor denies this account of Jaffa, but what he does relate is how he was led out of the ancient city by Arthur Ruppin (see panel 5), the ZO's chief land agent[98], to walk:

"over the dunes to the north of the town. When we had got well out into the sands — I remember that it came over our ankles — he stopped, and said, very solemnly: 'Here we shall create a Jewish city!' I looked at him with some dismay. Why should people come to live out in this wilderness where nothing would grow? I began to ply him with technical questions, and he answered me carefully and exactly. Technically, he said, everything was possible. Though in the first years communication with the new settlement would be difficult, the inhabitants would soon become self-supporting and self-sufficient. The Jews of Jaffa

[98] A Jewish-German economist and statistician who assured Weizmann that Palestine could "absorb large numbers of Jews in agriculture".

would move into the new, modern city, and the Jewish colonies of the neighbourhood would have a concentrated market for their products. The Gymnasium would stand at the centre, and would attract a great many students from other parts of Palestine and from Jews abroad, who would 'want their children to be educated in a Jewish high school in a Jewish city'".[99]

Weizmann referred to this as his "*first vision of Tel Aviv*". Two short years later, supported by a loan arranged by Ruppin, 66 families laid the foundations for the new Jewish town of Tel Aviv on the sand dunes just north of Jaffa. (In April 1950, the municipality of Tel Aviv-Jaffa was born.)

5

RUPPIN

Dr Arthur Ruppin (1876-1943) arrived in *Eretz Yisrael* in 1908, charged by the ZO to assess the potential for Zionist settlement. He became responsible for acquiring land and establishing Jewish settlements, which he accomplished most successfully. In 1926, Ruppin joined founded the sociology department at the Hebrew University of Jerusalem. Ruppin became known as "the Father of Zionist Settlement" and "the Father of Jewish Sociology".

ERETZ YISRAEL

For his tour of the Holy Land, Weizmann's guide was Joshua Chankin, who appeared to Weizmann to know every stone and blade of grass. They left Jaffa by horse-drawn buggy, travelling as far north as Metullah, which is today, as it has been since 1948, the most northerly point in Israel (in the pan-handle that is no more than a few kilometres from Lebanon and Syria on three sides). They turned south to Nazareth and the Jezreel Valley. Jerusalem followed, the condition of the Jewish Quarter of the Old City being for Weizmann utterly depressing. For generations, old Jews had gone there simply to await death, so

[99] *Trial and Error* (ibid)

as to ascend to heaven from Judaism's holy city. The whole Quarter was desperately poor and wretched. All around could be seen churches and mosques, but no Jewish buildings of any importance.

Jerusalem is a city, like Rome, of seven hills. Only one was bare — Mount Scopus. Weizmann looked upon and made plans for this hill. (Ruppin was to acquire it with funds from Russian Zionist, Isaac Goldberg, in 1916 — the year before Jerusalem fell into the hands of the British.)

Weizmann and Chankin took in Haifa and saw the splendid views from the Carmel Range of mountains. Further south in Rechovot, he met the Eisenbergs, a family whose *Aliyah* from Pinsk he recalled. He decided that, one day, he would make his home in Rechovot (as, in 1937, he did). In Rishon-le-Zion, he met the Gluskins, who had also come from Pinsk. None of the settlement towns funded by Baron Edmond — Rishon-le-Zion, Petach Tikvah and Ness Zionah, in the centre, or Rosh Pinah, Mishmar Ha-Yarden and Metullah in the north — impressed Weizmann, for, subsidised as they were, they could not be considered as examples of Practical Zionism. Weizmann wrote:

> *"I found Achad Ha'am's criticisms, his observations on the paralysing effect of the Baron's well-meant paternalism, thoroughly justified."*[100]

Back in Jaffa, Weizmann felt uncomfortable, if not a little fearful. The Arab population was palpably resentful of the Jews. Achad Ha'am had preceded Weizmann in 1891 and had written:

> *"... if the time comes when the life of our people in Erez Israel develops to the point of encroaching upon the native population, they will not yield easily their place."*[101]

Weizmann, too, sensed that, as *Aliyah* increased, Arab

[100] *Trial and Error* (ibid)

[101] *Chaim Weizmann: A Biography*, Norman Rose (ibid)

opposition to the Jews would also grow. He made a mental note to deal with the issue.

Despite all the negativity he felt, when, on his return to England, Vera demanded of her peripatetic husband: "*'Forget you are a Zionist and tell me what was so wonderful about Palestine'* he replied: *'It was magnificent.'* Vera, dissatisfied with this vague generalisation, persisted. *'The air,'* he expanded. *'It is difficult to understand without experiencing it. The air is crystal pure, so pure that you can look back over three thousand years of history.'*"[102]

In parallel with this romanticised view, Weizmann was convinced in his assessment that it would be the continuous practical work that would one day make the Jewish homeland in *Eretz Yisrael* a reality.

~~~

[102] *Chaim Weizmann: A Biography*, Norman Rose (ibid)
~~~

7

THE QUIET YEARS

In the year of Weizmann's first visit to *Eretz Yisrael*, 1907, the Wissotzky Tea Company recruited Achad Ha'am to run its London office. He and Weizmann picked up where they had left off in Berlin ten years earlier, the scientist going to London as often as he could afford the journey to stay with the philosopher. Weizmann's admiration for Achad Ha'am's high principles, his perfectionism and his insight was unqualified. Also, he was at his most relaxed when in Achad Ha'am's company.

In the years 1906 to 1914, the former bitter in-fighting within the Zionist movement had gone, along with Territorials. Synthetic Zionism had quelled the struggle between the Politicals and the Practicals. The members of the Democratic Faction, who had started out as a young splinter group, were gliding towards middle age. (In 1914, Weizmann turned 40.) The phenomenon of the pogrom, as a regular feature of Russian Jewish life in the Pale and further east in Russia itself, had largely consumed itself by 1907[103]; but the damage had been done and, between 1880 and 1914, some two and a half million Jews left the lands lying to the east of Europe. Palestine was not predominantly their destination, however.

THE LAND OF THE FREE

In October 1886, the Statue of Liberty had been dedicated on the eponymous island at the entrance to New York City, at the end of the long sea voyage from Europe. The Jewish-American poet, Emma Lazarus (1849-1887) had composed a message for the incomers, which was inscribed on the statue's base, the final words of which gained international fame:

[103] Only to arise again in the Ukraine after the Russian Revolution of 1917, some 100,000 Jews being murdered there between 1918 and 1921.

Give me your tired, your poor,
Your huddled masses yearning to breathe free,
The wretched refuse of your teeming shore.
Send these, the homeless, tempest-tost to me,
I lift my lamp beside the golden door!

In other words, the welcome mat was out at the threshold to the New World, and the free world, for Jews, amongst many others, including the Irish, Germans and Italians, who also sensed that the Land of the Free would be their land of opportunity. Those who did not wish to await the return of Russian slaughter, nor perhaps indefinitely the abandonment of repression and discrimination — it was at least a millennium old — took to the Atlantic and headed for emancipation, American-style. Zionism was the last thing on their minds. (The Jewish community of America would produce a large number of powerful personalities, some of whom would assist Weizmann's Zionist project, including Supreme Court Judge Louis Brandeis, Richard Gottheil, Rabbi Stephen S Wise of the Zionist Organization of America and Judge Samuel I Rosenman, whom we shall encounter later in these pages.)

ALIYAH

Immigration to the Holy Land had not completely shrivelled, however. In the First *Aliyah* (1882-1903) approximately 35,000 Jews, and in the Second *Aliyah* (1904-1914) approximately 40,000 more, arrived in *Eretz Yisrael*. Although the statistics vary according to sources, clearly the Holy Land was no longer attracting only those who anticipated an early death; rather those who would, with their offspring, build a new country. In any event, while the USA could absorb millions of immigrants, the days when the modern State of Israel would be able to do the same were almost half a century distant.

DR VERA WEIZMANN

Vera qualified to practise medicine in England in 1913. Amongst the first women doctors in Manchester, she became a medical officer of Manchester Corporation, responsible for the care of pregnant women and infants in their first year of life, practising in seven clinics. She developed advanced methods for monitoring infant diet and growth. In the course of her work, she met C P Scott, the editor of *The Manchester Guardian*, and it is claimed that she introduced him to her husband.[104]

DISAPPOINTMENT

Between 1905 and 1914, Weizmann published dozens of scientific papers derived from his work in his laboratory in Manchester and registered 21 patents.[105] By 1910, Weizmann greatly desired two prizes: a chair, as a professor of chemistry, and fellowship of the Royal Society. This latter would, if attained, confer great kudos on him and level the playing field with Perkin and others; but first he would have to become a naturalised Briton. He turned to Dr Gaster and others of influence to expedite his application and, in November 1910, Weizmann became a British citizen. Nevertheless, he failed to become elected a fellow of the Royal Society. If he was downhearted at this disappointment, it does not appear to have impeded his progress.

THE TENTH ZIONIST CONGRESS

The Tenth Zionist Congress was held in Basel in 1911. In at least a tacit acknowledgement of the work of Ben-Yehuda, the proceedings were, for the first time, conducted in Hebrew. Otto Warburg succeeded David Wolffsohn as President. Weizmann's formula for harmony in the movement, Synthetic Zionism, was formally adopted by Congress. There was much discussion of the practical work being done in *Eretz Yisrael* and of Zionist relations with the Arabs of Palestine.

[104] But others claim that Sacher made this all-important introduction.

[105] Source: Weizmann Archives.

THE WEIZMANN PROCESS

The 1911 Congress was quite agreeable for Weizmann, and professionally he was about to make greater progress than even he would be able to appreciate for several years.

Weizmann was investigating the uses of fermentation processes in a quest for synthetic rubber. To advance his knowledge of biological chemistry and bacteriology as special branches of his field of organic chemistry, he made several visits to the world-leading Pasteur Institute in Paris.

The large-scale production of rubber (that is, beyond the laboratory) requires, amongst other constituents, butanol (butyl alcohol), which was not readily available in large quantities. Weizmann began to experiment with producing butanol by fermenting bacteria with sugar. Eventually he discovered that maize[106] harboured bacteria. Next, he found that such bacteria could be encouraged to mutate into a fast-fermenting "soup". By distillation, the alcohol, the butanol and the acetone could be separated. Weizmann observed that the "soup" contained twice as much butanol as acetone and three times as much acetone as alcohol. (Even Weizmann had no inkling at this time the massive implications of his discoveries.)

Perkin was unimpressed, telling Weizmann to "pour it down the drain", and Weizmann endured some humiliation by Perkin[107] over the attempted, but abortive, application of fermentation chemistry to the commercial production of synthetic rubber. While at one time they had been close friends, Perkin and

[106] Maize is rich in carbohydrates and vitamins A, B & C. Today, thanks in large part to Chaim Weizmann, maize plants constitute the main subject material for the study of biochemistry and genetics. It is an important constituent in chemicals, explosives, paint, dyes, pharmaceuticals and solvents.

[107] Perkin witheringly referred to the outcome of Weizmann's work as "butyl futile".

Weizmann became adversaries; but Weizmann would prove the ultimate victor thanks to his self-belief and tenacity.

In December 1912, Perkin was appointed a professor at Oxford University. Weizmann expected to succeed to Perkin's Manchester chair, but it went to Perkin's brother-in-law, a mere readership in biochemistry being conferred on Weizmann.[108] For a brief moment, Weizmann thought to abandon his chemistry and to take a job:

> *"in the Zionist bureaucracy at Berlin. ... Vera, who could be stubborn, put her foot down. She had completed her medical examinations in Manchester and was not prepared to qualify again at Berlin. She told him so. Then she played her trump: 'You have already said that the road to Palestine is through London. Our road to Palestine will never go through Berlin.' Chaim did not speak to her for three weeks; but he stayed in Manchester: and, as a result, the world changed."*[109]

Shortly after that, Weizmann achieved his second doctorate, conferred by Manchester University, and he attained complete independence in his laboratory.

Weizmann continued developing his fermentation methodology. A bacterium emerged: "*Clostridium acetobutylicum*" (based on the name of the products used). This became known in scientific circles as "The Weizmann Organism" and his fermentation methodology became known as "The Weizmann Process".

They were set to change history.

---

[108] Weizmann confided to Vera that the incident had been driven by anti-Semitism and there may have been more of a trace of that; but there had also been a long episode of vying for the commercialisation of certain fermentation processes. Jehuda Reinharz covers the events in admirable detail in his *Chaim Weizmann: The Making of a Zionist Leader* (ibid).

[109] *Memoirs*, Israel Sieff (ibid)

8

THE APPROACH OF WAR AND THE SHELL CRISIS

THE MANCHESTER SCHOOL[110]

The Manchester School of Zionism evolved within a few years before the 1914 outbreak of the hostilities that were first called *"The Great War"*, then *"The War to End All Wars"* and finally (in 1939, on the outbreak of the Second World War) "*The First World War*". While in London, Jewry was fragmented, with rifts between the assimilationists and the Zionists, conversely in Manchester, both historically and later as galvanized by Weizmann's efforts, there was an almost complete unity of support for Zionism.

A formidable team of Manchester intellectuals and businessmen was about to leverage their talents way beyond their initial aspirations. The leader was undoubtedly Weizmann, but he was greatly assisted by Harry Sacher, Leon Simon, Samuel Landman and Norman Bentwich, each a considerable personality in his own right yet all becoming his disciples (with, as from 1913, Simon Marks and Israel Sieff) — and each of them had connections with the British establishment that would expand the group.

The Manchester School developed its work in what we would today see as a thoroughly modern manner:

> *"Propaganda was a priority for the group. Zionist education*

---

[110] The term *The Manchester School*, (otherwise *Manchester Liberalism*, *Manchester Capitalism* and *Manchesterism*) originally applied to the political, economic and social movements of the 19th century that originated in Manchester. The Free Trade Movement won acceptance of the argument (that has predominated for the last hundred years) that free trade, pursued democratically, leads to a more equitable society, and makes essential products available to all. Accordingly, Manchester was the natural home of those of a liberal frame of mind, such as that of C P Scott.

was at a low ebb at that time in England, and, in their opinion, what little material there was failed to properly root Zionist faith in Zionist philosophy and history. The result was their involvement in 'The Zionist Banner', which had been produced and printed by Joseph Massel since March 1910. Pamphlets were printed which discussed the main problems and gave essential information about Zionist history and activity, and propaganda work was also undertaken among the Jewish youth at the Universities."[111]

There would be help from beyond the Jewish community too.

THE POLITICIANS

In Protestant England, the British establishment of the early 20th century continued to hold the views of the proto-Zionists[112], especially within the Liberal party, which alternated with the Conservatives in government[113]. In 1895, Charles Prestwich Scott had been elected a Liberal MP for Manchester East. He was also the editor of *The Manchester Guardian*, the highly-respected and essentially-liberal newspaper, which gave him considerable influence in Parliamentary circles. Preoccupied with acquiring ownership of the newspaper he edited, Scott gave up his parliamentary career in 1906. Nevertheless, he retained his standing as an authoritative figure in the Liberal party in particular and in the establishment generally. He was to become a great ally of Weizmann.

The leading Liberal party figure was the mercurial David Lloyd George, known as "The Welsh Wizard" for his political skills (whom, or whose law firm, Herzl had consulted over the ill-fated Uganda Proposal). Lloyd George and Scott agreed on few issues

[111] The Centre for Jewish Studies of Manchester University: http://www.manchesterjewishstudies.org/manchester-school/

[112] See chapter 3.

[113] Although Disraeli had been a Conservative and was not the only such politician to incline towards the Jews.

but on Zionism, as sympathisers both, their views coincided.

In 1915, Lloyd George would be appointed Minister of Munitions and, from 1916, Prime Minister. In 1917, Arthur Balfour (whom Weizmann had met in 1906) would be Foreign Minister. From 1911 to 1915, Winston Churchill, whom Weizmann had first met in 1905, was First Lord of the Admiralty. Some explanation of the significance of that term, and of British history, is called for if the importance of Chaim Weizmann to the British Empire — and to the Balfour Declaration — is to be understood. First, however, it is necessary to appreciate what it was that stimulated Weizmann to aspire to seek Jewish redemption from senior British politicians and statesmen as war approached.

PARIS

In July 1914, Dr Chaim and Dr Vera Weizmann took their son, Benjamin, to cusp-of-war Europe. Weizmann met Baron Edmond de Rothschild in Paris the following month, just after war had been declared by Germany on France and by Britain on Germany and its allies, the Central Powers[114]. Weizmann reports on his meeting with the Baron:

> *"With real astonishment I heard him reiterate my own half-formulated views. Yes, he said, things looked black but we* [the Allies] *would win the war. And this was the time for us to act so that we* [the Jews] *might not be forgotten in the general settlement. He urged me, immediately on my return to England, to get in touch with British statesmen. It was his opinion — and I agreed with him — that the war would spread to the Middle East, and there things of great significance to us would happen."*[115]

With the Baron's words ringing in his ears, Weizmann met in

[114] Germany, Austria-Hungary, Bulgaria and the Ottoman Empire.

[115] *Trial and Error* (ibid)

London with Achad Ha'am, Leon Simon and Samuel Landman:

"We talked vaguely of great possibilities now opening, but no concrete plan of action emerged."[116]

Back home in Manchester, Weizmann spoke about these matters to Simon Marks and Israel Sieff, to whom he had been introduced by Sacher the year before. Highly successful businessmen, nationally respected for their trading and staff policies, they were fast turning a small family clothing company (which Marks' father had started in 1894 as a penny store in Leeds market) into a nationwide company which would have a presence in almost every British town. Both came from families in the Pale and lived in Manchester. If they were not avid Zionist activists before, they certainly were once Weizmann had worked his magic on them. The Manchester School of Zionism was evolving.

Towards the end of 1914, C P Scott at last entered Weizmann's life, by chance at a social gathering[117]. Weizmann writes that, had they not then met, he would soon have made a point of seeking out and introducing himself to Scott, whom he knew (almost certainly from Sacher) to be sympathetic to Zionist aspirations.

They agreed they needed a long discussion, so met up a few days later. When they did so, Weizmann explained to Scott the *"universal tragedy"* of the Jewish Question, the strains within the Zionist movement and the Zionists' *"hopes and aspirations for Palestine, of the little we had already done there, and of our almost Messianic dreams — such as they appeared then — for the future."*[118] According to Weizmann, Scott responded by promising to put Weizmann in touch with the Chancellor of the

---

[116] *Trial and Error* (ibid)

[117] Both Vera Weizmann and Harry Sacher separately claimed the credit for the introduction of the editor and the scientist.

[118] *Trial and Error* (ibid)

Exchequer[119], Lloyd George.

On 3 December, Scott announced to Weizmann, on his arriving in London: "*We're going to have breakfast at nine o'clock with Mr Lloyd George.*" Weizmann reports:

> *"There were present at this meeting, besides Lloyd George, Mr Scott and myself, Herbert Samuel, then the President of the Local Government Board under Asquith, and Josiah Wedgwood, then to me an unknown figure. I was terribly shy and suffered from suppressed excitement, knowing how much depended on this meeting.*
>
> ...
>
> *Lloyd George began to fire questions at me, about Palestine, about our colonies there, about the number of Jews in the country and the number who could go there. I answered as best I could. Then I had the surprise of my life when Herbert Samuel interposed some helpful remarks. I had been frightened out of my wits by his presence. It became clear that every person in the room was favourably disposed, and an atmosphere was created which warmed and encouraged me."*[120]

Plainly, the meeting with Lloyd George was a success, for not only did he promise to give the matter serious thought but also he suggested Weizmann meet with Balfour and Prime Minister Asquith. Weizmann did not say that he had already met Balfour in 1906, the night before his disastrous electoral defeat, as he "*thought that old history*".[121]

In order to reach Balfour, Weizmann spoke to his old friend and neighbour in Manchester, Professor Samuel Alexander, whom he knew to be well-acquainted with the Conservative party MP

---

[119] That is, minister of finance.

[120] *Trial and Error* (ibid)

[121] *Trial and Error* (ibid)

and former PM. Alexander duly made contact and heard back from Balfour:

> *"Dear Sam: Weizmann needs no introduction, I still remember our conversation in 1906."*[122]

When they met, Balfour told Weizmann:

> *"You know, I was thinking of that conversation of ours, and I believe that when the guns stop firing you may get your Jerusalem"* and later at Balfour's home they *"had a tremendous talk which lasted several hours."*[123]

Weizmann had an innate fear of the destructive effect that some Jews in high places, many of them opposed to a Jewish national home, could have on non-Jews. Accordingly, upon encountering Herbert Samuel at the Lloyd George breakfast, Weizmann was nervous about Samuel's potential negative influence. Weizmann was, therefore, both surprised and delighted to learn from Samuel that he was preparing a positive case for a Jewish state in Palestine to present to the Prime Minister. Weizmann writes:

> *"I received from Herbert Samuel a memorandum headed 'The Future of Palestine'. He goes on to argue at considerable length and with some vehemence in favour of the British annexation of Palestine, a country of the size of Wales, much of it barren mountain and part of it waterless. He thinks we might plant in this not very promising territory about three or four million European Jews and that this would have a good effect on those who are left behind.* [He added, a few weeks later:] *Curiously enough, the only other partisan of this proposal is Lloyd George, and I need not say he does not care a damn for the Jews or their past or their future, but thinks it will be an outrage to let the Holy Places pass into the possession or under the protectorate of*

[122] *Trial and Error* (ibid)

[123] *Trial and Error* (ibid)

'agnostic and atheistic' France."[124]

Thus it was that, as the Great War got underway, the Manchester School of Zionism, and key figures at the centre of the British government, were psychologically, not to say emotionally, primed to will a solution to the Jewish Question in the Holy Land.

THE BRITISH EMPIRE

Now it is necessary to appreciate the power of Great Britain in 1914, and how it almost became emasculated in 1915 — until rescued by Dr Chaim Weizmann.

At the start of the 20th century, the British Empire was at its zenith. The constituent parts of the Empire, and British spheres of influence, included territories as far flung as: much of West Africa and (as demonstrated by the Uganda Proposal) East Africa; Canada, Australia and New Zealand (independent dominions, but fiercely British in outlook and loyalty); several Caribbean islands, some parts of South America and the Falkland Islands, off the coast of Argentina; the Azores and other strategically-placed islands, including several in the South Seas of the Pacific Ocean; Singapore, Hong Kong and Burma; the jewel in the crown of the British Empire, India (which then included today's Pakistan and Bangladesh); and Gibraltar, Malta, Cyprus and Egypt in the Mediterranean.

The Suez Canal linked Britain with its eastern possessions and passed through Egypt, which, together with Britain, administered Sudan. Until after World War II, fully one third of the earth's land surface, as represented on maps and school books (those published in Britain, at least), was coloured red to signify British influence.

While over the centuries Portugal, Spain and later Holland had

[124] *Trial and Error* (ibid)

been great maritime nations, by the turn of the 20th century there was just one: Great Britain. To be, and remain, a great maritime nation — the only one with global reach — Britain required two navies: the merchant navy, for moving around the goods of and persons serving the Empire, and, for the protection of both Empire and merchant fleet, the Royal Navy. The latter was one of the most extensive and powerful institutions the world had ever seen. That did not mean, however, that it could not be challenged.

GERMANY

Germany did not become a unified nation until Bismarck brought that about in 1871[125]. Overnight, it became the most populous country in Europe, it faced both east (to Poland and Russia) and west (to France and Britain) and it had some overseas holdings, mainly a handful of colonies in Africa. In June 1888, Wilhelm II, on the death of his father, was anointed Kaiser (Emperor) of Germany and King of Prussia. Along with the crowned heads of many European countries (and Russia), Wilhelm was a descendant, and the eldest grandchild, of Queen Victoria, and looked on the more powerful and influential Britain with envy.

Bismarck had maintained a fragile balance of power between Germany, France and Russia, but there was in Germany both an innate antagonism towards Russia and growing popular resentment of the British Empire. On reaching the age of 75 in 1890, Bismarck resigned at the Kaiser's insistence. With the departure of the pacifist Bismarck, the Russians, fearful of a reversal of policy in Berlin, quickly aligned themselves with France. The slow but visible crumbling of the Austro-Hungarian Empire led to a series of interlocking mutual defence treaties being signed in the early years of the 20th century. By 1914, Germany was highly vulnerable. Of course, that state of affairs did not happen overnight but was built up over time. So, too, was

[125] See chapter 2.

the German Navy.

Wilhelm had started his rearmament programme in 1872 and by the outbreak of the Great War, over forty years later, Germany had many powerful naval vessels — modern, innovative and well-equipped. Germany's fleet was based mainly close to home, while both Britain and its main ally, France, had far-flung empires to protect. Britain had by far the most warships, almost double the number in the German fleet[126]. Of course, all of them had guns of varying sizes, all the guns fired shells and shells need explosives, not merely for their warheads but also as propellants.

THE NEED FOR EXPLOSIVES

Quite apart from the coming battles at sea, vast land armies of both sides were, within six months after the outbreak of hostilities, locked into trench warfare in northern France. Millions of troops faced each other, and would engage in dreadful combat with mass casualties on both sides. Before any charge from the trenches could be ordered, there would be days of massive bombardment of the enemy with field guns of varying sizes from simple trench mortars to massive howitzers. Every soldier had a rifle; some were issued with machine guns. All weapons need ammunition and, again, that means explosive propellants.

As was shown in the American Civil War, the winner of a war in modern times would be the one with the greater understanding of, and ability to undertake, the mass production of the means to wage war.

126 **COMPARATIVE NAVAL LINE-UPS, 1914**

Britain	France	Britain & France	Germany
609	399	1,008	334

DEATH KNELL OF THE OTTOMAN EMPIRE

In the summer of 1914, a series of events (which we need not consider here) led Germany to attack France, which had a decade-old mutual defence pact, the *Entente Cordiale,* with Great Britain. Britain declared war on Germany on 4 August 1914. Aligned with Germany was Turkey, and its Ottoman Empire that had dominated the Middle East for almost four centuries. On the evening of the first day of the war, Prime Minister Asquith announced that one British war aim would be the dismemberment of the Ottoman Empire, adding:

> *"It is the Ottoman Government, and not we, who have rung the death knell of Ottoman dominion not only in Europe but in Asia. The Turkish Empire has committed suicide and dug its own grave with its own hand."*[127]

The British War Cabinet first discussed Zionism and Palestine in November 1914, three months after Britain's declaration of war on Turkey. The Chancellor of the Exchequer, David Lloyd George, referred to the "ultimate destiny" of Palestine. Later Lloyd George assured Herbert Samuel that he was very keen to see a Jewish state established in Palestine. Samuel, in turn, later explained to Foreign Minister Edward Grey his aspirations for a Jewish state in Palestine, and its importance to the British Empire. Grey was fully receptive. An unremarked count-down had begun.

TRENCH WARFARE

As early as the end of 1914, the war was without movement. The trenches led from Belgium to the French-Swiss border, some 765 kms distant. The hunger for artillery shells was insatiable and the British guns were fast running out of anything to fire. The Royal Navy, too, was suffering from severe shortages of shells for its big guns. By May 1915, so serious was the shell

[127] Reported in The Times (of London) November 10, 1914.

crisis that most British cannon had been reduced to firing just four shells a day. It seemed the war would be lost, not in the trenches of Flanders in northern France, but in the factories of Great Britain.

It is trite to say: every army is condemned to fight the last war; but, for the conduct of the Great War, the British had developed new battlefield tactics of bombarding enemy lines with heavy artillery without respite before the troops would be ordered to "go over the top" and out of the foul and sodden trenches, where they had sat awaiting action for several weeks. That strategy had, however, been imperfectly developed in terms of ammunition for, as the British were about to discover — in the so-called Shell Crisis of 1915 — they were unable to produce sufficient shells for the guns of their land armies, let alone the Royal Navy also. The reason was that they lacked the means of production of the an essential constituent, cordite.

For a generation, cordite had been the British military's preferred propellant for its ammunition, since it is smokeless (so does not give away the shooter's position) and burns at a temperature that will not unduly overheat the gun barrel. For the continuous production of cordite, however, it was vital to enjoy a steady supply of acetone. Before the Great War, acetone was produced:

> *"mainly from refining minerals such as calcium acetate, which came from Germany and Central Europe. But now Germany was an enemy state, so Britain had to find another source of large quantities of acetone — and fast."*[128]

THE SHELL CRISIS

Following the disastrous Battle of Aubers Ridge in Flanders on 9 May 1915, in which British artillery had proved completely ineffectual in preparing the ground for the infantry's attack, *The*

---

[128] http://davidson.weizmann.ac.il/en/online/sciencehistory/scientific-context-balfour-declaration

Times of 14 May announced: *"Need for shells: British attacks checked: Limited supply the cause: A Lesson From France,"* and continued: *"The want of an unlimited supply of high explosives was a fatal bar to our success."*

Thanks to press freedom in the UK, the military crisis in France quickly led to a parliamentary crisis in London. The finger of blame having been pointed at the Liberal government, it quickly fell and a coalition government followed. Asquith, still the PM, created a new Ministry of Munitions and appointed Lloyd George to head it. Tasked with increasing the supply of artillery shells to the forces, the new ministry set about building munitions factories across the country and comprehensively putting the civilian economy onto a war footing.

Dr Chaim Weizmann, left to his own devices after the rift with Perkin and gaining autonomy in his laboratory, had, shortly before the outbreak of war, applied for a patent for *"Improvements in the Bacterial Fermentation of Carbohydrates and in Bacterial Cultures for the same"* (for which, in 1915, he was, as Charles Weizmann, granted British patent no: 4845[129]).

At the outbreak of war, British scientists were asked to notify the War Office of their work insofar as it could assist the war effort. Weizmann responded with information on the Weizmann Process. After the Shell Crisis hit, he was quickly invited to the Admiralty in London to attend, as Weizmann relates:

> *"a meeting with Sir Frederick Nathan, head of the powder department. He explained to me that there was a serious shortage of acetone, which was the solvent in making cordite. Without this solvent it would be necessary to make far-reaching changes in the naval guns. I was invited to work on this problem. For a few months I had to carry the double responsibility of teaching in Manchester and putting up a pilot plant in London. My week was split into two parts: four days at the university, three in London. I travelled*

[129] https://patents.google.com/patent/GB191504845A/en

backwards and forwards by night, to save time. It was nerve-racking, and not too productive. And so the university was requested to relieve me of most of my teaching work, and I was engaged by the Government. To finish the business, my new employers brought me into the presence of the First Lord of the Admiralty, who was at that time Mr Winston Churchill [whom Weizmann had met in Manchester in 1905]*."*

Weizmann describes Churchill as: *"brisk, fascinating, charming and energetic"* and continues: *"Almost his first words were: 'Well, Dr Weizmann, we need thirty thousand tons of acetone. Can you make it?' Weizmann replied: '... if I were somehow able to produce a ton of acetone, I would be able to multiply that by any factor you chose. Once the bacteriology of the process is established, it is only a question of brewing. I must get hold of a brewing engineer from one of the big distilleries, and we will set about the preliminary task. I shall naturally need the support of the Government to obtain the people, the equipment, the emplacements and the rest of it. I myself can't even determine what will be required.'*

'I was given carte blanche by Mr Churchill and the department, and I took upon myself a task which was to tax all my energies for the next two years, and which was to have consequences which I did not then foresee.'"[130]

THE SOLUTION OF THE SHELL CRISIS

Weizmann found that his Process, of acetone production based on corn, would indeed work on an industrial scale. Employing the Process, under Weizmann's guidance and management, some 600,000 pounds of acetone a year were produced, enough to satisfy the British forces' massive demand for cordite. Shell production rose from 500,000 units in the first five months of the war to 16.4 million in 1915 — that is from 100,000 monthly at first to 1.4 million per month, once the Weizmann Process was

[130] *Trial and Error* (ibid)

fully underway.

As the war ground on, Britain started to run short of food and required all of her corn for foodstuffs. Accordingly, the manufacture of acetone was transferred to Canada, where the British government (in the guise of British Acetones Limited) operated the Weizmann Process from August 1916 until the War's end in November 1918. There, 6 million pounds of acetone and about twice that amount of butanol, were produced. By 1917, thanks to the new munitions factories and the women that worked in them — and Weizmann — the forces of the British Empire were firing more than 50 million shells a year. By the end of the war, the British Army alone had fired 170 million shells.

"Charles" Weizmann filed, at the USPTO, on 26 December 1916, US patent no: 1,315,585[131]: *"Production of Acetone and Alcohol by Bacteriological Processes"* (as to which see panel 6) and, on 1 May 1918, US patent no: 1,437,697[132]: *"Fermentation Process for the Production of Acetone and Butyl Alcohol"*. What those titles fail to disclose are their colossal military, political and diplomatic significance, possibly unique in the history of patents — and as the story of one man's unique accomplishments.

6

THE ROBUSTNESS OF THE ALL-IMPORTANT PATENT

Weizmann improved his financial standing over the years by the sale of his patents, the most important of which was almost certainly that for the *Production of Acetone and Alcohol by Bacteriological Processes* (mentioned above), which he sold to Guaranty Trust Company of New York and the Butacet Corporation.

In 1931, this became the subject of litigation in a patent

[131] https://patents.google.com/patent/US1437697A/en

[132] https://patents.google.com/patent/US1437697A/en

infringement action. The Delaware U.S. District Court handed down its judgment[133] to the effect that the "*process of the Weizmann patent is a bacteriological fermentation process for the production of acetone and butyl alcohol. ... Weizmann was not the first to produce acetone and butyl alcohol by a fermentation process. He made no such claim.*

Mere production of limited quantities of acetone and butyl alcohol by a fermentation process was not the problem with which Dr Weizmann was dealing. The problem with which he was dealing and successfully solved was that of isolating a particular bacteria or a culture containing some particular bacteria that would produce butyl alcohol and acetone in commercial quantities better than any other known bacteria.

Weizmann discovered a particular species of bacteria new to bacteriologists and invented the process of successfully employing them. This task called for the exercise of inventive genius. He obtained his patent, not for the bacteria per se, but for a process which consists in the employment of certain bacteria to produce large yields of acetone and butyl alcohol under aerobic or anaerobic conditions."

While it cannot be said that Weizmann single-handedly won the Great War for Great Britain, it is plain that he alone may have prevented British defeat in 1915[134]. He thereby came, not merely to the notice, but indeed to the rescue, of the Empire, the country and three major political figures: Balfour, Churchill and Lloyd George. The first two had met him a decade previously and not forgotten him; while he had met Lloyd George the year before. All had Zionist sympathies. The question now was how to create a new, three-way, synthesis: between Weizmann's attainments for the British war effort, the Zionist inclinations of the British political establishment for the solution to the Jewish Question

[133] http://law.justia.com/cases/federal/district-courts/F2/54/400/1498055/

[134] We cannot know whether the alternative of redesigning and reworking all Britain's guns and cannon to suit another propellant could have been achieved in time to save them but it seems unlikely.

and the ambitions of the Manchester School of Zionism.

CODA: The eleven year old Chaim Weizmann had foretold that the path to Zion would pass through England; now the redemptive scientist and inspirational Zionist had the opportunity to fulfil his own childhood prediction.

9

WHAT MANNER OF REWARD?

An oft-quoted exchange between Balfour and Weizmann runs as follows:

> Balfour: "Dr Weizmann, how can the Crown reward you for your invaluable work for the Admiralty?"
>
> Weizmann: "The only reward I desire is a homeland in Palestine for the Jewish people."

but it seems that this story is apocryphal for, according to Weizmann himself:

> *"Lloyd George, in his War Memories, dates his acquaintance with me, and his interest in our movement, from the time ... when I came to work for the Ministry of Munitions, and centres the relationship on the subject of my chemical work for the Government during the second half of the war. His narrative makes it appear that the Balfour Declaration was a reward given me by the Government when Lloyd George became Prime Minister, for my services to England. I almost wish that it had been as simple as that, and that I had never known the heartbreaks, the drudgery and the uncertainties which preceded the Declaration."*[135]

On the other hand, Weizmann clearly appreciated, as he confided to Dorothy de Rothschild that, if he were to be successful in his employment with His Majesty's Government, *"it would help our Palestinian work very considerably."*[136]

While the outcome was sometimes in doubt and the route to Jerusalem was an exceedingly complex one, if Weizmann did question whether there was a direct line from him to the Declaration, he will have been in a minority of one. At the very

---

[135] *Trial and Error* (ibid)

[136] *Chaim Weizmann: A Biography,* Norman Rose (ibid)

least, the Balfour Declaration was catalysed by the chemistry behind the mass production of acetone — the Weizmann Process — and the chemistry between him and many key figures that was, in each case, engendered by his charm. They were the essential factors that led to the all-important 67 word letter from British Foreign Minister, Balfour, to Lord Walter Rothschild of 2 November 1917.

By September 1915, Weizmann had resigned from Manchester University and moved to London. Weizmann was retained under contracts with two government departments to advise on the production of acetone, and was provided with a well-equipped laboratory in the prestigious Lister Institute in London, where he could conduct constant testing for quality control of the large-scale acetone production. In addition, in 1916, he was appointed superintendent of His Majesty's government's laboratories.

ZIONISM AND OPPOSITION TO ZIONISM

Detractors of Weizmann's efforts claim that it was merely because it served the interests of the British Empire to have the Jews emplaced at the far end of the Mediterranean Sea, east of the Suez Canal, and that all it took was for Allenby to conquer Jerusalem and the Jews were assured of their homeland. The reality was not only much more complex but also securing the Declaration was the result of immense efforts by the Manchester School, those whom they recruited to their cause and the extraordinarily focussed leadership and unremitting efforts of Chaim Weizmann.

There were many who were not so recruited — Jews in the communities mainly of London (but elsewhere in the UK, too) and some in the upper echelons of the establishment. They may not have been motivated by ill-will but there was unquestionably, in the breast of Jewish opposition, a broad sinew of selfishness. They did not wish to be accused of dual loyalties, nor did they wish to appear ungrateful to their British hosts who had given them a tolerant home in an intolerant world, and they certainly did not wish to be expelled from Britain to Palestine; but they could have given no thought for the welfare of millions of other Jews who had not been so fortunate as to make it to the United Kingdom or (for there was similar opposition there) the United States of America. Weizmann and his colleagues would have to fight those tendencies all the way.

Likewise, while the Manchester School identified and recruited many non-Jewish actors of goodwill towards their Zionist project, there were many more Gentiles who, for reasons ranging from ignorance to hostility, opposed the concept of a Jewish Homeland.

THE GENTILE SUPPORTERS

One Gentile, however, who was fiercely supportive of Jewish ambitions for Palestine was C P Scott. In March 1915 (that is before the Shell Crisis exploded onto the scene), Weizmann wrote to *The Manchester Guardian* owner-editor, as follows:

> *"The British cabinet is not only sympathetic towards the Palestinian aspirations of the Jews, but would like to see these aspirations realised. I understand Great Britain would be willing even to be the initiator of a proposal to that effect at the peace conference. But at the same time Great Britain would not like to be involved in any responsibilities. In other words, they would leave the organisation of the Jewish commonwealth as an independent political unit entirely to the care of the Jews. At the same time there is a view prevalent that it is not desirable that Palestine should belong to any great power"*

which shows both Weizmann's thinking at the time and the confidence that he was able to place in Scott.

Other great collaborators were to follow. Chief Secretary to the Cabinet, Sir Mark Sykes, a Conservative party politician and diplomatic adviser, particularly with regard to the Middle East, was to become central to Zionist ambitions. Sykes was introduced to Weizmann by Leopold Greenberg, the editor of the *Jewish Chronicle* in January 1917[137] and went on to guide Weizmann through the bureaucracy with which he would be confronted on an escalating basis.

The very mention of Sykes and others, such as Leopold Amery[138] (assistant secretary to the British War Cabinet in 1917 and one of the authors of the Balfour Declaration), William Ormsby-Gore (Parliamentary Private Secretary to Lord Alfred Milner and assistant secretary in the War Cabinet, with whom Weizmann struck up a personal friendship), Lord Milner himself (a key figure in the War Cabinet) and Sir Ronald Graham (a senior official in the Foreign Office), demonstrates that a wide network of high-level relationships was created, each personality destined to play a vital rôle in what would follow, and all bound together by the force of Weizmann's personality.

THE SYKES-PICOT AGREEMENT

Pursuant to British interests in the Middle East, as discussed in cabinet in November 1914, negotiations with their French allies got underway the following year. The initially secret Sykes-Picot Agreement of 16 May 1916 was formulated between Sir Mark Sykes and French lawyer and diplomat, François Georges-Picot, formerly a French Consul in Beirut. The signatories were Britain and France, while (pre-Soviet) Russia assented to it.

By the relevant provisions of the agreement[139]:

1. *France would acquire Lebanon and the Syrian shoreline;*
2. *Great Britain would acquire southern Mesopotamia, including Baghdad, and also the Mediterranean ports of*

---

[137] *Balfour and Weizmann: The Zionist, the Zealot and the Emergence of Israel*, Geoffrey Lewis (Continuum UK, 2009).

[138] His mother having been Jewish, he appears successfully to have kept his antecedents from his contemporaries.

[139] Just as would, at Yalta in 1944, Churchill, Roosevelt and Stalin carve out areas of influence after World War II.

Haifa and Acre;

3. *between the French and the British acquisitions there would be a confederation of Arab states or a single independent Arab state, divided into French and British spheres of influence; and*
4. *Jerusalem, because of the holy places, would be under an international régime.*
5. *Russia would have had Istanbul, the Turkish Straits and Armenia.*
6. *Within the delineated areas, the controlling powers were free to determine state boundaries.*

There was, however, nothing that would guarantee that the British would not, at the last moment, having conquered Palestine, deliver the nascent protectorate to the Arabs. Colonel T E Lawrence (Lawrence of Arabia)[140] had passed on promises on behalf of the British government to those Arabs who had, behind his flag, supported the British war effort in the region by sparking and pursuing the Arab Revolt to drive the Ottomans out of the Arabian Peninsula and the province of Syria. Some formal declaration of intent in favour of the Zionists was required (not that they knew of the Sykes-Picot danger at this time) if they were not to be overlooked.

ORGANISING THE ZIONISTS

Weizmann's time was greatly taken up with his three government contracts and the development of the relationships with the brilliant array of personalities that we have reviewed, so as to ensure that the prospect of a Jewish homeland in Palestine would emerge. The ground would need careful preparation. Accordingly, as he reports:

---

[140] The flamboyant T E Lawrence, or "Lawrence of Arabia", a junior British intelligence officer from Cairo, envisioned an independent post-war pan-Arabian state.

> *"Early in the spring of 1916 I called together the Manchester Zionists in a little room on Cheetham Hill and put the situation before them. I told them of my talks with Edmond de Rothschild, with Achad Ha'am, with Herbert Samuel and, above all, with the British statesmen. With the support of the Manchester Zionists I went to London, and there talked with Joseph Cowen, the chairman of the English Zionist Federation. We decided, as a first step, to publish a little book on Zionism. For, apart from a few pamphlets, mostly out of date, and some reports of the Congresses, there was nothing that could be put into the hands of British statesmen."*[141]

A political committee was formed, consisting of Nachum Sokolow, Joseph Cowen, Dr Gaster and Herbert Bentwich of the ZF, working in close consultation with the Rothschilds, Herbert Samuel, Achad Ha'am and, of course, Chaim Weizmann.

Thus was born and published — first in 1916 and then in successive print runs, hungrily consumed by Jew and Gentile alike — *Zionism and the Jewish Future*[142], edited by Harry Sacher. The twelve page introduction was written by Chaim Weizmann.[143]

In 1916, the burden of the preparatory work increased to the point where the facilities of the ZF needed to be recruited. An office was opened in Piccadilly, in the heart of London, and Simon Marks was released from the British Army to run it. Weizmann continues:

> *"The little office in Piccadilly became an important centre*

[141] *Trial and Error* (ibid)

[142] The whole pamphlet may be read at: https://archive.org/details/cu31924083937684

[143] Other contributors included Nachum Sokolow, Albert M. Hyamson, Dr Gaster, Leon Simon, R. Gottheil of (New York), S Tolkowsky, S Brodetsky, B Benas and Norman Bentwich.

> *towards which gravitated everything in Zionist life. .... A small group crystallised which gradually constituted itself a political committee. To it came those members of the Zionist Executive who passed through London. We had with us Achad Ha'am, Harry Sacher (who was now living in London), Israel Sieff, some Palestinians like Aaron Aaronson*[144]*, Tolkowsky and Dr Oettinger, who were extremely valuable because of their knowledge of Palestine and of its economic and agricultural possibilities and problems. ... From time to time we had the benefit of the advice of Herbert Samuel, of James de Rothschild, and of other members of the House of Commons. Later we had the help of Sir Alfred Mond....*"[145]

The Piccadilly office first published a periodical on 26 January 1917: *"Palestine"*. The object was, as Israel Sieff relates:

> *"to publicise the Zionist cause, and to try and impress everybody with the importance and resources of British Zionism. We were a lobby. We called ourselves the British Palestine Committee, and the office, the Palestine Bureau. Simon* [Marks] *and I put up the money, Harry Sacher edited the journal...*"[146]

It may now be clearly seen that the Balfour Declaration did not just materialise one fine day from a clear blue sky. Work that was wide-ranging and detailed was required — and it was just beginning.

GETTING INTO TOP GEAR

In the month of February of the fateful year, 1917, in which he

---

144 See also chapter 12 regarding *Nili*.

145 *Trial and Error* (ibid). In 1926, Mond created Imperial Chemical Industries (IC), one of the world's largest industrial corporations at the time.

146 *Memoirs*, Israel Sieff (ibid)

became the President of the ZF, Weizmann attended what he referred to as the *"first full-dress conference leading to the Balfour Declaration"* with Dr Gaster, Lord Walter Rothschild[147], Herbert Samuel, James de Rothschild, Nachum Sokolow, Joseph Cowen, Herbert Bentwich, Harry Sacher and Sir Mark Sykes, who attended in a private capacity, his cards doubtless pressed hard against his chest.

Two main points were agreed:

1. *no internationalisation (save for the Holy Places), but a British protectorate with full rights for the Jewish nation; and*
2. *the emergent Jewish homeland to be that of the "nation" and in Palestine alone, so that the Jews who went to Palestine would belong to the Jewish nation (and not become Arabs, Druses or Britons).*

Sykes spoke at length of the difficulties which confronted the ZF, but confirmed that he was lending the Zionists his diplomatic skills. Weizmann continues:

> *"Sir Mark began by revealing that he had long considered the question of Palestine and the Jews, and that the idea of a Jewish Palestine had his full sympathy; moreover, he understood entirely what was meant by 'nationality,' and there was no confusion in his mind on that point. His chief concern, at the moment, was the attitude of the Powers. ... Italy, he said, went on the principle of asking for whatever the French demanded. And France was the real difficulty. He could not understand French policy. The French wanted all Syria and a great say in Palestine. Sir Mark then went on*

---

[147] Lionel Walter Rothschild, 2nd Baron Rothschild, Baron de Rothschild, FRS (8 February 1868 - 27 August 1937), was a British banker, politician, zoologist, a scion of the Rothschild family and Conservative Member of Parliament for Aylesbury from 1899 until 1910. As an active Zionist and close friend of Chaim Weizmann, he worked on the evolving drafts of the Balfour Declaration.

to speak of the Arab problem, and of the rising Arab nationalist movement. Within a generation, he said, the movement would come into its own, for the Arabs had intelligence, vitality and linguistic unity. But he believed that the Arabs would come to terms with us — particularly if they received Jewish support in other matters."[148]

Utterly lacking in experience (except where Sykes could assist) in diplomacy, public administration or taxation, the little band at the ZF had only their experience as professionals, businessmen and thinkers upon which to draw. Nevertheless, they were able to give a good impression of how the Jewish state might look: democratic; rooted in the rule of law; a thrusting ambition to develop infrastructure, industry and agriculture; locally autonomous; supportive of institutions, existing and projected; and a right of citizenship for Jews from all over the world — a fair description of today's Israel. A first formal memorandum was prepared and delivered in February 1917 to Sir Mark Sykes, who took it to the British government.

There followed what would today be described as a media blitz, led by *The Manchester Guardian*, to prepare public opinion.

The following month, March, Weizmann spoke with Balfour, by then the British foreign minister, who explained that the French were indeed causing difficulties. In fact, much of the Zionist effort was calculated to avoid French involvement in Palestine for it was feared that they would not permit the emergence of a Jewish culture, the French believing their own to be universally supreme.

Then came what appeared to Weizmann to be the bombshell of 16 April 1917: Weizmann learned of the Sykes-Picot Agreement from C P Scott, who heard of it in Paris, and that:

"France was to obtain, after the war, not only northern

---

[148] *Trial and Error* (ibid)

> *Syria, but Palestine down to ... Lake Tiberias, ... the rest of Palestine ... to be internationalised."*[149]

While the agreement did not in fact (or in the end) so provide, the French would always have to be accommodated and they were not known for their flexibility.

AMERICA ENTERS THE WAR

Another ground-shaking event had occurred ten days earlier: on 6 April 1917, America entered the war. British Foreign Minister Balfour went to Washington DC. Given the arrangements for the future joint conduct of the war that would have to be planned, it is impressive that Zionism was on the agenda. As Weizmann reports:

> *"On April 20, Mr Balfour arrived in America on a special mission, and almost immediately met Justice Louis D Brandeis at a party at the White House. Mrs Dugdale, Balfour's biographer, reports ...Balfour remarked ... that Brandeis was in some ways the most remarkable man he had met in the United States. It seems, from such notes of these conversations as survive, that Balfour pledged his own personal support to Zionism. He had done it before to Dr. Weizmann, but now he was British Foreign Secretary. Mr Justice Brandeis seems to have become increasingly emphatic, during the course of the British Mission's visit, about the desire of American Zionists to see a British Administration in Palestine"*

which was to prove invaluable at the eleventh hour.

Given the rate of acetone production by the Weizmann Process was keeping the British war machine well supplied with cordite and shells, and the goodwill of the politicians at the very core of government, what could possibly go wrong?

---

[149] *Trial and Error* (ibid)

10

THE DECLARATION DECLARED

THE ASSIMILATIONISTS LASH OUT

In May 1917, the stresses within Anglo-Jewry fractured publicly. Those who had always been opposed to the Jewish Question being solved by the provision of a Jewish Homeland in Palestine secured the publication in *The Times* (presumably expecting a more accommodating stance than might have been provided by *The Manchester Guardian*) of a statement *"violently repudiating the Zionist position, and urging the Government against favourable action on our demands."*[150] They asserted that, being merely a religious community, the Jews could not claim a national home for themselves, so that:

> *"the most that could be demanded for the Jews of Palestine was enjoyment of religious and civil liberty, 'reasonable' facilities for immigration and colonisation, and 'such municipal privileges in towns and colonies as may be shown to be necessary.'"*

The timing — as the eleventh hour was perceived to be approaching — was intended by the assimilationist Jews to inflict maximum damage upon the Zionists, so the attack had to be answered promptly and effectively. Letters from the Ashkenazi and Sephardi Chief Rabbis, from Lord Walter Rothschild and from Dr Weizmann were published in *The Times*.

The treasonable attack on Zion by the assimilationists was, perversely, helpful, as it stimulated Weizmann and his colleagues to get the matter concluded. They agreed that, there having been considerable and sufficient discussion, the time had come for the government to come out openly with a declaration of its Palestine policy.

---

[150] *Trial and Error* (ibid)

Weizmann called on Sir Ronald Graham on 12 June and gave him detailed information indicating that in Germany[151]:

> *"orders have been given to treat Zionism as an important political factor in* [German] *policy ... Weizmann 'concluded by urging very strongly that it was desirable from every point of view that His Majesty's Government should give an open expression of their sympathy with, and support of, Zionist aims and should publicly recognize the justice of Jewish claims on Palestine.'"* [152]

Graham replied that it was plain that the government had already indicated its support[153] and the ball was plainly in Balfour's court. On 19 June, Weizmann and Lord Walter Rothschild met Foreign Minister Balfour. He asked that they prepare for his consideration some form of declaration.

Then a wild card was played. Brandeis tipped off Weizmann that an American delegation, en route to Palestine, might interfere with British plans, since its members might be more assimilationist than Zionist.

---

[151] The Germans were neither disinterested nor uninterested in Palestine. In 1898, Theodor Herzl had met the German Emperor Wilhelm II at the entrance to the *Mikveh Yisrael* agricultural college during Herzl's only visit to Palestine and, at the outbreak of war, the *Teknikum* technical college in Haifa had placed itself under German protection. Germany and Turkey were allies and Allenby's army was well short of Jerusalem in June 1917.

[152] *Britain and the Arab Middle East: World War I and its Aftermath*, Robert H. Lieshout (I B Tauris & Co Limited, London & New York, 2016). According to the publisher: *"Robert H. Lieshout is Emeritus Professor of International Relations at Radboud University in the Netherlands. He has published widely on the theory and history of international relations.... This book is based on extensive archival research spanning several decades, work completed with Elie Kedourie."*

[153] In *Trial & Error* (ibid), Weizmann appears to place this episode a year earlier; but the reader may conclude that the Lieshout/Kedourie version is the more accurate one.

Weizmann duly reported this to the British Government and they entrusted to him the task of dealing with it. Weizmann was despatched on a secret diplomatic mission to Gibraltar in early July, with all manner of papers and a security detail, to intercept the Americans. Weizmann must have done his job well for, after listening to him, the delegation promptly returned to the United States without embarking on the crossing of the Mediterranean. This episode serves to show how well-entrenched were both the Zionist project and Weizmann himself within the British government by this stage.

On his return, the first draft declaration, in course of preparation while Weizmann was away, was finalised. The draft, delivered to Balfour on 18 July, read as follows:

> His Majesty's Government, after considering the aims of the Zionist Organisation, accept the principle of recognising Palestine as the National Home of the Jewish people and the right of the Jewish people to build up its national life in Palestine under a protection to be established at the conclusion of peace, following upon the successful issue of the war.
>
> His Majesty's Government regard as essential for the realisation of this principle the grant of internal autonomy to the Jewish nationality in Palestine, freedom of immigration for Jews, and the establishment of a Jewish National Colonising Corporation for the re-establishment and economic development of the country.
>
> The conditions and forms of the internal autonomy and a Charter for the Jewish National Colonising Corporation should, in the view of His Majesty's Government, be elaborated in detail and determined with the representatives of the Zionist Organisation.

Weizmann writes that, after a month, he concluded that both the Foreign Office and the Prime Minister had approved the draft and all that remained was approval by the Cabinet, some members of which, as they had told Weizmann, were in agreement with the draft.

Several more weeks elapsed and there was still no word from the Cabinet. Weizmann made enquiries and learned that there had been a Cabinet meeting on 3 September, but Lloyd George, who was recovering from illness, and Balfour, who was on vacation, had both missed it. Edwin Montagu[154] — a notorious Jewish assimilationist — newly-appointed as a junior cabinet member, had contrived to attend the War Cabinet meeting and secured the dropping of the matter from the agenda, asserting that the Jews were members of a religion and were not a nation. The Cabinet had decided to adjourn further consideration until US President Wilson expressed his view on the Palestine issue.

A BARRAGE OF TELEGRAMS

Robert Cecil, representing Balfour, cabled the president's assistant, Colonel House[155]:

> *"We are being pressed here for a declaration of sympathy with the Zionist movement and I should be very grateful if you felt able to ascertain if the President favours such a declaration."*

As explained, from an American standpoint by Professor R N Lebow[156]:

[154] A nephew of Herbert Samuel, but with conflicting views on Zionism.

[155] A most complex man, Colonel House manipulated President Wilson for some weeks to the detriment of progress toward the Balfour Declaration. His close relationship with Wilson came to an end when House allowed the French to eviscerate the Germans over reparations at Versailles. (Many see that as the first step on the road to Nazism.)

[156] Richard Ned Lebow: American political scientist Professor of International Political Theory of Ivy League Dartmouth College and King's College London.

> *"When Balfour returned to London* [from his vacation], *he was surprised to hear that Wilson had not given his approval when consulted. His spirits dampened, Balfour informed Weizmann and Rothschild that the case had been 'decided against the Zionists.' Discouraged though he was, Weizmann refused to admit defeat. He began a campaign to have the Cabinet restore the Palestine question to the agenda and let loose a barrage of telegrams to Brandeis and the American Zionists imploring them to obtain Wilson's approval."*[157]

We see here the typical Weizmann: faced with disappointment, he confronts it head-on and redoubles his efforts, undiminished in either enthusiasm or energy. Weizmann and Lord Rothschild decided they must meet with Balfour. The foreign minister saw Weizmann on 19 September and Rothschild three days later, telling each of them that his views remained unaltered by Montagu's interference. Some further text was prepared and Weizmann sent a further cable to Brandeis, as follows:

> "Following text declaration has been approved [by the] Foreign Office and Prime Minister and submitted [to the] War Cabinet:
>
> 1. His Majesty's Government accepts the principle that Palestine should be reconstituted as the National Home of the Jewish people.
> 2. His Majesty's Government will use its best endeavours to secure the achievement of this object and will discuss the necessary methods with the Zionist Organisation."[158]

suggesting that the approval of this formula by Brandeis and the

---

[157] *Woodrow Wilson and the Balfour Declaration,* Richard Ned Lebow (The Journal of Modern History Vol. 40, No. 4, The University of Chicago Press, 1968)

[158] *Trial and Error* (ibid)

President would be of the greatest assistance.

Lebow continues:

> *"Weizmann, aided by Mark Sykes ... was fighting to have the Palestine question restored to the Cabinet agenda, but Lloyd George, still recuperating from his illness, was inaccessible until the end of September.*
>
> *On the twenty-eighth* [September] *C. P. Scott, editor of The Manchester Guardian, had breakfast with the prime minister and brought Weizmann along with him just in case the prime minister cared to see him. Lloyd George was agreeable, and Weizmann was able to convince him of the need to restore the Palestine question to the agenda."*[159]

There followed another Cabinet meeting on 4 October, at which it was suggested that both the Zionists and the assimilationists should be given a final opportunity to present their respective cases. Montagu again engineered his attendance and made an impassioned plea against the Declaration. It was decided that Weizmann should, despite its being most irregular (as he was not a Member of Parliament, let alone in the government), be invited to address the War Cabinet directly — but he was nowhere to be found. Montagu once more held sway and prevailed over Balfour. The issue was postponed yet again.

THE GERMAN SPECTRE

That may have been the end of the matter (for the Imperial War Cabinet had other, more urgent, business than this) were it not for press speculation that started appearing (whether originating from and leaked by Weizmann, Graham or elsewhere, we shall never know) that the German enemy was about to declare themselves in favour of Zionism. The rumour was taken seriously and the Cabinet was stung into action:

> *"Balfour cabled House* [on 6 October] *that, 'in view of*

[159] *Woodrow Wilson and the Balfour Declaration,* Richard Ned Lebow (ibid)

reports that the German Government are making great efforts to capture the Zionist Movement, the question of a message of sympathy with the movement from Her Majesty's Government has again been considered by the Cabinet.'"[160]

Weizmann's barrage of cables continued with one to Brandeis, on 9 October, that the Cabinet had approved the following wording:

"His Majesty's Government views with favour the establishment in Palestine of a National Home for the Jewish race and will use its best endeavours to facilitate the achievement of this object; it being clearly understood that nothing shall be done which may prejudice the civil and religious rights of the existing non-Jewish communities in Palestine, or the rights and political status enjoyed in any other country by such Jews who are fully contented with their existing nationality and citizenship."[161]

Three paragraphs had been replaced with one but progress had to be made, so Weizmann continued his cable:

"Most likely shall be asked to appear before the cabinet when final discussion takes place in about a week. It is essential to have not only President's approval of text, but his recommendation to grant this declaration without delay. Further your support and enthusiastic message to us from American Zionists and also prominent non-Zionists most desirable to us. Your support urgently needed."[162]

It was considered too risky to seek a return to the first draft yet, on reflection, the most recent was considered not quite acceptable. Weizmann therefore suggested some minimal subtle, but important, changes, thus:

---

[160] *Woodrow Wilson and the Balfour Declaration*, Richard Ned Lebow (ibid)

[161] *Woodrow Wilson and the Balfour Declaration*, Richard Ned Lebow (ibid)

[162] *Trial and Error* (ibid)

His Majesty's Government view~~s~~ with favour the establishment in Palestine of a National Home for the Jewish ~~race~~ people, and will use ~~its~~ their best endeavours to facilitate the achievement of this object, it being clearly understood that nothing shall be done which may prejudice the civil and religious rights of the existing non-Jewish communities in Palestine, or the rights and political status enjoyed in any other country by ~~such~~ Jews ~~who are fully contented with their existing nationality and citizenship~~ in any other country.

On 13 October:

"Wilson, his mind made up, wrote House: 'I find in my pocket the memorandum you gave me about the Zionist Movement. I am afraid I did not say to you that I concurred in the formula suggested from the other side. I do, and would be obliged if you would let them know.'"[163]

Three days later, the Secretary to the Cabinet received a cable from Colonel House to the effect that he had :

"put information before President, who approves it but asks that no mention of his approval shall be made . . . as he has arranged that American Jews shall ask him for his approval, which he will give publicly here."[164]

FINALLY, THE DECLARATION

On 26 October, Lord Curzon circulated to War Cabinet members a memorandum "*The Future of Palestine*", which questioned many aspects of the proposed Jewish homeland. Sykes responded with a note of his own refuting Curzon's arguments.

---

[163] *Woodrow Wilson and the Balfour Declaration*, Richard Ned Lebow (ibid)

[164] *Woodrow Wilson and the Balfour Declaration*, Richard Ned Lebow (ibid)

THE BALFOUR DECLARATION

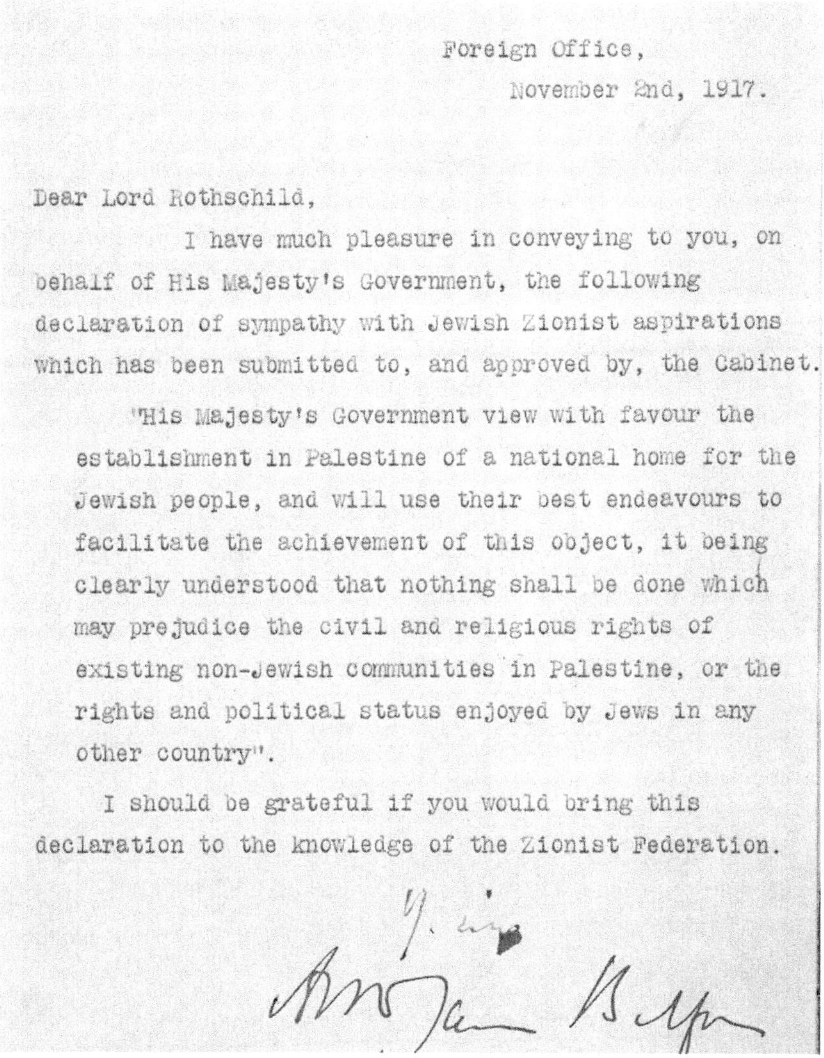

Foreign Office,
November 2nd, 1917.

Dear Lord Rothschild,

I have much pleasure in conveying to you, on behalf of His Majesty's Government, the following declaration of sympathy with Jewish Zionist aspirations which has been submitted to, and approved by, the Cabinet.

"His Majesty's Government view with favour the establishment in Palestine of a national home for the Jewish people, and will use their best endeavours to facilitate the achievement of this object, it being clearly understood that nothing shall be done which may prejudice the civil and religious rights of existing non-Jewish communities in Palestine, or the rights and political status enjoyed by Jews in any other country".

I should be grateful if you would bring this declaration to the knowledge of the Zionist Federation.

Arthur James Balfour

The all-important cabinet meeting (the relevant extracts being set out in Appendix 2) was held at noon on 31 October. Balfour suggested that all were *"now agreed that from a purely diplomatic and political point of view it was desirable that some declaration favourable to the aspirations of the Jewish nationalists should now be made"* and that the declaration once given would serve as *"extremely useful propaganda both in Russia and America"*. Whether this was, for Balfour and Lloyd George, truly their priority or merely a way of convincing the others not to delay any further is less important than the outcome.

The Balfour Declaration (see above) was finally issued but, as Churchill was to say, on a different subject and at a later juncture: *"... this is not the end. It is not even the beginning of the end. But it is, perhaps, the end of the beginning."*[165]

The War Cabinet authorised Secretary of State for Foreign Affairs Balfour to *"take a suitable opportunity of making the following declaration of sympathy with the Zionist aspirations"*. Two days later that opportunity was found.

Five days later, Lenin's Bolsheviks were swept into power in the Russian October Revolution. The Sykes-Picot Agreement was disclosed by *Izvestia*[166] and *Pravda*[167] on 23 November 1917 and published in *The Manchester Guardian* three days later (Weizmann having learned of it in April from C P Scott).

As for opposition to the Declaration, the British assimilationists had been beaten[168]; but the Palestinian Arabs were becoming

---

[165] From a 1942 speech by Winston Churchill concerning the Second Battle of El Alamein, when the British army began to turn the tide of WWII against the Germans.

[166] The official mouthpiece of the Kremlin.

[167] The official newspaper (mouthpiece) of the Communist Party of the Soviet Union.

[168] Although as late as 1921, the ZO in London was careful not to offend the assimilationists more than could be helped. Weizmann's team in San Remo received a communication from their London office seeking the publication of a statement that *"in reply to enquiries Zionist Organisation emphasizes fact that Zionist programme does not involve political allegiance to Government Palestine from Jews Diaspora"*. Source - *Weizmann Archives: San Remo/6-571A.TIF*

attentive to the rival entity that was already in their midst, and recently accorded some form of status by those who were on the point of taking Jerusalem. It was, therefore, to the Arabs that Weizmann, to his credit, would soon turn his attention.

CODA: Weizmann berates himself for not having been available, by a quirk of fate, when the War Cabinet sent for him to address them on 4 October (not least because he was just down the corridor in the office of Ormsby-Gore); but perhaps it makes no difference, given that the Declaration has come in for much criticism as it stands. A form that would more trenchantly have supported Zionist aspirations, and that did not mention *"the existing non-Jewish communities in Palestine*" (as in the final form but not the first draft of 18 July), would hardly have generated less condemnation by those who opposed — and even now oppose — the Declaration.

If there is any precedent in history for such a document as the Balfour Declaration, it is not immediately apparent; but in any event the expression of support for the return of an ancient people to their ancestral homeland after almost two millennium is truly momentous. Further, it was essentially the result of one man's magnetism, focus and drive.

~~~
~~~

11

A CHRISTMAS PRESENT FOR THE BRITISH

THE WAR CABINET MINUTES[169]

Between 31 October and 2 November 1917, the British resolved upon, prepared and then delivered to the ZF the Balfour Declaration. They had thereby willed a "national home for the Jewish people" in Palestine; but could they deliver? An important question, to which the minutes of three further contemporaneous War Cabinet meetings provide clues to the answer.

The seminal 31 October 1917 War Cabinet [261] minutes contained this compelling item:

> *5. The Director of Military Operations informed the War Cabinet that the preliminary marches of General Allenby's troops, in connection with the forthcoming offensive, had been very satisfactorily carried out. He further indicated on a map the line that the offensive would take.*

The War Cabinet [262] minutes for 1 November included this:

> *9. War Cabinet 261, Minute 5, the Director of Military Operations reported that General Allenby had carried out his attack in accordance with the plans explained on the previous day, had captured Beersheba and was continuing his advance. The progress had been satisfactory, and water could now be obtained in the neighbourhood in which our troops were operating.*

There were two War Cabinet meetings on 2 November 1917, one at 11:30 hours [263] and the other at 18:00 hours. Although Sir Mark Sykes emerged from one of them (it is not clear which) with the all-important letter addressed to Lord Rothschild, duly signed by Foreign Minister Balfour, neither the Zionists nor

[169] See: http://filestore.nationalarchives.gov.uk/pdfs/large/cab-23-4.pdf

Palestine were mentioned in the minutes of either — apart from this (minuted for the earlier one):

> *7. War Cabinet 262, Minute 9, the Director of Military Operations reported that General Allenby's troops had established themselves to the north of Beersheba. General Allenby was completing his preparations before resuming the offensive.*[170]

BRITISH INTERESTS IN THE MEDITERRANEAN

Gibraltar, which controls the entrance to the Mediterranean, was brought under British control with the Treaty of Utrecht in 1713. Malta, an island set in the centre of the Mediterranean, has for centuries enjoyed great strategic importance as a naval base. Moving inexorably eastward, the British took control there pursuant to the Treaty of Paris in 1814. Further east, Cyprus, sitting squarely between Turkey and Egypt, fell under British influence by way of a lease granted at the Congress of Berlin in 1878. Finally, Egypt fell under British domination in 1882. Accordingly, in terms of Palestine, it was plain in 1914 that the British were coming — hence Asquith's declared war aim of the destruction of the Ottoman Empire.

THE SUEZ CANAL

It is said that there was, in antiquity, a waterway from the Mediterranean Sea to the Red Sea, though it had been lost for centuries. In the early 16th century, the Venetians had wanted to

---

[170] These minutes provide a complete answer to the assertions of ex-Mossad spymaster, Efraim Halevy reported at:
http://www.jpost.com/Israel-News/Ex-Mossad-chief-Jewish-spies-were-instrumental-in-Balfour-Declaration-500553:
to the effect that intelligence supplied by Aaron Aaronsohn had an influence on extraction from the War Cabinet of the Balfour Declaration (in dilution of the work of Weizmann). The timing alone disproves it, for the sources of water identified by Aaronsohn could not have been of importance to Allenby until his push out of Egypt, which was manifestly after the 31 October 1917 decision to issue the Declaration.

re-establish it; but, after the Ottoman's conquest of Egypt in 1517, the dead hand of their empire fell on the region and the lost channel.

In late 1798, during Napoleon's campaign in Egypt and southern Syria (or Palestine), the French general sent archaeologists, scientists, cartographers and engineers to seek out the ancient passage and, after he had crowned himself Emperor in 1804, he planned to connect the two seas. While few still thought the Earth was flat, Napoleon was credulous enough to accept reports that there was a difference in the sea levels as between the Mediterranean Sea and the Red Sea. The plan was accordingly abandoned.

In 1830, a report to the British government stated there could be no such thing as a difference in altitude between any two places at sea level, so a canal joining the two seas was feasible; but no further attention was given to the matter in London. It was the French Suez Canal Company that constructed the canal, the British government opposing it throughout.

The canal opened under French control in November 1869 — the first ship through the Canal, however, being British — but, with the costs at double the original estimate, the Suez Canal Company ran into financial difficulties.

The Canal soon proved itself to be a boost to world trade. With its interests in east Africa, India and Australasia, it was plain what Britain had to do. With finance from the London Rothschilds, Prime Minister Disraeli, acting alone in something akin to a corporate dawn raid, gained effective control of the Suez Canal for Great Britain in November 1875. No one had a greater interest in the Canal in any event — 80% of its traffic was British — for passage along it, rather than round the Cape of Good Hope at the most southerly point of South Africa, reduced the sailing time from Britain to the Far East by several weeks. This was one British asset that had to be preserved at all costs, and to secure its newly-acquired Canal, the British quickly subjugated Egypt, and made it into a major strategic and military base.

At the start of World War I, the very length of the canal appeared to Germany and the Ottoman Empire to represent the weak link in British communications. The British, however, doggedly and successfully defended its strategically-vital waterway. In March 1916, the British-Egyptian Expeditionary Force was formed to push east out of Egypt, through the northern section of the Sinai Peninsula, towards and into Turkish-controlled Palestine.

An understanding with Britain's ally, France, with its own interests in Palestine and Syria, became urgent. By May 1916, Sir Mark Sykes, who had studied the political problems of Mesopotamia and Syria, had forged his (then secret) Sykes-Picot Agreement with François Georges-Picot: upon the successful outcome of the war in the region, Britain would occupy Iraq and Palestine (southern Syria) while Lebanon and Syria (proper) would fall under French control.

THE CONQUEST OF JERUSALEM

In February 1917, the Sinai Desert was secured by the Expeditionary Force and the Palestine campaign began at once. A series of battles to the detriment of the Turkish army along the Mediterranean coastline brought Beersheba, Gaza and Jaffa under Allenby's control. Then (after the end of October 1917), with the capture of the road from Beersheba through Hebron and Bethlehem, together with substantial Ottoman territory south of Jerusalem, the ancient city itself was within reach.

British Army General Edmund Allenby entered the Old City of Jerusalem on 11 December 1917, through the Jaffa Gate. He did so on foot, rather than riding on horseback or in a military vehicle, in order to show respect for the Holy City. This further success for the Palestine Campaign greatly boosted the morale of the British Empire. In London, Prime Minister David Lloyd George felt able to describe the capture of Jerusalem as *"a Christmas present for the British people"*.

Jerusalem, a city held holy by the three great Western monotheistic religions, was under Christian control for the first time in seven hundred years. The Jews had already been waiting a further twelve centuries, but the Balfour Declaration held out the hope that their long exclusion was about to end. Five weeks after the signature of the Balfour Declaration, the British were on the tip[171] of their ability to deliver on it.

~~~

[171] It would be several months before the Turks capitulated completely.
~~~

12

THE ZIONIST COMMISSION

The Balfour Declaration of the British Government of November 1917 was the cause of great celebration for the vast majority of Jews everywhere. The fact that it was the British who conquered Jerusalem just over a month later only added to the general jubilation.

THE OCTOBER REVOLUTION

October 1917, too, had been a momentous month for many Jews. The previous February had seen the first of two revolutions that were conclusively to change the face of Russia. The first need not detain us, save to say that it ended hundreds of years of tsarist rule. In the second, the October Revolution, Vladimir Ilyich Lenin led the Bolsheviks to power. In the sealed train in which he had been despatched by the Germans to Russia, of the 29 comrades who accompanied Lenin, 17 were Jews. Around 10% of the communist political elite of some 3,000 at the start of the Revolution were Jews. Many Jews throughout Russia and the Pale of Settlement (as for the population size, see Panel 7 below) were communist activists or sympathisers. They could not imagine that life could be as bad in a communist future than it had been under the tsars (but they did not then know the capacity for cruelty of Joseph Stalin.)

7

THE JEWS OF SOVIET RUSSIA

Precise figures of the numbers of Jews within the Russian sphere of influence at the time of the Revolution are hard to establish with certainty:

- The American Jewish Year Book for 1919 suggests that some four million Jews were living in the Pale and Russia[172], extrapolated thus:

---

172 http://www.hillel.org/docs/default-source/historical/american-jewish-year-

Estonia:	7,500
Latvia	150,000
Lithuania	250,000
Ukraine	3,300,000
	3,707,500
Soviet Russia:	200,000
Total:	**3,907,500**

- *The American Jewish Year Book Statistics of Jews for 1927-8,* gives alternative and greatly-elevated figures (again extrapolated)[173].

Estonia	4,566
Latvia	95,675
Lithuania	155,125
Ukraine	1,795,540
Russia (RSFSR)	518,260
Russia (RSFSR) in Europe	2,662,139
Russia (USSR)	2,820,429
Russia (USSR) in Asia	114,953
Siberia	44,725
	8,211,412
Poland	2,854,000
Total	**11,065,412**

- A final source to be considered is the redoubtable author, Irving Howe, who writes[174] as follows:-

"The Pale of Settlement comprised that area of czarist Russia in which the Jews were legally authorized to settle. The Pale covered an area of about 386,000 square miles, from the Baltic Sea to the Black Sea. By 1897, slightly less than 4,900,000 Jews lived there, forming 94 percent of the total

book-(1920-1921).pdf?sfvrsn=2

173 The *American Jewish Year Book for 1927-8, Statistics of Jews* by H S Linfield, PH D, Director, Department of Information and Statistics of The Bureau of Jewish Social Research
http://www.ajcarchives.org/AJC_DATA/Files/1927_1928_7_Statistics.pdf

174 In "*World of Our Fathers: The Journey of the East European Jews to America and the Life They Found and Made*", Irving Howe, NYU Press, 2005

> Jewish population of Russia and about 12 percent of the population of the area"

which suggests that the correct figure by the time of the October Revolution was well below eleven million and more like four to five million Jewish souls in Russia.

In the end, the exact numbers do not matter for this purpose: no one, not even Dr Chaim Weizmann, a product of the Pale, thought that they might all somehow be settled in Palestine.[175] The establishment of the Soviet Union in 1923 meant that the fate of all its Jews was as securely sealed as were its borders to the West.

THE GERMAN COLLAPSE

The Americans had, in April 1917, declared war on Germany, but not on its allies and, therefore, not on Turkey. Accordingly, the US military was mobilised to fight only on the Western Front, in France. There was no large standing army in an America that had emerged from the devastating Civil War only a half century earlier, whose default foreign policy was normalcy (isolationism) and whose rôle as "The World's Policeman" was still thirty years into the future. After the declaration of war on Germany, almost three million men had to be conscripted from scratch. Only a full year later did large numbers of American troops start to arrive in France but, once they did, they landed at the rate of some 10,000 a day.

It was clear from America's entry into the war that there could be only one outcome: certain defeat for the Germans. The Russian withdrawal from the hostilities following the Soviet takeover, releasing to the German lines on the Western Front many divisions from the Russian Front, could not alter the inevitability of the Allies' victory. The Germans, already suffering exhaustion, hunger — not to say famine, as a result of the blockade of the German ports by the British Royal Navy —

[175] Although, as we shall see, he did envisage, when presenting the case for Palestine at Versailles, that one million might.

and a breakdown of morale, swiftly collapsed. A general armistice took effect at 11th hour of the 11th day of the 11th month of 1918.[176] A pre-arranged luncheon for that day for Weizmann at 10 Downing Street, the prime minister's official residence, with Lloyd George went ahead regardless. Such was Weizmann's *"unique access to the British Government"*[177], engendered by both the debt that British military survival owed to him, by virtue of his fixing the 1915 Shell Crisis, and his bewitching and tenacious personality.

THE ZIONIST COMMISSION

Back at the end of 1917, so far as the British were concerned, having issued the Balfour Declaration, and expecting to conquer, with the French, the whole Middle East region, they could not sit back and await events, any more than the Zionists. Those who had brought the Declaration about took great pride in what they achieved and wanted to see effect being given to it. Accordingly, even though the war was not yet over, at the instigation of Dr Chaim Weizmann, the Zionist Commission was formed.

Before plans for Palestine's development could be made, information about its condition was required but sorely lacking. What was known was that the land was largely desert and the general belief in those days was that it must therefore be infertile. Jerusalem was, compared to any of the greater or lesser capitals of Europe, a village, and Tel Aviv (still in its first decade) consisted of only around one hundred homes. The whole *Yishuv* (after a depletion of a third in the Great War, mostly by reason of the deportation of young men) consisted of no more than 60,000 souls in a total population of around 800,000 in Palestine.

---

[176] Regarded to this day by the British people as the moment of remembrance for their fallen soldiers.

[177] *Chaim Weizmann: A Biography By Several Hands* (ibid) per Tosco R. Fyvel, author and political writer.

Sir Mark Sykes made the travel plans to Palestine for the representatives of the Allied Powers. The Russians, no longer being in a state of war absented themselves. That left Great Britain, France, Italy and the USA. (The Americans were offered two representatives and availed themselves of one, Isaac Zar.[178])

The Zionist Commission was comprised of, for the British, Weizmann, Israel Sieff (the celebrated M&S mogul went as Secretary to the Commission and Weizmann's personal assistant), Joseph Cowen, Leon Simon and Dr David Eder (destined to be Weizmann's representative in Palestine); for the French, an assimilationist Jew, Sylvain Lévi, and James de Rothschild, a son of Baron Edmond; and for the Italians, Marco Levi Bianchini, a Jewish psychiatrist. Before long, Weizmann concluded that the French were there to protect Baron Edmond's interests, and legacy, and the Italian to explore his country's trading opportunities in Palestine.

As Weizmann was leaving London in March 1918, he was honoured with an audience with King George V. The British monarch, a cousin of the soon-to-be defeated German Emperor, Wilhelm II, was concerned about the fate of their common cousins, the Russian branch of the vast Victorian family, the Romanovs, who had been taken captive by the Bolsheviks.[179] Nevertheless, Weizmann was accorded a courteous and sincere royal farewell for his momentous trip (another example of Weizmann's unique access to the establishment) and *"the King talked with great interest and knowledge of the Commission's plans and prospects, and wished him every success."*[180] The journey was to take several weeks, including a layover of nearly a month in Alexandria, Egypt.

---

[178] See Chapter 19.

[179] All seven were, with some loyal household members, brutally murdered by Bolshevik troops in Yekaterinburg on 17 July 1918.

[180] *Memoirs*, Israel Sieff (ibid)

THE *YISHUV*

It may safely be assumed that nowhere was news of the Balfour Declaration greeted more warmly than in the *Yishuv*. The war had been devastating for the Jews of the Ottoman Empire in general and for those in the Yishuv in particular. Jews in Palestine who originated from enemy states — mostly Russia — were either exiled from Palestine or conscripted into the Turkish army, but to do back-breaking work such as road building.

In February 1915, Ze'ev Jabotinsky[181] and Joseph Trumpeldor set out to form a military unit, the Zion Mule Corps, comprised of Russian Jewish émigrés from Palestine, to support British efforts to liberate the region from the Ottoman Empire. By the end of March 1915, 500 Jewish volunteers from among the *Yishuv* deportees in Egypt had started training. Between April 1915 and January 1916, 562 of the then 650-strong muleteers, participated in the disastrous Gallipoli campaign. (See panel 8).

8

CHURCHILL AND GALLIPOLI

> Churchill, having met with Weizmann in the spring of 1915, as First Lord of the Admiralty, drew most criticism for the Gallipoli rout of British forces by the Turks in November 1915. He resigned from the government and, as a self-imposed penance, went to fight with the Allies' soldiers in France. In July 1917, he returned to government, and the Cabinet, as Minister of Munitions. Accordingly, at the times that were relevant to Weizmann, Churchill, a Zionist sympathiser and an admirer of Weizmann, was on the scene.

For the *Yishuv*, the War was especially hard in a Palestine deprived of manpower generally and youth in particular. There was an extra existential worry: which side — the Allies or the

---

[181] Ze'ev Jabotinsky, the Russian Jewish Revisionist-Zionist leader, author, poet and orator, has been described as *"one of the most colourful, if erratic, of the early leaders of Zionism in Palestine." Memoirs*, Israel Sieff (ibid)

Central Powers — would better serve their ultimate interests or, perhaps more to the point, prevail? (David Ben-Gurion and Yitzhak Ben-Zvi were among those who discovered that they had initially backed the wrong horse.[182])

Some of those who resented the oppressive Turks, organised themselves into an underground espionage unit, *Nili*[183], to collaborate with the British in support of their war efforts. British intelligence, however, failed to respond until the leading *Nili* figure, Aaron Aaronsohn (see panel 9), made it to London and met Sir Mark Sykes. After that, *Nili* began to make headway but it was decided, fatefully, that intelligence would be sent by to the British by carrier pigeon. In late 1917, one of the pigeons was caught by the Turks who (or whose German allies) decrypted the coded message it bore, even though it comprised Hebrew, Aramaic, French and English. The spy network was then swiftly uncovered, the *Yishuv* disassociated itself, and Na'aman Belkind was captured by the Turks and tortured. Finally, the Turks arrested numerous people from Zichron Yaakov, including Aaron Aaronsohn's sister, Sarah. After suffering several days' torture, she chose suicide. Belkind and others were hanged. Her brother, Aaron, was destined never to

[182] Ben Gurion and Ben-Zvi were not the only ones to fail to back the British from the outset. Of Weizmann's twelve living siblings, probably none is more intriguing than his sister Mina. She was born in 1890 and is reported to have: "*emigrated to Palestine before the* [Great] *war, and was trained as a doctor. She spied on behalf of the Germans (her handler was a guy named Curt Max Prüfer, whom she was rumored to be having a fling with) in Egypt, working at British hospitals in Cairo and Alexandria, and got caught in .... 1916 when, after escorting a wounded French soldier to Rome, she was observed meeting with the German ambassador to Italy. Initially exiled to Malta, she was deported to prison in Moscow, and then got sent to Vienna in a prisoner exchange in August 1918.*" She died aged 35 and is reportedly buried in Jerusalem.
http://1914-1918.invisionzone.com/forums/index.php?/topic/190918-mina-weizmann/

[183] An acronym for the Hebrew phrase *Netzah Yisrael Lo Yishaker* - "The Eternal One of Israel Will Not Be False." (Samuel I, 15:29).

return to *Eretz Yisrael.*

9

AARONSOHN AND AGRONOMY

Aaronsohn was, long before he arrived in London, a luminary, as a leading expert on wheat. In 1906, aged 30, having previously botanically-mapped Palestine and the surrounding territories, he discovered wild emmer (*Triticum dicoccoides*) near Rosh Pinah. He branded this the "mother of wheat" as he believed it was the same species as that grown in the early Neolithic period. Agronomists and anthropologists applauded his discovery and overnight he became an international celebrity. He toured America, where he impressed Louis Brandeis, Felix Frankfurter and Henrietta Szold. Back home in Palestine, he set up an agricultural research station with a wide range of specimens of geological and botanical interest. More recently, modern science (using genetic-engineering techniques) has confirmed that wild emmer is indeed an ancestor of most domesticated wheat strands cultivated on a large scale today.

Aaronsohn accompanied Weizmann at the post-War Paris Peace Conference. Later, in May 1919, his plane disappeared en route from England and all on board were presumed to have perished in the English Channel.[184]

In August 1917, a battalion designated The Jewish Legion was officially formed as part of the 38th Battalion of the Royal Fusiliers. It included British volunteers and a large number of Russian Jews, as well as members of the former Zion Mule Corps (plus, a little tardily, Ben-Gurion and Yitzchak Ben-Zvi, who signed up in the USA in 1918[185]).

PALESTINE AND PROTOCOLS

The condition of the *Yishuv* that greeted Weizmann in April

[184] Life is harsh: Twenty-three years later, the same fate befell Weizmann's younger son, Michael Ezer, an RAF pilot, in the Bay of Biscay.

[185] See chapter 19.

1918 was wretched and depressing. Over the course of the war, by reason of deportations, emigration, economic depression and disease, the Jewish population in Palestine was reduced to poverty and despair — and by a third in number.

Not only was this the scene that greet Weizmann; it was also plain to him that he had arrived in a war zone. Some troops were being sent back to Europe to replenish the great losses suffered there (the Americans only just beginning to make their presence felt). That placed extra pressure on those who remained and were still fighting the Turks. General Allenby was not over-impressed by the sheaf of letters of introduction that Weizmann handed to him on arrival. The general's foremost concern was that the majority of the indigenous population — the Arabs — should not be unduly disturbed by the incoming Europeans (by which he presumably meant Jews).

On arrival, the Commission's members were taken to British Army's headquarters at Ramle, some 20 kilometres south-east of Tel Aviv, where they were initially deprived of any freedom of movement. The harsh realities of war meant a distinct absence of home comforts and little by way of communications. Soon, however, Weizmann was able to work his magic on Allenby and, after only a few days, the Commission's members were given travel passes, a car, fuel and telephone access.

Allenby's unstiffening did nothing to improve the atmosphere in the military headquarters, which was unmistakably hostile to the Commission. Weizmann supposed it was evidence of an innate prejudice against the *Yishuv* and its pitiful condition rendered by the war. He soon found there were other influences at work.

Weizmann formed an early connection with Brigadier-General Sir Wyndham Henry Deedes who passed him some reading material. Weizmann turned over the pages with increasing bafflement and asked Deedes for an explanation. Deedes told him that what he held was an extract from *The Protocols of the Elders of Zion* (the Russian canard that alleged that the Jews were omnipotent and in pursuit of world domination) and that many of the British officers in Palestine not only had similar copies but also were gullible enough to believe what they read. (The fact that the supposed overarching power of the Jews had not benefitted the poverty-stricken *Yishuv* did not appear to have crossed their minds.)

Given Western antipathy to the Bolshevik Revolution — the British intervened on the side of the Mensheviks, opposing Lenin's Bolsheviks, in the Russian Civil War that was on-going at this time — the narrative of *The Protocols*, and the belief that the Bolsheviks and the Jews in Revolutionary Russia were one and the same, fed into the natural prejudices of some in the military. (It was not until 1921 that Philip Graves, an Irish writer and journalist writing in *The Times*, exposed *The Protocols* as an anti-Semitic fraud.[186])

Irrespective of the ambient hostility, the Commission, operating under the auspices of His Majesty's Government, got down to and steadily expanded its work. After some initial surveys, and the resettling of Jews who returned from their exile by the Turks, the Commission set up offices for the promotion of agriculture, education, land acquisition, housing, finance, immigration and statistics.

Weizmann, in a letter to Vera of 26 May 1918 (the full text being at Appendix 3), describes how he worked some more on Allenby, that he had a two hour conversation with the general and that he *"found him to be an understanding, friendly and sympathetic man"*. He reported that Allenby was invited for the weekend to be the *"guest of the Jerusalem Jewish community"*, during which Weizmann:

> *"presented A*[llenby] *with a tiny Torah. He was touched and*

[186] In *Warrant For Genocide*, Penguin Books, (1970), Oxford don, Norman Cohn, explains that the Protocols appear to have plagiarised *Dialogue aux Enters*, a critique by French lawyer Maurice Joly of 1864 of Napoleon III and his régime.

was actually moved to tears and he replied with a very friendly speech; afterwards there was a tea with music and everything went like clockwork. Everybody went away delighted. It was a magnificent Jerusalem display."

Finally, Weizmann informed his wife:

"tomorrow I'm going with [William Ormsby-]*Gore to Hedjaz, that is to Aqaba, from there to Amman, to the Arab army headquarters for an interview with Feisal, the son of the Sherif of Mecca. This is a difficult journey, which will take altogether (there and back) about 2 weeks."*[187]

EMIR FEISAL

Weizmann had not forgotten his discomfort at the palpable hostility of the Arabs towards the Jews in Jaffa on his first visit a decade earlier, and was all too aware that the Commission's very presence had awoken a dormant Arab consciousness about their situation in Palestine. The following commentary paints a picture that would almost certainly have become plain to contemporary observers:

"[the] *Zionists were .. in a difficult position because numerous local groups had already been formed with the intent of stopping Jewish immigration to Palestine. One set of these groups were the Muslim-Christian Associations. Formed in late 1918 in the major cities of Palestine, these associations were generally comprised of wealthy and established notables who presented a united front in opposition to Zionism, though internally they often did not agree on other aspects of the region's political future. Other regional groups ... were generally composed of "the young Arab intelligentsia" and were similarly anti-Zionist, though they too were often not in total agreement about what to request beyond the cessation of Zionism. Despite their internal differences, opposition to Zionism provided these*

[187] Source: *Weizmann Archives - Feisal/16-427.TIF*

groups with a central organising principle."[188]

In anticipation of these developments, in May 1918, in order to try to build some bridges with the Arabs, and with the full support of Allenby, Weizmann went with Ormsby-Gore to meet Emir Feisal, putative King of the Arab Kingdom of Syria. British Colonel T E Lawrence was fighting alongside Feisal and they were encamped at Ma'an, about 120 km north-east of Aqaba[189] and 40 km to the east of the Red Rose city of Petra, in Transjordan. Weizmann hoped to construct an understanding with Feisal about a joint future for the Arab Kingdom and a Jewish home in Palestine.

According to Weizmann, the discussions (through a translator) were constructive. Weizmann and Feisal discussed future cooperation between the *Yishuv* and the indigenous Arabs of Palestine. Weizmann:

> *"explained to him the mission on which I had come to Palestine, our desire to do everything in our power to allay Arab fears and susceptibilities, and our hope that he would lend us his powerful moral support. ... I stressed the fact that there was a great deal of room in the country if intensive development were applied, and that the lot of the Arabs would be greatly improved through our work there."*[190]

To return, the arduous journey of several days had to be repeated just as laboriously, and all for talks that had lasted but a few hours. Weizmann believed that he had made progress with

---

188 *The Zionist Commission and the Jewish Communities of Greater Syria in 1919*, Andrew J. Patrick, Assistant Professor of History, Tennessee State University, Jerusalem Quarterly 56, 2014. Dr Patrick writes: "*The Middle East was reborn in the wake of World War I*".

189 A flight today of an hour to Eilat, in the same Gulf of Aqaba, was for Weizmann and Ormsby-Gore a tortuous passage of a week across deserts and in rusty, leaking ships.

190 *Trial and Error* (ibid)

someone of bourgeoning influence in Palestine. The very fact that the Emir received and parleyed with Weizmann is evidence that the latter was already being treated like an international statesman and the leader of a state for the Jews that had just taken its first steps to reality.

Less than six months later, in October 1918, the Arab and British forces of Feisal and Lawrence took Damascus, thus ending the Ottoman domination of some 450 years in Syria.

The Zionists were encouraged by Feisal's clearly-stated hopes, as reported by *The Times* on 12 December 1918:

> *"The two main branches of the Semitic family, Arabs and Jews, understand one another, and I hope that as a result of interchange of ideas at the Peace Conference, which will be guided by ideals of self-determination and nationality, each nation will make definite progress towards the realisation of its aspirations. Arabs are not jealous of Zionist Jews, and intend to give them fair play and the Zionist Jews have assured the Nationalist Arabs of their intention to see that they too have fair play in their respective areas. Turkish intrigue in Palestine has raised jealousy between the Jewish colonists and the local peasants, but the mutual understanding of the aims of Arabs and Jews will at once clear away the last trace of this former bitterness, which, indeed, had already practically disappeared before the war by the work of the Arab Secret Revolutionary Committee, which in Syria and elsewhere laid the foundation of the Arab military successes of the past two years."*[191]

Later that month, Weizmann met again with Emir Feisal, rather more comfortably, in London. A form of agreement was prepared which provided that:

> *".. the Arabs would recognise the Balfour Declaration and*

[191] *"Jews And Arabs In Syria: The Emir Feisul Looks To A Bright Future"*, The Times, December 12, 1918.

would encourage Jewish immigration and settlement in Palestine. Freedom of religion and worship in Palestine was set forth as a fundamental principle, and the Muslim holy sites were to be under Muslim control. The Zionist Organisation promised to look into the economic possibilities of an Arab state and to help it develop its resources."[192]

Weizmann and Feisal met for the final time on 3 January 1919 to sign what augured to be, for both Arab and Jew in Palestine, as a province of Syria, a mutually-beneficial agreement, the Feisal-Weizmann Pact[193]. It guaranteed the Jews the right to immigrate freely into Palestine and settle there, with a concomitant assurance that Arab tenant farmers would be protected and assisted economically. Feisal, however, added one highly significant condition to the agreement, which Weizmann could hardly resist, in these terms:

"Provided the Arabs obtain their independence as demanded in my Memorandum dated the 4th of January, 1919, to the Foreign Office of the Government of Great Britain, I shall concur in the above articles. But if the slightest modification or departure were to be made [in relation to the demands in the Memorandum], *I shall not be bound by a single word of the present Agreement which shall be deemed void and of no account or validity, and I shall not be answerable in any way whatsoever."*

Feisal's memorandum — which demanded Arab autonomy in the territories which, it was anticipated, the British and French would control by the end of the war — was addressed to the British. They, however, were unable to deliver what Feisal

---

[192] Israeli Ministry of Foreign Affairs: http://www.mfa.gov.il/mfa/foreignpolicy/peace/mfadocuments/pages/the%20weizmann-feisal%20agreement%203-jan-1919.aspx

[193] The full text may be seen at: https://israeled.org/resources/documents/emir-feisal-chaim-weizmann-correspondences/

sought, for it was the French who were accorded control of Syria pursuant to the Sykes-Picot Agreement. Whether or not the French knew about the condition that Feisal had imposed (and it may reasonably be assumed that they did), they ignored it. Feisal arrived in Damascus before the French but was ejected by them. The Arabs did not get their Syrian autonomy and the Feisal-Weizmann Pact was doomed never to take effect. Nevertheless, Weizmann may properly be credited with having signed the first agreement between Jewish interests in Palestine and the Arabs.[194] (See also panel 10.)

10

WEIZMANN AS STATESMAN

Israel Sieff provides a vital insight to Weizmann's accomplishment with the Feisal-Weizmann Pact:

"This was a period of immense and delicate diplomatic activity in which Weizmann showed himself a genius, and, in my view, single-handedly conjured a Jewish state out of the air. To understand the real nature of his achievement it is essential to understand the dilemma indeed, the set of dilemmas he was in. First, his only real power was in what he could actually bring about — he had no authority other than his achievement. Unless he could dominate world Zionism, and in particular command American Zionist financial support, he could not bring a Jewish state into being.

On the other hand he could only keep up his position as leader of World Zionism and mesmerise the American Jews into giving him the money by bringing the Jewish state into being. With only the Balfour Declaration behind him, and with the Sykes-Picot Agreement hanging over him, he had to convince Feisal on the one hand and the American Jews on the other that he, Weizmann, represented a strong and viable Jewish state. He had

[194] The others were the Armistice Agreements (1949), the Camp David Accords (1978), the Egypt–Israel Peace Treaty (1979), the Oslo Accords (1993), the Israel-Jordan Peace Treaty (1994) and the Camp David Summit (2000) all signed on behalf of the State of Israel. Then, in August 2020, came the Abraham Accords between Israel and the UAE and Bahrain.

to behave towards the British Government as though World Jewry were at his back, giving him plenary powers.

To leading militant Zionists on the other hand, he had to pretend that his power was very limited so that they would not try to push him further than the British Government could stand. Much bluff and counter-bluff was required. In 1919 Weizmann behaved as though he had a great Jewish state behind him. In fact all he had, if he had been asked to show, was his handful of Manchester friends ...!"[195]

~~~

[195] *Memoirs,* Israel Sieff (ibid)
~~~

13

DECLARATION - AND INDISPENSABILITY - CONFIRMED

THE PARIS PEACE CONFERENCE

The formal end of the First World War did not come with the cessation of hostilities, nor with the several armistice agreements that followed, but with a series of peace conferences. The most significant was the Paris Peace Conference, the start of which was postponed until Lloyd George obtained a renewed mandate from the British electorate at a general election. On 14 December 1918, the British duly returned the Welsh Wizard as prime minister, so proceedings could begin at the Palace of Versailles, near Paris, in January 1919.

The further recognition of Weizmann as a statesman, this time on the world stage, may be seen in his attendance in Paris as a member of the ZO. Weizmann's ZO colleagues were, even before his return from Palestine, busily engaged in preparation for the Paris Peace Conference.

For the purposes of the conference, the victorious allies' foreign ministers[196] formed the "Council of Ten". Various states or "powers" were invited to present their cases to the Committee. One set of sessions was set aside for "Powers with Special Interests". One such was Syria, whose case was put by Mr Chekri Ganem on 29 January 1919. He spoke, one might think very reasonably, as follows:

> *"there are few small nations who have suffered so much as the people of Syria.*
>
> *The members of the Conference are asked to decide, conscientiously and after due consideration of the facts:*
>
> *(1) Whether Syria can be constituted, within its natural frontiers, into a democratic State distinct from the other*

[196] The British Council members being Balfour and Lord Milner.

Arabic — speaking countries.

(2) Whether that State can be left to itself from the time of its creation, or whether it will require the external support of a highly civilised Power.

(3) What should be the nature of such support, and by what Power should it be rendered? If the first of these three points is decided in the affirmative, it will necessitate arriving at a decision on the others — namely, whether Syria is entitled to a free existence, and whether you will grant it to her." [197]

Ganem concluded with commendable humanity by referring to Palestine (which under the long Ottoman years had been part of Greater Syria), as follows:

"Palestine is incontestably the Southern portion of our country. The Zionists claim it. We have suffered too much from sufferings resembling theirs, not to throw open wide to them the doors of Palestine. All those among them who are oppressed in certain retrograde countries are welcome. Let them settle in Palestine, but in an autonomous Palestine, connected with Syria by the sole bond of federation. Will not a Palestine enjoying wide internal autonomy be for them a sufficient guarantee?

If they form the majority there, they will be the rulers. *If they are in the minority, they will be represented in the government in proportion to their numbers.* [Emphasis added.]

Is it necessary, in order to establish them, to dismember Syria, to take from it its means of access and its historic safeguard against any invasion (which always took that route), and to constitute a State in the midst of a country

[197] Minutes of The Paris Peace Conference, 1919: http://digicoll.library.wisc.edu/cgi-bin/FRUS/FRUS-idx?type=div&did=FRUS.FRUS1919Parisv03.i0005&isize=M

which, as a consequence, would be hostile to them?"[198]

In short, the Syrians proposed a federation between Syria and Palestine and accepted that, should the Jews "*form the majority there, they will be the rulers*" (possibly believing — though one hopes that this is not too unfair or cynical — that such a disproportionate growth in the Jewish population was unlikely).

The Zionists accorded by implication the status of a "power" were invited to put their case on 23 February 1919.

Weizmann relates the testimony of his colleague, Nahum Sokolov, as follows:

> *"Mr Sokolow delivered a very short, concise speech upon the first point, namely, the historic claim of the Jewish people to Palestine, and referred to the favourable declarations which had been made by the various governments on this subject. He described the immemorial attachment of the Jewish people to Eretz Israel, and explained how local Jewish questions, in whatever countries, really turned upon Palestine: on these grounds, he continued, we demanded the foundation of a Jewish National Home in Palestine. From where I stood I could see Sokolow's face and, without being sentimental, it was as if two thousand years of Jewish suffering rested on his shoulders. His quiet, dignified utterance made a very deep impression on the assembly."*[199]

Then Weizmann addressed the Council of Ten. He pointed out that the war had left the Jewish people comparatively weaker than any other people in the world. He anticipated there would be mass movements of Jews but that:

> "[the] *Great Powers would naturally scrutinise every alien who claimed to enter their countries, and the Jew would be*

---

[198] Minutes of The Paris Peace Conference (ibid)

[199] *Trial and Error* (ibid)

regarded as a typical wandering alien. As a result the Jews would find themselves knocking around the world, seeking a refuge and unable to find one. The problem, therefore, was a very serious one, and no statesman could contemplate it without being impelled to find an equitable solution.

In his opinion, the solution proposed by the Zionist Organisation was the only one which would in the long run bring peace, and at the same time transform Jewish energy into a constructive force, instead of its being dissipated into destructive tendencies or bitterness.

Palestine possessed great possibilities. The country was not very densely populated: There were some 600,000 to 700,000 people occupying 40,000 square kilometres, which gave a population of 10 to 15 per square kilometre. On the other hand, in Lebanon, which resembled it in many aspects, the density of the population was 160 per square kilometre. Consequently, in Palestine there was room for an increase of at least four to five million people, without encroaching on the legitimate interests of the people already there.

The Zionists wished to settle Jews in the empty spaces of Palestine, organising the settlements to be created by the expenditure of their own money and the exercise of their brains."[200]

Weizmann sought a resolution that Great Britain, as the incipient Mandatory Power should:

(a) Promote Jewish immigration and close settlement on the land, the established rights of the present non-Jewish population being equitably safeguarded.

(b) Accept the co-operation in such measures of a Council representative of the Jews of Palestine and of the world that may be established for the development of the Jewish National Home in Palestine and entrust the

---

[200] Minutes of The Paris Peace Conference (ibid)

organisation of Jewish education to such Council.

(c) *On being satisfied that the constitution of such Council precludes the making of private profit, offer to the Council in priority any concession for the development of natural resources which it may be found desirable to grant.*[201]

and he concluded by saying that he:

> *"spoke in the name of a million Jews who ... were waiting the signal to move. It would be the duty of the Zionist Association to organise immigration successfully, but the Jewish leaders would be faced with a far greater catastrophe if they found themselves unable to tell their people to wait until they received the signal. For the fulfillment of their plans the Jewish Associations required the support of the Great Powers, and in full hope they left their case in their hands."*[202]

The Zionists emerged from this (and the next following conference at San Remo) seemingly receiving all that they had hoped for. The Arabs, however, were not so well-treated, for, according to historian Edwin Black[203]:

> *"... at the Paris sessions, the French snubbed Feisal. ... the French were uninterested in relinquishing their designs on greater Syria, especially since the Lebanon region was overwhelmingly Maronite Christian. ... France then began a disingenuous diplomatic process with the Arabs — the legacy of which would last many generations.... Feisal summarily left Paris for Syria to claim his nation."*

---

[201] Minutes of The Paris Peace Conference (ibid)

[202] Minutes of The Paris Peace Conference (ibid)

[203] New York Times best-selling and award-winning author of *IBM and the Holocaust*. Writing in the Jerusalem Post of August 6, 2009 an article adapted from *"Banking on Baghdad, Inside Iraq's 7,000-Year History of War, Profit and Conflict"*, Edwin Black (2004) John Wiley & Sons.

The Treaty of Sèvres of 10 August 1920 formalised the partitioning of Palestine (pursuant to the Sykes-Picot Agreement) and the ultimate destruction of the Ottoman Empire. All non-Turkish territory was relinquished to the Allies, mainly the British Empire, the French Republic and Italy. The principal result was the creation of the British Mandate over Palestine and that of the French over Syria and Lebanon.

The French refused to grant independence to the Arabs and ejected Feisal, who repudiated the Feisal-Weizmann agreement, the Feisal pre-condition having been breached. For balance, it should be said that doubt has since been cast on the ability of Feisal to speak at that time for the Arabs in Damascus let alone those in Palestine. (Feisal himself, a member of the Hashemite tribe, was granted a large compensation package: the British installed him as the King of Iraq. His brother, Abdullah, was later accorded Transjordan by the British. (See the coda to this chapter.))

THE LEAGUE OF NATIONS

The League of Nations was constituted at Paris as first global intergovernmental organisation, charged to maintain world peace. Following the Treaty of Versailles (the formal outcome of the Paris Peace Conference) and the Treaty of San Remo, the League of Nations granted Great Britain on 24 July 1922 a mandate for full powers of legislation and administration in Palestine. The preamble of the mandate document[204] incorporated the Balfour Declaration word for word, reciting:

> *"Whereas the Principal Allied Powers have also agreed that the Mandatory should be responsible for putting into effect the* ***declaration originally made on November 2nd, 1917****, by the Government of* [Great Britain]*, and adopted by the said Powers, in favour of the establishment in Palestine of a national home for the Jewish people, it being clearly*

[204] For the full text of the document see: http://avalon.law.yale.edu/20th_century/palmanda.asp

understood that nothing should be done which might prejudice the civil and religious rights of existing non-Jewish communities in Palestine, or the rights and political status enjoyed by Jews in any other country." [Emphasis added.]

This then was the culmination of all of Weizmann's efforts so far: full international recognition by the League of Nations, in granting the mandate to Britain, of the Balfour Declaration, which he and only he could have wrested from the grip of the most powerful country in the world, over the Palestine that they conquered in the Great War, their potential loss of which he had averted in 1915. It is, when all the surrounding geo-political considerations are stripped away, as great an achievement by the force of personality of one man as might be found in all the chronicles of politics and diplomacy.[205]

Ominously, the Arabs' rejection of the understanding with the Zionists as expressed in the Feisal-Weizmann Pact (following the French rejection of Feisal) was to be merely the first of many setbacks that practical Zionism encountered on entering its British Mandate phase. Soon pogroms would despoil the Holy Land, as the Arabs appreciated the meaning of the Balfour Declaration. In grim lockstep, the British sought to abandon it and ever more aggressively supported not the evolution of the

---

[205] Some writers, for example Martin Kramer* (who teaches Middle Eastern history at Shalem College in Jerusalem and is the Koret Visiting Fellow at the Washington Institute for Near East Policy), has urged that the contribution of Nahum Sokolow, who worked on the French, Italians and Americans, should not be overlooked. There were other heroes of diplomacy, too, but none nor all of them together can dilute the supreme achievements of Weizmann in London and Palestine in 1917 and 1918, as confirmed at Sèvres and San Remo.

https://mosaicmagazine.com/response/2017/06/how-the-balfour-declaration-became-part-of-international-law/

https://mosaicmagazine.com/essay/2017/06/the-forgotten-truth-about-the-balfour-declaration/

"national home for the Jewish people", as mentioned in the Balfour Declaration, but the local Arabs who were increasingly violently opposed to it.

CODA: Contrary to popular belief, the frontiers of Mandatory Palestine were not definitively recognised at San Remo. According to the preamble of the Mandate, there was entrusted to the British:

> *"the administration of the territory of Palestine, which formerly belonged to the Turkish Empire, **within such boundaries as may be fixed by them**"*. [Emphasis added.]

The position crystallised in 1921 when, at the behest of Winston Churchill, as Secretary of State for the Colonies, Transjordan was created at the expense of what was to have been Palestine in full. Today, Transjordan is the modern state of Jordan, bestowed (like Iraq) by the British upon leaders of the Hashemite tribe.

Few Israelis regret the removal of the immensely larger Transjordan (90,000 km^2) from the future Jewish homeland and state (21,000 km^2). It was in 1948, and has been since, hard enough to preserve the integrity of the borders of modern day Israel — achieved very largely by its short lines of communications and supply — without the burden of the vast deserts and remote frontiers of Transjordan, contiguous for thousands of kilometres with those of its neighbours, Iraq, Syria and Saudi Arabia. They would surely have presented Israel with its first territorial retreat, or worse.

~~~
~~~

14

FROM EUPHORIA TO ANGUISH

THE WEIZMANN RESIDENCE

The year after World War I ended, Weizmann, with several government contracts and 54 patents providing him and Vera with a standard of living that they would not have dared hope for five years earlier, bought a house at 16 Addison Crescent in the Royal Borough of Kensington and Chelsea (always one of central London's wealthiest boroughs). His portrayal of the visitors to their home is perhaps an ingenuous affirmation of his ability to attract to himself personalities from across a wide spectrum, thus:

> *"That house was for thirty years the centre for all who were interested in, or connected with, Zionism and Palestine. Statesmen like Lord Balfour, General Smuts, Lord Cecil, Leon Blum, Mr Philip Kerr; soldiers like Meinertzhagen, MacDonogh, Wyndham Deedes, T E Lawrence, Orde Wingate; Zionists like Bialik, Shmarya Levin, Feivel and Jacobson; American friends and supporters like Felix Warburg, Louis Marshall, Stephen S Wise, Louis Lipsky, Morris Rothenberg, Ben Cohen and others; Palestinians visiting London, like Ruppin and Arlosoroff — all passed through Addison Crescent and all enjoyed my wife's warm and unobtrusive hospitality. In this home our boys grew up; here they spent their holidays and brought their friends; and here we stayed until the outbreak of the Second World War."*[206]

THE WILDERNESS YEARS

The Wilderness Years is a term used[207] to encapsulate the

---

[206] *Trial and Error* (ibid)

[207] By Martin Gilbert, Churchill's official biographer until his death in 2015. See *Winston Churchill: The Wilderness Years*, Martin Gilbert (Pimlico Press, 2004). The term depicted the years 1931 to 1940 in which Churchill was unable to make any impact on the UK political scene mainly owing to the

period, 1931 to 1940, in which Winston Churchill was unable to influence events in Britain as he had in the past, and would again. His was the lone voice in the bleak, opaque wasteland that was the appeasement disposition of the British Parliament. Seemingly, there, only Churchill could see the approaching disaster that Hitler represented.

Weizmann saw the future through the same prism as Churchill. With apologies on behalf of one great man to another, the author considers that the term applies equally aptly to Chaim Weizmann, though his period in the wilderness, in which he was the titular head of Zionism yet less and less able to provide it with direction, started earlier and ended later.

While Weizmann served as president of the ZO from 1920 to 1931 and then again from 1935 until he resigned (after what amounted to a vote of no confidence in him) at the 22nd Zionist Congress in 1946, if he had a fault, it was that he allowed himself to be perceived as being too close to the British. The complaint was not without merit, but he saw himself as a conduit between his own people and those from whom he had wrought his great political achievement in 1917. It was that close association with the British oppressors of the *Yishuv* under the Mandate, which culminated in his 1946 effective ejection from office (on the very eve, of course unknowingly, of his three great diplomatic coups with US President Truman).

THE MANDATE SOURS

The high point of British altruism towards the Jewish people came with the British Mandate — its initiation and not its implementation, which was to prove another matter entirely. In 1922, the League of Nations granted the Palestine Mandate to

---

divergence between the conventional European view prevalent in Westminster at the time and that of Churchill - that appeasing Hitler would end in a devastating war. In short, his greatest triumph was yet to come, as Britain's wartime leader. Weizmann, too, had further political achievements ahead of him.

Britain. It took effect on 29 September 1923, the Mandate document (faithfully restating the Balfour Declaration) serving as the legal constitution for the conduct of the affairs of the territory under the control of the British following their dismantling of the Ottoman Empire.

What happened next was something akin to buyer's remorse: the British soon began to wish that they had never bought into Palestine in the first place. Gone were the high-minded ideals of Protestant Zionism, and gone too was the steadfast cohort of British politicians who had given impetus to the Zionist dream. By the late 1920s, Sir Mark Sykes[208], Balfour, Lloyd George, Ormsby-Gore and the others had left the scene. They were replaced by a new generation of politicians, devoid of empathy with the motivations of the former ensemble who had been willing servants of Weizmann's passion.

For the *Yishuv*, the euphoria that greeted the Balfour Declaration and the establishment of the Mandate was to turn into the misery, privations and violence of the Mandate period.

A CONSTRUCTIVE START

It had started well. In April 1920, free elections were held for the Assembly of Representatives of the Palestinian Jewish community. Herbert Samuel was appointed the first Palestine High Commissioner and took up office the following June. Weizmann was almost contemporaneously elected President of the ZO. The two men, both Jewish and both Zionists, had enjoyed a constructive working relationship from 1916. The whole *raison d'être* of the Mandate was to be productive and to make progress, and they set out, with their parallel portfolios, to pursue that ideal.

In April 1925, Lord Balfour attended the opening ceremony of

---

[208] Sykes colourful life was ended tragically and anti-climatically in his hotel room in Paris, where he succumbed to the great post-war Spanish Influenza pandemic on 16 February 1919.

Weizmann's signature project within the *Yishuv* — the Hebrew University of Jerusalem[209], for which Weizmann had undertaken the (for him) disagreeable task of fundraising (something else at which, despite his distaste for it, he excelled). The *kibbutzim* and the *moshavim* increased their agricultural yields year on year, and significant infrastructure starts were made.

THE ARAB TRADITION

Sadly, the bulk of the Palestinian Arabs came from a different tradition. They had been comfortable with their quiet life, unchanged throughout the generations. To the extent that Palestine had been settled at all in the centuries of Ottoman neglect, its inhabitants (apart from the elderly Jews awaiting their own demise in the Holy City) were largely Arab goat-herds and shepherds, content to mind their flocks and to live on a subsistence basis on the land, but generally without title to it. Their absentee landlords, living in Syria or Turkey, had no objection to leaving swathes of Palestine open and available to them.

Boundaries and fences were virtually unknown in rural Palestine. Accordingly, since proprietorial rights had never been a matter that entered the contemplation of the Arab mind, the purchase of spaces around, and sometimes under, them was a threat to their traditional lifestyle. They had not asked to be dragged into the 20th century. Their Oriental outlook was different from that of the Westerners suddenly not only mushrooming in their midst but also given official standing. The Muslim masters in Constantinople had been replaced by Christian ones in London. Associated Jewish immigration was a significant added issue, which came to be seen as an existential threat.

A GREAT HELP TO THE ARABS

If Weizmann was the champion par excellence of the Zionists,

---

[209] See further at chapter 18.

Colonel T E Lawrence was hardly less of campaigner for the Arabs, with whom his credentials were well-established (if sometimes overstated). He had fought with Emir Feisal in the Arab Revolt against the Ottoman Empire from 1916 through the Arabian Peninsula by way of Aqaba to Damascus. His part in the Arab Revolt and his liaison rôle with the British during the Sinai and Palestine military campaigns earned him his colourful reputation and the sobriquet: Lawrence of Arabia. Weizmann writes of him:

> *"I had met Lawrence fleetingly in Egypt, with Allenby, and later in Palestine. I was to meet him quite often later, and he was an occasional visitor to our house in London. His relationship to the Zionist movement was a very positive one, in spite of the fact that he was strongly pro-Arab, and he has mistakenly been represented as anti-Zionist.* ***It was his view — as it was Feisal's — that the Jews would be of great help to the Arabs, and that the Arab world stood to gain much from a Jewish Homeland in Palestine****".*[210] [Emphasis added.]

Corroboration of this view is provided by Martin Gilbert[211] writing of Lawrence and Churchill:

> *"Lawrence, like Churchill, saw virtue in the Zionist enterprise. His friendship with the Arab leaders with whom he had fought during the Arab Revolt was paralleled by his understanding of Zionist aspirations, and his keenness to see the Zionists help the Arabs forward in Palestine - and elsewhere in the Middle East - to modernity and prosperity.*
>
> *On the first anniversary of the Balfour Declaration in November 1918, Lawrence told a British Jewish newspaper: 'Speaking entirely as a non-Jew, I look on the Jews as the natural importers of western leaven so necessary for*

[210] *Trial and Error* (ibid)

[211] The late and greatly missed official biographer of Winston Churchill.

> *countries of the Near East.'"*[212]

and by Cecil Bloom[213] who wrote:

> *"Lawrence had his own plans for the Middle East in which he envisaged the Zionists playing a major role. He and other British diplomats, including Sir Mark Sykes and William Ormsby-Gore, believed that Zionist and Arab interests could be brought together to achieve a progressive political and economic development of the Middle East"* [214]

and Weizmann is surely confirmed in it by the agreement with Emir Feisal, the genesis of which Lawrence had witnessed (and he claims to have helped facilitate) in the Transjordan desert north of Aqaba. Wyndham Deedes, in letter to Weizmann of 14 July 1919 referred to his negotiations with Feisal at Aqaba as: "*your most statesmanlike stroke*".[215]

The vexing French refusal to give Feisal control of Syria extinguished whatever Arab goodwill Weizmann had been able to engender; and he was never able to identify any successor to Feisal in Palestine or elsewhere on whom he could work his magic.

IMMIGRATION ISSUES

At first, the British administration, consistent with their mandate, encouraged Jewish immigration into Palestine. This was soon curtailed as the local Arab population raised the tempo

---

[212] *"leaven"*: a pervasive influence that modifies something or transforms it for the better. Writing in *Churchill and the Jews*, Martin Gilbert (Simon & Schuster UK Limited, 2007) was, until his death in 2015, Sir Winston Churchill's official biographer.

[213] Cecil Bloom: a researcher and writer on Jewish history, music and literature.

[214] In *T. E. Lawrence and Zionism - Jewish Historical Studies*, Cecil Bloom (Jewish Historical Society of England, Vol. 38, 2002).

[215] Source - *Weizmann Archives: Feisal/3-520.TIF.* Deedes went on to be Chief Secretary to High Commissioner Herbert Samuel.

and volume of their protest — often accompanied with extreme violence[216] — against the *Yishuv*, who were seen as (and resented for) making very significant progress with the development of their Palestine project, building new settlements and expanding their modern city of Tel Aviv.

Confronted by continuing and escalating civil unrest, the British clamped down on Jewish immigration so that, while Jews continued to arrive, increasingly they had to do so illegally and in far fewer numbers than were at first desirable and later, as Nazism began to take hold in Europe, essential.

With the leaders of the Arabs unequivocally opposed to the national home for the Jews envisioned by the Balfour Declaration, and the *Yishuv* vigorously pursuing it, the British found themselves less and less able, or willing, to carry out their mandated mission. They severely restricted Jewish immigration in an effort to placate the Arabs, just when the Jews needed it most. This led to the formation of Jewish activism — direct action against the British. To find a solution, several commissions were established[217], the most significant of which

---

[216] For those readers not too circumspect about using Wikipedia as a source, a list of terrorist actions between 1920 and the 1946 bombing by the Jews of the King David Hotel is available at: https://www.wikiwand.com/en/List_of_killings_and_massacres_in_Mandatory_Palestine

[217] In all, there were seven commissions of inquiry in Mandated Palestine:

- The King-Crane Commission (appointed by the United States), 1919;
- The Haycraft Commission of Inquiry, 1921;
- The Shaw Commission (Commission on the Palestine Disturbances), 1929
- The Peel Commission (Palestine Royal Commission), 1937;
- The Woodhead Commission (Palestine Partition Commission), 1938;
- The Anglo-American Commission (Anglo-American Committee of Enquiry Regarding the Problems of European Jewry and Palestine), 1946; and
- UNSCOP (United Nations Special Committee on Palestine), 1947.

was the Peel Commission.

THE PEEL COMMISSION

Between 1936 and 1939 there was a second Arab Revolt, this time against the British administration of Mandatory Palestine. The Arabs demanded independence and the end of Jewish immigration. In the wake of the clashes, the Peel Commission was set up to investigate the causes of unrest. It arrived in Palestine in November 1936. Weizmann addressed the Commission, in the light of the growing Nazi menace (as Churchill might have done), saying that there were six million Jews in Europe *"for whom the world is divided into places where they cannot live and places where they cannot enter"* and urging that the gates of Palestine be opened for them.

The Commission concluded that the national aspirations of the Arabs and the Jews were:

> *"incompatible. The Arabs desire to revive the traditions of the Arab golden age. The Jews desire to show what they can achieve when restored to the land in which the Jewish nation was born. Neither of the two national ideals permits of combination in the service of a single State."*[218]

The Commission's recommendation was effectively a two-state solution (so often urged on the parties today), called Partition. Land in the north of Palestine, where Jews were already in the majority would become a Jewish state, while the territory to the South would form an Arab state, and there would have to be population transfers between the two. The British mandate would effectively end, except — anticipating competing Jewish and Arab claims upon it — in respect of Jerusalem.

The Partition idea united the Arabs and the *Yishuv* only in their parallel dismissals of it. Weizmann alone was unequivocally convinced that Partition offered new hope to the Zionist

[218] http://www.jewishvirtuallibrary.org/text-of-the-peel-commission-report

movement. (Ben-Gurion's alleged acceptance of Partition at that time is the subject of intense debate by scholars based on a letter he wrote to his son and a passage within it that had been scribbled out.)

THE WHITE PAPER

The notorious "White Paper" policy statement of 23 May 1939 followed, limiting Jewish immigration to 75,000 over five years, with further immigration to be decided by the Arab majority — and this on the very cusp of the locking-up in wartime Nazi-dominated Europe of the six million Jews to whom Weizmann had referred when giving evidence to the Peel Commission. The war that Churchill and Weizmann had long foreseen was less than four months away.

WORLD WAR II

With the intervention of World War II the following September, the resolution of the Mandate problem was put on hold. Arab sympathies were with the Germans, but the *Yishuv* resolved to follow the dictum of Jewish Agency leader, Ben-Gurion: *"We must assist the British in the war as if there were no White Paper and we must resist the White Paper as if there were no war",* throwing themselves into the British war effort; no less Weizmann, who became an honorary adviser to the British Ministry of Supply. Further, he resumed his research into the development of synthetic rubber, intensified once the Japanese entered the war and swept across the Pacific region. Just as Germany had complete control over acetone in WWI, now the Japanese rendered inaccessible to the Allies the usual sources of rubber in the Malaya that they wrested from the British in February 1942.

It is not the purpose of this work to consider all that Weizmann endured, or even the difficulties over which he prevailed, in the quarter century between 1921 and 1946. Since it is the writer's purpose to consider in depth only Weizmann's matchless contributions to Zionism and Israel, it is to those that we now return.

CODA: There was much inter-communal violence between Jew and Arab in the inter-war years, to the distress of both sides and the British authorities. If the reader regards the deprivation of a Palestinian Arab state as the necessary consequence of the Balfour Declaration or that constant mutual enmity between Arab and Jew is inescapable, he may see in Appendix 4 the author's personal views to the contrary.

~~~
~~~

15

THE RUBBER CRISIS

The adage, that history repeats itself, but never quite in the same way, may be a cliché but, in the case of Dr Chaim Weizmann, it is entirely appropriate. The problem that was acetone in the First World War became that of rubber in the Second.

THE RISE OF THE RIGHT

The Great War ended with the Versailles and other treaties of 1919 to 1922. Within twenty years, World War II had erupted. Some consideration of how that arose is required.

The Germans were very severely punished by the reparations imposed on them at the insistence of the French at Versailles.[219] Next, in the USA, following the Roaring Twenties, came the Wall Street Crash and the Great Depression, which affected all the economies of the western world. In Germany in the 1930s, a downtrodden, dispirited people (after suffering, too, massive hyperinflation in the early 1920s and wide-scale unemployment after that) were ready to experiment with anything that might lift them out of their abasement — even *Nationalsozialismus* (National Socialism), otherwise "Nazism", as from 1933.

The Nazis, under Hitler and his henchmen, with their concept of racial purity — and superiority — told the German people that they were entitled to conquer Europe and (their undoing) Russia for *lebensraum* (living space). Hitler launched a war of aggression invading Poland in September 1939, and the British declared war on Germany two days later.

In June 1941, Hitler ordered the German army, closely followed by the SS and Hitler's killing machine, to invade Russia. Millions of Jews became fatally trapped behind German lines in Poland, the Baltic States, Ukraine and western Russia. The

[219] And as a result of the neglect of Colonel House - see chapter 10.

Holocaust followed, with the destruction of the *heim* and *yiddishe* culture, along with the lives of six million Jews, and millions of others. Yet, in their policy of adamant aggression and unrestrained cruelty, the Germans were not alone.

Totalitarian fascism had erupted before that of Germany in Mussolini's Italy (from 1925) and Franco's Spain (from 1936-39). In the 1930s, however, in the Far East, nothing matched the feral aggression inflicted by the Japanese in their invasion of Manchuria in 1931 and, on a wider scale, China from 1937. The territorial ambitions of the Japanese were, however, not limited to China, despite its vastness. By the summer of 1941, the Japanese occupied also the whole of French Indochina (today's Vietnam, Cambodia and Laos). The Pacific Ocean — some 30% of the globe — connected Japan with its conquests, past and projected; but it was not the domain of the Japanese alone.

Whereas America was instinctively opposed to imperialism and colonialism (in the shape of the Dutch East Indies, French Indochina and the British Empire), it nevertheless had its own interests, commercial and strategic, throughout the Pacific area. (Some referred to this as "America's Empire".) For the protection of those interests, the USA maintained naval and other military bases in the Pacific, most notably at Honolulu in the Hawaiian islands.

The USA sought to restrain Japan but, on 7 December 1941, in a devastating surprise attack, Japanese carrier-based torpedo- and bomb-carrying aircraft attacked and dismembered the US Navy's Pacific Fleet at Pearl Harbor, Honolulu. With that, the conflict provoked by the Germans two years earlier became truly global.

LOSS OF ACCESS TO RUBBER

Long before World War II, Henry Ford had given the American people affordable mobility and independence with the Model T automobile. Millions were sold, and each car rolled out of the showroom on four rubber tyres. By the late 1930s, the United

States was using half the world's supply of natural rubber, most of it coming from Southeast Asia.[220]

When the USA was plunged into war in late 1941, it was appreciated that its demand for rubber would be immense: for a military airplane, half a ton; for a tank, one ton; for a battleship, 75 tons. Every soldier required 32 pounds of rubber for footwear, clothing and equipment — and millions of soldiers had to be kitted out.

It soon became clear that, with their swift subjugation of the whole Far East and Pacific regions, the Japanese had brought under their control, and deprived the USA of access to:

> *"90 percent of the natural rubber supply. At this time, the United States had a stockpile of about one million tons of natural rubber, a consumption rate of about 600,000 tons per year, and no commercial process to produce a general purpose synthetic rubber."*[221]

The UK's 1915 Shell Crisis had become the USA's 1942 rubber crisis. Weizmann's progress towards manufacturing acetone on an industrial scale had been in the pursuit of synthetic rubber. The Weizmann Process was crucially relevant again.

THE WEIZMANN PROCESS AGAIN

Weizmann had first met the colossus of US politics, Franklin Delano Roosevelt (popularly known as FDR) in February 1940. Their conversation had been about the White Paper, but ended inconsequentially. Whether they discussed Weizmann's scientific work with acetone and rubber is not known but likely

---

[220] See: https://www.acs.org/content/acs/en/education/whatischemistry/landmarks/syntheticrubber.html

[221] See https://www.acs.org/content/acs/en/education/whatischemistry/landmarks/syntheticrubber.html

for, two years later, after Pearl Harbor, FDR sent for Weizmann to assist with the US quest for synthetic rubber.

Weizmann's journey in response to FDR's request was delayed by tragedy. Shortly after the president's invitation reached Weizmann, his younger son, Michael, a Royal Air Force pilot, was reported missing-in-action over the Bay of Biscay, west of German-occupied France and he was soon presumed dead. No family can recover fully from a loss of that nature but life, perforce, carries on and, within a month, Weizmann's sense of duty propelled him to undertake the passage to America.

Immediately prior to his departure, in March 1942, Weizmann called into number 10 Downing Street, to see Britain's formidable war-time prime minister, Winston Churchill, in yet another example of Weizmann's unique access to the British Government. The political leader of United Kingdom and the British Empire and that of the Jewish people — more than half of whom were by then staring into the Nazi abyss — spoke about the purpose of Weizmann's journey to America. Churchill went on to tell Weizmann that he was still thinking about Zionist ambitions. He spoke of a post-war plan to make the ruler of Saudi Arabia, Ibn Saud:

> *"lord of the Middle East — the boss of the bosses — provided he settles with you. It will be up to you to get the best possible conditions. Of course we shall help you. Keep this confidential, but you might talk it over with Roosevelt when you get to America. There's nothing he and I cannot do if we set our minds on it."*[222]

After arriving in Washington DC, Weizmann met with FDR but found he was unable to broach the subject of the Middle East, and no doubt thought Churchill would find his own opportunity to mention his Saudi plan to his American counterpart. Following a short conversation about the rubber crisis,

---

[222] *Trial and Error* (ibid)

Weizmann left the Oval Office to try to contribute to its solution. He thought that what should be done:

> "*was to ferment maize — of which millions of bushels were available in the United States and Canada — and convert it into butyl alcohol and acetone by my process, which was established and working on a large scale in various parts of America. The butyl alcohol could without difficulty be used for the making of butylene and the butylene easily converted into butadiene, the basis for rubber. I knew that large quantities of butadiene were already being made out of oil, but the trouble was, as far as I could gather, that the butadiene so produced was not pure, and the purification was slow and costly, whereas the butylene produced by my process was chemically pure, and would lend itself more easily for conversion into a purer form of butadiene.*"[223]

VICE-PRESIDENT WALLACE

Of course, the US became aware of its emergent rubber crisis immediately war was visited upon them by the Japanese, and had not been awaiting Weizmann's arrival before starting to seek a solution. The American approach was through its gigantic oil industry, much to Weizmann's frustration.

Weizmann quickly found an ally in FDR's vice-president, Henry A Wallace, who was a plant geneticist and fully acquainted with Weizmann's work. Wallace was regarded as "*with the exception of FDR, the most popular Democrat in the country.*"[224] He had been FDR's Secretary of Agriculture in the 1930s and had sent Walter C Lowdermilk to examine soil conditions in several countries, including British Mandatory Palestine. Lowdermilk reported back, as he later wrote:

> "[after] *1,000 years of deterioration* .... [in] *some 50 years of*

---

[223] *Trial and Error* (ibid)

[224] According to the biographer of Harry S Truman in *Truman*, David McCullough, Simon & Schuster (1992).

reclamation of both the highlands and the lowlands by relatively small groups of Jewish settlers ... Petah Tikva became the first settlement to conquer the deadly foe of malaria, by planting Eucalyptus .... in the swamps to absorb the moisture, draining other swamps, importing large quantities of quinine, and developing rich agriculture and citriculture. ... [becoming] *the largest of the Jewish rural settlements, supporting 20,000 people."* [225]

Lowdermilk had told Wallace that with innovative farming methods the Holy Land could absorb four million Jewish refugees. This contrasted sharply with British and Arab claims that the country was already overcrowded. Wallace came to see the Jewish pioneers as American-style frontiersmen, but with biblical overtones.

As to the rubber crisis, as Wallace warned him would be the case, Weizmann was unable to breach the walls of the American oil companies. They were determined, whether they knew of the Weizmann Process or not, on a different route to salvation: creating synthetic rubber by the development of petroleum by-products. Under the direction of Bernard M Baruch[226], over 50 industrial plants were set up to produce the monomers and polymers required for the manufacture of synthetic rubber, and the Americans soon surmounted their difficulties.

In that environment, it is impressive that Weizmann made any impact whatsoever but he did find opportunities to contribute to the US war effort: solving both the problem of mixing hard and soft rubbers for the inner tube, and issues with the hard outer parts of tyres by extending the Weizmann Process to the

[225] *Palestine, Land of Promise*, Walter Clay Lowdermilk (Harper New York, 1944)

[226] Baruch (1870 –1965) was a Jewish American financier, stock investor, philanthropist, statesman and consultant to presidents from Woodrow Wilson to Truman.

condensation of acetone and acetylene. According to Wallace:

> *"The world will never know what a significant contribution Weizmann made towards the success of the synthetic rubber programme at a time when it was badly bogged down and going too slowly."*[227]

Weizmann's attention was in any event being drawn to the Western Desert of Egypt, where the armies of Britain and Germany faced each other. The British were dug in at El Alamein, little more than 100 km west of Alexandria. Facing them there, the German general, Rommel, widely regarded as one of the best generals of any army in the war, was threatening Egypt and the Suez Canal.

There had been little if any good news for the Allies and the Jews since the start of the war and now disaster threatened them both. Should Rommel, followed by the SS and the Gestapo, break through the British lines (in the pursuit of Middle East and Persian Gulf oil), the whole *Yishuv* would fall under a sentence of death, like their brothers and sisters in eastern Europe.

EL ALAMEIN

There were two battles of El Alamein. In the first (1-27 July 1942), after retreating from Libya into Egypt, the British held firm, but needed significant resupply. The second saw the long-awaited turning point of the war, for Churchill reinvigorated the British forces with the appointment of the swash-buckling General Sir Bernard Law (Monty) Montgomery. Of course, morale alone could not win battles and Monty knew that. Accordingly, while at the end of July 1942 the initiative lay with him, he awaited resupply before resuming the hostilities.

Weizmann writes that he secured a meeting with the American Chief of Staff, General George Marshall, to provide him with a fresh perspective on the vital importance of what was about to

[227] *Chaim Weizmann: A Biography By Several Hands* (ibid) by Ritchie Calder.

take place in the Western Desert and the repercussions beyond:

> "*I explained what faced us if the needed munitions did not reach the British in time. General Marshall listened gravely and attentively, said very little, made notes of what I told him, and thanked me for the information. The story of how the supplies were rushed across the Atlantic and Africa, of how they arrived in the nick of time, of how the tide was turned at the last moment, has been told many times.*"[228]

The details of the second battle of El Alamein are complex, but the main reason for the success of the British may be seen in one set of statistics: by the time Monty was ready to attack, on 23 October, in pursuit of the destruction of Rommel's 547 tanks, he had under his command 1,029 tanks, fully 422 (25%) newly supplied by the Americans.

Whether Weizmann's plea was pivotal to the decision to send the matériel to the British is somewhere on a scale from doubtful to unknown, but the passage from *Trial and Error* is included to show that Weizmann's "*unique access*" was not restricted to the British establishment. That the American Chief of Staff would find the time to see the British scientist, and Zionist, suggests that he was aware of Weizmann's international reputation.

As for Wallace, he was too clever, too left-wing in his views and too outspoken to last as vice president. He was ousted by the Democratic Party before the electioneering that would lead to FDR's fourth term. Wallace's replacement was to be the little-known Harry S Truman.

~~~

[228] *Trial and Error* (ibid)
~~~

16

IN THE GIFT OF TRUMAN I - THE NEGEV

To say that Harry Truman was not a politician in the mould of the titan of American politics that was Franklin Delano Roosevelt is to be not only honest (and kind) but also reflective of how the president thought of his running-mate and then deputy: between FDR's January 1945 inauguration and his death four months later, the president met with his vice-president only twice.

WALLACE REPLACED

By July 1942, the Democratic party grandees had taken against Vice President Wallace. Later, things deteriorated further because the vice president would not be restrained from making a series of public speeches that infuriated all except those on the extreme left. Moves were afoot to replace Wallace at the July 1944 Democratic National Convention with the less outspoken Truman. That this was not the popular choice in the country may be seen in the results of a Gallup poll taken just before the Convention: 65% of those surveyed favoured Wallace and only 2% Truman.

FDR had contracted poliomyelitis in 1921 at the age of 39, which condemned him to a wheelchair for the rest of his life; but he did not let that prevent him becoming one of the greatest of the US presidents of modern times. Nevertheless, as the pressures of the Great Depression, the New Deal, Pearl Harbor and all-out war — and a lifetime as a chain smoker — took their toll, so FDR's health deteriorated. He went into the 1944 presidential campaign suffering from multiple heart-related issues and, by then, all within the Washington Beltway, and many beyond, appreciated that whoever would be nominated as vice president would, before long, succeed FDR as the next president of the USA. Despite all this, Truman was nominated as FDR's running mate.

PRESIDENT TRUMAN

Contrary to all expectations, Roosevelt (with Truman alongside) comfortably won the 1944 election with 432 out of the 531 electoral college votes and 53.4% of the popular vote. The two men were sworn into their respective offices on 20 January 1945. FDR succumbed the following 12 April, whereupon Truman became the leader of the Free World. He had no vice president[229] so, recognising his own inexperience in foreign affairs, Truman relied exclusively for those matters on his appointee as Secretary of State, General George Marshall, known by then to many as the "greatest living American".[230]

Truman may have been chosen because he was not Wallace — not as intellectual and without the wealth that Wallace had generated through his industrialising agricultural techniques. Truman was a quiet man, who had spent most of his youth on the family farm near Independence, Missouri. He saw combat in France as an artillery officer in World War I and returned to his home state after the war.

While few had high hopes for Truman — and, assuredly, FDR was a hard, arguably the hardest, act to follow[231] — as president, Truman made some decidedly momentous decisions and few have doubted their appropriateness. Most significantly, Truman

---

[229] The Twenty-Fifth Amendment to the US Constitution, 1967, provided that such a vacancy in the office of Vice President should be filled by the President's nominee.

[230] Attributed to Dean Acheson and Presidents Roosevelt and Truman - see *Harry S. Truman: A Life*, Robert H Ferrell (University of Missouri Press, 1994)

[231] FDR was the only president to serve more than two terms. The Twenty-Second Amendment to the American Constitution, passed by Congress in 1947, and ratified by the states on 27 February 1951, provides: *No person shall be elected to the office of the President more than twice, and no person who has held the office of President, or acted as President, for more than two years of a term to which some other person was elected President shall be elected to the office of the President more than once.*

did not shrink from twice using over Japan the atomic bomb. Its first deployment claimed 90,000-145,000 lives in Hiroshima on 6 August 1945. He decided upon its second use, too, three days later, taking a further 40,000-80,000 lives in Nagasaki. He thereby brought to a swift end World War II that, it may fairly be assumed, would have continued for at least another year as the Allies sought to subdue the Japanese in their home islands, at the cost of probably a million (and possibly millions of) lives. Those decisions of Truman took courage.

While, plainly, Truman could make brutal choices, he also understood compassion and, after World War II, he approved the launching of the Marshall Plan that (contrary to the French policy of punishing the Germans at Versailles in 1919 for the First World War, so hastening the Second) rebuilt the devastated post-World War II Europe — including Germany. Around $12 billion[232] was invested in the infra-structure and economies of Western Europe. (The countries of Eastern Europe were not the recipients of Marshall Aid, as they fell behind what Churchill described as an "Iron Curtain" drawn by Stalin from Stettin in the Baltic to Trieste in the Adriatic.)

Then there was the Truman Doctrine, which he announced to Congress in March 1947. Its purpose was the containment of Soviet Russia's geopolitical expansion during the Cold War, for which Congress granted economic and military aid to Greece and Turkey; and, consistent with his Doctrine, Truman faced down the Soviets with the Berlin Airlift of 1948-9. Before that came up, there was the problem of Palestine.

TRUMAN AND JACOBSON

Three decisions of great significance to the Zionist cause fell to Truman. Without his having taken them in the way that he did, the creation and continuation of the State of Israel may well have faltered. Unlike Wallace, Truman is not known to have had any

---

232 About $124 billion in 2017.

appreciation of Zionism, before he met Chaim Weizmann at any rate, but he did have some early exposure to the Jewish mind.

In 1917, at his army training camp before his departure for France, Truman ran the base canteen. According to Truman's biographer, David McCullough:

> *"In addition to his regular duties, he had been assigned to run the regimental canteen ... To help make the operation a financial success (as most Army canteens were not) Harry took on a partner, Sergeant Edward Jacobson, a former clerk in a Kansas City clothing store.* [Truman wrote to his wife, Bess]: *'I have a Jew in charge of the canteen by the name of Jacobson and he is a crackerjack,' ... as if that were all the reason anyone would need to expect a profitable outcome. And it was indeed Jacobson who ran things, as Harry was always first to acknowledge.*
>
> *To finance the canteen every man in the regiment was assessed $2, which produced an instant capitalisation of $2,200. In no time Truman and Jacobson had a "grand, rushing" business, taking in $500 to $900 a day. A barbershop and a tailor shop were added. After six months business was so successful overall that the canteen paid dividends of $10,000, which made Truman and Jacobson extremely popular and led them to conclude they were an unbeatable business combination. Some of the other officers began kidding Harry, calling him a 'lucky Jew' and 'Trumanheimer.' 'I guess I should be very proud of my Jewish ability,' he said."*[233]

Not unexpectedly, one might think having read all that, after the war, Truman and Jacobson set up in partnership together. They opened a small clothing store in Kansas City and became life-long friends.

With Jacobson running the store, Truman was able to enter

[233] *Truman*, David McCullough (ibid)

public life, joining the Democratic Party and being elected a county official in 1922. By 1934, he was a US Senator and, from March 1941, he headed up the Truman Committee, charged with identifying and remedying waste and inefficiency in Federal wartime contracts; and Truman acquired national prominence. His friendship with Jacobson was to become as important to Zionism as would have been a lifetime's devotion to the movement.

After the full horrors of the Holocaust had been revealed towards the end of World War II, Truman's sympathies were with the Jews. As McCullough writes:

> *"... in 1943, he had said everything 'humanly possible' must be done to provide a haven for Jewish survivors of the Nazis"* and reports that *"his own belief* [was] *that Palestine was the answer"*.[234]

CONFLICTING PRESSURES

Truman was not alone in holding those views in post-World War II America: a Jewish homeland in Palestine was supported by most Americans, Jewish and otherwise. Of course, with another election approaching in 1948 (electioneering begins mid-term at the latest in America) and his approval ratings as low as 36%, Truman recognised that the Jewish vote was important to him. Inevitably, his political enemies would accuse him of supporting the Zionist cause purely for electoral purposes; but Truman was not so persuaded of the need to placate or attract the Jewish electorate that he did not vacillate over Palestine wildly — and alarmingly, to supporters and detractors equally.

The reasons for Truman's equivocation were many and diverse. First, the State Department (like the Foreign Office in London) was instinctively more warmly disposed to the Arabs than to the Jews. This is not the place to explore the historical reasons for this inbuilt bias but one explanation was plain: while the Jews

---

[234] *Truman*, David McCullough (ibid)

(save for certain individuals) had always been without power, Arab nations controlled most of the world's proven oil reserves. Having said that, when he was reminded by his Defence Secretary: *"of the critical need for Saudi Arabian oil, in the event of war, Truman said he would handle the situation in the light of justice, not oil."*[235] Yet, the State Department's policy was in line with that of the Europeans, 80% of whose oil came from the Gulf Arabs. All those parties *"favoured a United Nations Trusteeship over Palestine until the contention between Arabs and Jews could somehow be resolved"*.[236] Such a resolution, being impossibly distant and indeterminate[237], would be the worst possible outcome for Weizmann and the Zionists, who were beginning to embrace Partition.

Palestine was not, of course, the only, and not even remotely the most pressing, item in the president's in-tray. World War II over, the Soviets were threatening expansion at the cost of freedom all over Europe, and another major conflagration did not seem impossible. There were precious few troops that were not already deployed, given that many were still in Japan and much of the Far East, and many others were stationed in West Germany (East Germany having fallen into the hands of the Russians), where they faced a massive Soviet army.

With that background, Truman found exhausting the constant communications bombardment under which he came from Jews, and every Jewish interest group, to see through Partition at the United Nations ("UN"). It also had the self-defeating effect of negating any desire he might have had to make decisions to please the Jewish lobby in advance of a looming election. At the same time, he was being pummelled by both the State Department and the Defense Department, the former telling him that the Arabs complained they were being *"made to pay for the*

[235] *Truman,* David McCullough (ibid)

[236] *Truman,* David McCullough (ibid)

[237] It is still awaited at the time of writing.

crimes of Adolph Hitler" and the latter *"fearing an 'oil-starved' war"*.[238] Both sets of pressures were conspiring to defeat Weizmann's enduring ambition for a Jewish state.

THE SUN SETS ON THE BRITISH EMPIRE

The British Empire, for two centuries known as the empire on which the sun never sets, was at its zenith before World War I; but by the end of World War II Britain was, financially, totally drained. Indeed, Britain was so destitute that in 1946 it gratefully accepted a loan of $4.33 billion[239] from its former American colonies. A certain amount of British retrenchment was called for. In any event, the continuation of the Empire was no longer practical, given that many, if not most, constituent parts were pushing hard for their independence.

Unlike the French, who fought, and bled, for years to maintain their hold on their north African and south-east Asian colonies, the British adopted a post-war, post-colonial policy of peaceful disengagement in favour of stable, non-Communist governments. The first and greatest task was disentanglement from India. The granting of Indian independence in 1947 caused massive population movements — of millions — to and from Pakistan to its west, and East Pakistan, today's Bangladesh, to its east. Next in line was Palestine, where the British were assailed by both Arab and Jew alike. After thirty unhappy years, in which the elation of the Balfour Declaration had become a burdensome source of misery to all, the British had had enough.

THE MANDATE

On 26 June 1945, the Charter of the United Nations was signed. A new International Trusteeship system for application to *"territories now held under mandate* [meaning under the auspices

---

[238] *Truman,* David McCullough (ibid)

[239] Equivalent to some equivalent to £27bn at the time that the final repayment instalment was made in 2009.

of the League of Nations]" was created.

The British Palestine Mandate had become widely unpopular in Britain. While the British Labour Party had promised before the 1945 election to allow mass Jewish migration into Palestine, once in power it went back on its word.

With the remnants of the Holocaust desperate not to remain on the soil of the European/Russian landmass soaked with the blood of six million Jewish dead, hundreds of thousands of desolate, just-about-surviving Jews clamoured to enter Palestine. Having endured years of abuse imprisoned in concentration camps (few had survived the extermination camps), they were now languishing in Displaced Persons (DP) camps, mainly in the hostile environments of Germany and Austria.

The romanticism of the Protestant Zionists having long-since evaporated, British political hearts were hardened against the Jews. Many of those who had survived the devastation of the Holocaust risked drowning by crossing the Mediterranean largely in unseaworthy vessels. Some even touched the soil of the Holy Land, but only fleetingly, before they were returned by the British ghoulishly to Europe or interned in camps on the British-controlled island of Cyprus, tantalisingly just 275 kms east of the port of Haifa. In post-World War II Palestine itself, the British forces made little if any effort to control marauding Arabs, concentrating their efforts on hampering self-defence by the *Yishuv*. As a result, anti-British Jewish militancy — and Jewish terrorism directed against the British military — increased to the point where not even 100,000 British troops could subdue Palestine.

PARTITION

It was time for the appointment of yet another commission and, in 1946, an Anglo-American Committee of Inquiry was set up. It concluded its work with the recommendation that 100,000

Jewish refugees from Europe be admitted into Palestine[240], while opposing the establishment of either an Arab or a Jewish state. (Truman infuriated the British by unilaterally and publicly endorsing the Committee's recommendation.) The British and the Americans met again in London and agreed upon the division of Palestine into Arab and Jewish provinces — what was called Partition (and is today called a Two State Solution).

As with the Peel Commission's suggestion a decade earlier, the Jews and the Arabs of Palestine at last found something they could agree upon: they were of one mind in rejecting the Partition proposal. So too did the Americans. At that stage, few Zionists saw the opportunity that Partition offered them. One who did was Chaim Weizmann.

Weizmann had been the first Zionist leader to accept the idea of the partition of Palestine. In January 1937, the idea had been put to him firstly in a secret session of the Peel Commission. He brought it before the 20th Zionist Congress in Basel the following August. The proposal was, in the time-honoured traditions of Zionist Congresses, deeply divisive; and the resolution that was passed on the subject both rejected it and left the door open.

Fast forward ten years to 18 February 1947 and the British Foreign Secretary announced that the British accepted that they were unable to resolve the differences between the Jews and the Arabs in Mandatory Palestine. They referred the matter to the UN.

UNSCOP

In May 1947, yet another inquiry was launched: the United

[240] According to the United States Holocaust Memorial Museum: "*With over 80,000 Jewish DPs in the United States, about 136,000 in Israel, and another 20,000 in other nations, including Canada and South Africa, the DP emigration crisis came to an end. Almost all of the DP camps were closed by 1952.*" https://www.ushmm.org/wlc/en/article.php?ModuleId=10005462

Nations Special Committee on Palestine ("UNSCOP"), which proceeded to take evidence in Palestine and in the US. Weizmann played his part in this, too, for he gave evidence to UNSCOP in Jerusalem and later at the UN at Lake Success, New York.

As fate determined, some members of UNSCOP were present on the dockside in the port of Haifa when over 4,500 Jewish DPs, and would-be immigrants into the Palestine from which Britain sincerely wanted to depart, were forcibly removed from the ship, *Exodus*, by British soldiers, only to be deported back to Germany.

The Arab Higher Committee boycotted UNSCOP on the basis that the Palestinian Arabs' natural rights were self-evident and should automatically be recognised by the UN. The UNSCOP membership was unimpressed: not one of them endorsed the One State Solution sought by the Arab Higher Committee.

The UNSCOP report was delivered to the UN on 3 September 1947. It recommended to the UN the Plan of Partition with Economic Union. There were to be independent Arab and Jewish states, with special provisions for the neutrality of Jerusalem and the preservation of Palestine's economic unity. The General Assembly of the UN was to consider and vote on the matter in November 1947. The British announced their intention to withdraw from Palestine completely by 1 August 1948.

The Zionists frantically threw themselves into the process of lobbying every member of the UN that was not manifestly hostile. As a young Zionist diplomat, Abba Eban, recalled:

> *"We took the list of undecided countries and began to seek ways of influencing them. How shall we influence Liberia? They say that the American Firestone Company carries weight there. How to reach Firestone? How shall we approach the President of the Philippines? Is there any Jew who knows him? How can we influence Haiti, which was*

still straddling the fence?"[241]

Weizmann was brought over from London, where he had been preparing to leave for his home in Rechovot. Norman Rose reports that:

> *"Weizmann played his part, despatching last-minute appeals to the French, the Indians, and the Filipinos. 'Our fate is still hanging in the balance,' he wrote to Henry Morgenthau, Jr. 'Could* [you] *help us with Greece or with the Philippines or with Haiti. Mr Sumner Welles has promised to do something with Greece.'"* [242]

On 5 October 1946, the day after *Yom Kippur*, in a dawn-to-dusk operation, the Jewish Agency established eleven new *kibbutzim* in the Negev. Weizmann declared that the new settlements would *"have greater political significance than a hundred speeches about resistance."*[243]

THE NEGEV

If there were to be Partition, there would have to be a map showing what territory was to be apportioned to which party. At this point, we should remind ourselves that the land over which the Jews and the Arabs were locked in dispute — and combat — was (and is today) no greater in expanse than the Principality of Wales, the Italian island of Sicily or the American State of New Jersey. The small area that was proposed for Partition in favour of the Jewish homeland may not have been viable for an independent state but the Jewish Agency accepted the plan. As was their custom, the Arabs rejected it. The Jews believed, as Weizmann said, it is better to have fifty percent of something than a hundred percent of nothing. For the Arabs it was a zero

[241] *Chaim Weizmann: A Biography*, Norman Rose (ibid)

[242] *Chaim Weizmann: A Biography*, Norman Rose (ibid)

[243] *Chaim Weizmann: A Biography*, Norman Rose (ibid)

sum game.

The largest part of the area allocated to the Jews was the Negev. That area, 13,000 km^2 and 55% of today's State of Israel, was all desert and commonly believed incapable of supporting either agricultural or urban development.[244] The Jews were to have, at the southernmost tip of the Negev, access to the Gulf of Aqaba (through which Weizmann had passed to meet Emir Feisal in 1918) and the shipping routes to the East.

As the UN General Assembly vote approached, some of the American delegates (State Department men), looking at the map, and disregarding that fact that the Negev was virtually barren, decided that the Jews were receiving too much land. They prepared to amend the plan by removing the Negev from the Jewish sector.

Writing the epilogue to *Trial and Error* in August 1948, Weizmann remarks about the Negev with typical acuity:

> *"At present it looks a forbidding desert, and the scene of desolation masks the importance of the region. But with a little imagination it becomes quite clear that Aqaba is the gate to the Indian Ocean, and constitutes a much shorter route from Palestine to the Far East than via Port Said and the Suez Canal."*[245]

The incipient state would have been hopelessly stunted without the Negev so, on hearing of the redrawn lines, Weizmann left his colleagues in New York and set out for Washington DC.

It should be remembered that, by this time, Weizmann had resigned his presidency of the ZO, his eyesight was failing, his

---

[244] The Israeli State has shown that neither assumption was correct.

[245] Today, Israeli exports to the Far East, as with so many other places, are growing strongly. Without egress through the Gulf of Eilat, that trade would be severely hindered.

general health poor and his home, where he truly would have preferred to have been, resting and regaining his strength, was in Rechovot in *Eretz Yisrael*. It was a week before his seventy-third birthday. Notwithstanding all that, Weizmann recognised that his commitment to his life's mission was undiminished.

FIRST SECRET MEETING WITH TRUMAN

Weizmann was received at the White House by President Truman, according to Weizmann, *"with the utmost cordiality"*.

> *"They ... met secretly in the White House* [on 19] *November 1947 ... and the effect on Truman was nearly as pronounced as it had been on the British Foreign Secretary, Lord Balfour, thirty years earlier. Spreading a map on Truman's desk, Weizmann ... fascinated the former Missouri farmer with the agricultural possibilities in the Negev Desert, the future control of which was still at issue."*[246]

Weizmann told Truman that the Negev as a whole would be a vital part of the Jewish state, explaining:

> *"The northern part ... is beautiful country. It needs water, of course, which can either be brought from the north, as projected in the Lowdermilk scheme, or provided locally by desalting the brackish water which is found in abundance in these parts."* [247]

Weizmann described the desalinisation experiments at the Daniel Sieff Institute at Rechovot, where drinking water was even then being extracted from briny water economically for supply to settlements in the Negev[248], and he read from a specially prepared memorandum on the Negev (see panel 11), in

---

[246] *Truman, David McCullough* (ibid)

[247] *Trial and Error* (ibid)

[248] Today, Israel is, irrespective of rainfall, or the absence of it, self-sufficient in water, thanks to the development of its desalinisation technology.

which there are references to Aqaba. The Israeli city of Eilat did not even amount to the five huts that were established in the 1948 War of Independence.

11

THE NEGEV MEMORANDUM

> Aqaba, which is found on the southern end of the Negev and the Red Sea, represents the only outlet for the Jewish state to the Indian Ocean, India, the Far East, Australia and New Zealand. For the Jewish state this outlet will be one of the important routes for commercial relations with that part of the world. The Jewish state, in order to absorb the refugees coming from Europe, will have to do its utmost to develop its industrial and commercial capacities and in this connection the importance of Aqaba is much greater than just a piece of land on the Red Sea.
>
> Aqaba has played an important rôle in Jewish history from the early days of the Jewish Kingdom, and the UNSCOP report giving this place to the Jewish state has recognised the historic connections of the Jews with this part of the Red Sea.
>
> Aqaba, in the hands of the Arabs, may be a permanent threat in the rear of the Jewish state. The Arab States have an outlet to the Red Sea and the Gulf of Aqaba through Transjordan, Egypt and Saudi-Arabia.

Truman was persuaded, and pledged his support for the inclusion of the Negev in the Jewish state with the words: *"You can bank on us."*[249] He gave his delegates at the UN no room for doubt, and the Negev was restored to the Jewish section on the Partition map. Weizmann wrote, *"I was extremely happy to find that the President read the map quickly and clearly"*[250], somewhat modestly, one might think: had Weizmann not met and worked on Truman, there would have been no Jewish (now, Israeli) Negev and effectively no Israel. After the meeting, it was to be in Jewish hands and the viability of the state stood a chance. That Chaim Weizmann alone was indispensable to that

---

[249] *Truman,* David McCullough (ibid)

[250] *Trial and Error* (ibid)

outcome is beyond argument.

The UN vote took place on 29 November 1947, broadcast by radio to the world: the counting of the votes took three minutes, agonising for the Zionists but the most productive moments of their lives — indeed, of the previous two millennia of Jewish history. Partition was passed by 33 votes in favour (including both the US and the Soviet Union), 13 against (the Arabs unanimously rejecting it) and 10 abstentions. Jews worldwide rejoiced.

CODA: Whereas Weizmann had been the pivotal influence upon the British government that granted the Balfour Declaration thirty years earlier — the first seminal, defining achievement — with Truman he was to be required to work his magic a second time, and within a period of six months. Two further defining and vital achievements were required of the ageing and ailing, recently ousted-Zionist leader. Of course, Weizmann could not know that and in December 1947 he returned to the Dorchester Hotel in London, en route (so he thought) to Rechovot.

~~~
~~~

17

IN THE GIFT OF TRUMAN II

PARTITION AND RECOGNITION

After the passing of the Partition resolution by the UN, the Jews and the supporters of Israel saw a grim future for the *Yishuv*: a few hundred thousand Jews confronted by a million local Arabs, whose strength would be augmented by the armies of five Arab nations, from as far afield as Iraq, such was the determination of the Arabs to snuff out the life of the Jewish State at the moment of its birth. Indeed, long before the May 1948 British departure, and the Israeli Declaration of Independence, the War of Independence was effectively underway. By the end of 1947, the battle for Palestine had begun in earnest, with Arabs attacking Jews in their towns and settlements and the British turning a blind eye to the fighting, until, that is, the *Yishuv* tried to defend itself or retaliate. Then the British were motivated to act — against the Jews.

LOBBYING TO SAVE THE *YISHUV*

Truman was on the receiving end of constant lobbying[251] to make ready to defend the *Yishuv* at a time when, just two years after World War II had ended, there was the constant threat from the Soviet Union of renewed hostilities in Europe. To have issued a general call-up to augment the army would have been political suicide for Truman, who faced an election at the end of 1948. Equally, not to show real support for the *Yishuv* would lose him the support of New York (where alone there were two and a half million Jews), Philadelphia and Chicago, to mention but a few areas of concentrated Jewish votes.

TRUSTEESHIP RE-EMERGES

Truman was at a loss to know which way to turn. He retreated

[251] In late 1947, Truman received more than 100,000 letters and telegrams concerning Palestine - *Truman,* David McCullough (ibid)

into his shell, refusing to see any members of the Jewish lobby. On one occasion involving in-fighting between opposing teams within the White House, Truman snapped. He stood up and exclaimed, *"Oh, hell, I'm leaving!"*[252] Then the vacillation became an inclination to retreat from his former pro-Jewish State policy and allow the status of Palestine to return to its default mode of Trusteeship. At least that way he would not have to stand up to Secretary of State Marshall and the State Department. They had started to work for it.

The American Zionists and the *Yishuv* team at the UN could see the push for Trusteeship. The State Department was proposing to table a resolution at the UN to that effect, to reverse the November 1947 vote of the General Assembly. The Zionist team at the UN was not short of talent, but there was amongst them (and, equally, in Tel Aviv) no recognisable statesman, and certainly no one who had the ear of the American president. There was only Chaim Weizmann and he was in London, fatigued, unwell, with failing sight and preparing to return to Rechovot. Nevertheless, it was plain that Truman needed stiffening and only Weizmann could generate within him the necessary resolve.

RETURN TO NEW YORK

In January 1948, Chaim Weizmann was asked to return to New York. Initially, he declined for personal reasons. Meyer Weisgal, Weizmann's assistant, tells us[253] that he had made his mind up that Weizmann should receive more than a casual request and demanded a proper appeal. On 23 January, a Western Union cablegram[254] arrived in London from the Zionist delegation in New York (see panel 12).

---

[252] *Truman,* David McCullough (ibid)

[253] *Meyer Weisgal ... So Far,* Meyer Weisgal (Weidenfeld and Nicolson, 1971)

[254] Source - *Weizmann Archives: Jacobson E/1-2812.TIF*

12

PLEA TO RETURN TO NEW YORK

CABLEGRAM NEW YORK JANUARY 23,1948

CHAIM WEIZMANN
DORCHESTER HOTEL
LONDON

IN VIEW WORSENING SITUATION PALESTINE AND FACT THAT COMMISSIONS ARRIVAL NOT IMMINENT PERSONALLY ADVISE YOU IF POSSIBLE RECONSIDER DECISION TO GO JANUARY STOP NO CONDITIONS EXIST THERE CONSTRUCTIVE POLITICAL ACTIVITY EVERYTHING DEPENDING UPON OUTCOME SECURITY NEGOTIATIONS HERE LAKE SUCCESS AND WASHINGTON STOP MOST CRUCIAL PHASE OF ALL NOW APPROACHES HERE IN WHICH WE KEENLY MISS YOUR PRESENCE ADVICE ACTIVITY INFLUENCE AFFECTIONATELY

AUBREY EBAN

Once again, out-of-office, unwell, of failing sight, but his sense of purpose undiminished — and plainly without a substitute — Weizmann undertook yet another cross-Atlantic journey. Hearing, on arrival, that Truman refused to see him, he checked into the Waldorf-Astoria Hotel in New York to recuperate — and to await destiny's call.

According to Truman's biographer again:

> *"A secret paper from George Kennan's Policy Planning Staff recommended no further support for partition. A report from the new Central Intelligence Agency concluded that partition would not work and urged reconsideration. More important to Truman were the views of George Marshall who, at a meeting of the National Security Council on February 12, had said the United States was 'playing*

with fire while having nothing with which to put it out.'"[255]

Truman was again asked to see Weizmann and once more refused point-blank.

ENTER EDDIE JACOBSON

In the event, it was Eddie Jacobson, Truman's former partner and friend of thirty years whom fate, and the President of the Bnei Brith movement, called upon. Was Jacobson able to assist? He was prepared to try, and wrote to Truman on 20 February imploring the President to receive Chaim Weizmann. Truman's reply took a week to reach Jacobson: there was nothing to discuss as the situation was "*not solvable as presently set up.*"[256]

Refusing to give in, Jacobson flew to the nation's capital and walked into the Oval Office on Saturday, 13 March, uninvited. After a little small talk, Jacobson raised the question of Palestine. Truman turned his back on Jacobson and said he would not discuss Palestine, Jews, Arabs or the British. He had decided to leave matters to the UN. According to McCullough, Truman thought both he and Jacobson were being used by the Jewish lobby and he:

> "*... spoke bitterly of the abuse he had been subjected to, of how 'disrespectful and mean' certain Jews had been to him. Jacobson thought suddenly and sadly that 'my dear friend, the President of the United States, was at that moment as close to being an anti-Semite as a man could possibly be ...'"*[257]

Then, seemingly at a total impasse, Jacobson was hit by inspiration to play a final card:

> "*'Harry, all your life you have had a hero* [Andrew

[255] *Truman,* David McCullough (ibid)

[256] *Truman,* David McCullough (ibid)

[257] *Truman,* David McCullough (ibid)

Jackson[258]] .... *I too have a hero, a man I never met, but who is, I think, the greatest Jew who ever lived .... I am talking about Chaim Weizmann. He is a very sick man, almost broken in health, but he traveled thousands of miles just to see you and plead the cause of my people. Now you refuse to see him just because you are insulted by some of our American Jewish leaders, even though you know that Weizmann had absolutely nothing to do with these insults and would be the last man to be party to them. It doesn't sound like you, Harry, because I thought you could take this stuff they have been handing out. ...'"*[259]

SECOND SECRET MEETING WITH TRUMAN

That did the trick. Truman agreed to meet Weizmann but (yet again) secretly. Accordingly, after dark on Thursday, 18 March, Dr Chaim Weizmann was once more led into the White House through the East Gate. Even — rather, especially — the State Department knew nothing of the clandestine encounter.

What Weizmann wanted was an irrevocable US commitment to the Partition plan that had been passed by the General Assembly of the UN the previous November. The encounter ended with Truman giving his word that he would not depart from that policy. Indeed, he: "*gave his visitor a specific commitment. He would work for the establishment and recognition of a Jewish state, of which the Negev would be a part.*"[260]

BLACK FRIDAY

Ill-advisedly, Truman neglected to contact Secretary of State Marshall, who was on the West Coast, to tell him what had occurred and what he, the president, had decided. Nor did he tell

---

[258] American soldier/statesman, seventh President of the United States, from 1829 to 1837, and founder of the Democratic Party.

[259] *Truman,* David McCullough (ibid)

[260] *Chaim Weizmann: A Biography By Several Hands* (ibid) by Abba Eban.

anyone else at the State Department or amongst the US delegation at the UN.

The following day, Black Friday, as it was to become known, the American ambassador to the UN, in ignorance of the Oval Office discussion, told the General Assembly that the US *"recommended abandoning the partition plan and called for a temporary UN "Trusteeship" over Palestine ...* [to] *give all sides in the Palestine controversy time to cool down".*[261]

At that, the whole of America, from Congress to the Bnei Brith and coast-to-coast, was in uproar. The press had a field day, saying that the president and the administration were untrustworthy. Of course, no one felt more confused and let down than Chaim Weizmann. The next day, 20 March, Truman awoke and discovered from the Saturday newspapers what had occurred on Black Friday. *"The first I know about it is what I see in the papers! Isn't that hell? I'm now in the position of a liar and a double-crosser."*[262]

Then another blow: in Los Angeles, Marshall held a press conference, declaring he considered Trusteeship over Palestine "*the wisest course*", for he had, he said, recommended it to the president and the president had approved it.

Truman went into vacillation mode again. He held a press conference in which he said *"Trusteeship did not necessarily 'prejudice the character of the final political settlement.' Was he then in favour still of partition at some future date? 'That is what I am trying to say here as plainly as I can'"*[263] — but apparently it was not plain and it was unconvincing.

FROM PARLIAMENT – A DATE

[261] *Truman,* David McCullough (ibid)

[262] *Truman,* David McCullough (ibid)

[263] *Truman,* David McCullough (ibid)

In a debate in the British House of Lords on the Palestine Bill, on 7 April, a Labour (government) peer, stated:

> *"In the discussions which are now proceeding in New York preliminary to the special session of the Assembly, our representative has been instructed to make it clear that British troops will not be available after May 15 to support any policy upon which the agreement of both Arabs and Jews has not been obtained. We have given of our best to Palestine and it has brought us little reward. Our Mandate has proved a thankless and ultimately an impracticable responsibility. In the nature of things, neither Jews nor Arabs have been satisfied that their rights and claims have been fully acknowledged by the Mandatory Power. They have not felt able to take genuine responsibility for administration, or to acknowledge their differences and find mutual accommodation. No one can expect us to carry this burden indefinitely, and we have given ample warning of the circumstances in which we propose to relinquish it."*[264]

Suddenly, there was a date: 15 May 1948.

THE FIRST TO RECOGNISE ...

The British would leave Palestine to its fate on 15 May 1948, so that should be the date by which the Jewish state would be born.

Inspiration now hit Weizmann: he had to persuade the President that the USA should not only recognise the Jewish state (as the president had indicated at their 18 March meeting) but also should be the first country to do so. That, more than anything else, would be a public demonstration of the viability of the Jewish state at the point of its birth. Weizmann decided to wait till the last moment to wring that gesture out of Truman. First, the president had to find his way, or be steered, back to his promise to support Partition.

---

[264] http://hansard.millbanksystems.com/lords/1948/apr/07/palestine-bill

Truman was struggling with his conscience and the way he had seemingly misled Weizmann. With exquisite timing and phrasing, on 9 April, Chaim Weizmann wrote to the President:

> "*thanking Truman for 'the personal kindness which you have so often shown me' and for 'the sympathetic interest which you have constantly devoted to the cause of our people,' he stressed the gravity of the moment and Truman's own historic rôle in it"* and continued: ***'The choice for our people, Mr President, is between statehood and extermination.*** *History and providence have placed this issue in your hands and I am confident that you will yet decide it in the spirit of moral law.'"*[265] [Emphasis added.]

Two days later Truman confided in Jacobson that he had resolved to recognise the Jewish state. On this occasion, Truman was determined not to let the State Department know his thinking; yet State had not given up. In a cable of 22 April 1948, Undersecretary of State Robert Lovett told Nahum Goldmann, president and founder of the World Jewish Congress, that he was ready to disseminate a white paper that would "*do great harm to the Jews*" by releasing anti-Semitic documents, if Israel prevented the truce by declaring independence on its own terms.[266]

Whether or not Jacobson kept Truman's decision from his hero, Weizmann was, in any event, to hear of it from another source, Judge Samuel I Rosenman. One of President Truman's closest

---

[265] *Truman, David McCullough (ibid)*

[266] According to the Jewish Telegraphic Agency: Rafael Medoff, the director of The David Wyman Institute for Holocaust Studies discovered the cables while conducting research for his recently released book, *"Herbert Hoover and the Jews: The Origins of the 'Jewish Vote' and Bipartisan Support for Israel."*
http://www.jta.org/2012/04/26/news-opinion/united-states/cables-reveal-1948-threats-from-state-dept

political advisers[267], he told Weizmann on 23 April that Truman had had made up his mind to keep his word, for he had learned that:

> "[t]*he President would like to find his way back to the United Nations resolution. If the General Assembly session could be surmounted without reversing partition and if a Jewish state was declared, the President would recognise it immediately. Thus fortified by international legitimacy the new State could fight for its survival, not as an unregarded outcast, but as a member of the international family.*"[268]

Weizmann learned from the same source that Truman stipulated that he should remain in America, as the president wished to deal with the Zionists (and the Jewish lobby), if at all, through Weizmann alone. Of course, Weizmann stayed in New York as the president required. (The consequences would be eternally injurious to his reputation.[269])

On 29 April, in London, the House of Commons passed into law the Act terminating the British Mandate as at midnight on 14/15 May 1948. In Palestine, the British military would continue to be nothing but obstructive towards the *Yishuv* and supportive of the Arabs.

In the meantime at the UN, the US delegation declared (doubtless at the behest of Truman) that it would abstain from its own Trusteeship proposal, which was duly retracted; but with only two weeks left before the British were to withdraw and the new state declared, there was maximum anxiety as to what could

---

[267] Rosenman was said to be *"a willing victim of Weizmann's personal spell"*. *Chaim Weizmann: A Biography By Several Hands* (ibid) by Abba Eban. Judge Rosenman was said to have coined the historic phrase "New Deal" for FDR, for whom he had written nearly all of FDR's speeches. He remained close to Truman, writing many of his speeches, too.

[268] *Chaim Weizmann: A Biography By Several Hands* (ibid) by Abba Eban.

[269] As described at the end of chapter 20.

go wrong. Weizmann had not forgotten how the Balfour Declaration was almost lost (twice) with eleventh hour objections from Montagu, a Jew, turning the British War Cabinet against it. Would some Jewish leader, or even some-one in the *Yishuv*, get cold feet — not least at the prospect of invasion by five Arab Armies — and seek a postponement or, worse, make another attempt at a Trusteeship?

In early May, Moshe Shertok was despatched by Weizmann from the UN to Tel Aviv, to advise Ben-Gurion and his team to reject fresh warnings from Secretary of State Marshall against proclaiming the State. "*Weizmann pursued him to the airport with an entreaty, 'Don't let them weaken, Moshe, it is now or never.'*"[270]

According to Norman Rose, with only two days of the Mandate left:

> *"When the Yishuv's provisional cabinet agonised over whether or not to declare independence, Ben-Gurion sought Weizmann's advice. His reply was blunt, in style, and in Yiddish: 'What are they waiting for, the idiots?'"* [271]

Weizmann's fears proved well-founded. The fact that BG had to ask Weizmann for guidance shows that he was dithering. In the event, the vote went 6-4 in favour of statehood. What would have happened had one vote gone the other way and it had all come down to Ben-Gurion's casting vote, we shall, fortunately, never know.

That same day, 12 May, a final strategy conference was held at the White House to discuss immediate recognition of the new, but as yet unnamed, Jewish state. The battle lines were drawn

[270] *Chaim Weizmann: A Biography By Several Hands* (ibid) by Abba Eban.

[271] Meyer Weisgal, quoting the same reportage as to the words used, claims that the messages were passed through him. (*Meyer Weisgal ... So Far*, Meyer Weisgal (ibid).

between Marshall and the State Department, still seeking a return to Trusteeship, and Truman (whose electoral popularity ratings were languishing around 35%), resolute that the president alone should make foreign policy, to which the State Department should give effect. The heated discussion passed boiling point and Marshall even threatened to vote against the President in the election looming in the autumn (although it was unclear at that stage whether he would have broken the tradition of secrecy of the ballot). Truman remained impassive to the end of the meeting, but the risk that Marshall might resign was unmistakeable. That would have been a disaster for Truman's electoral hopes.

One day before independence would be declared, in his final gambit which he had been saving for over a month, Weizmann wrote to Truman (doubtless emboldened by what he had heard from Jacobson and Rosenman, but leaving nothing to chance), as follows:

DEAR MR PRESIDENT: May 13, 1948

The unhappy events of the last few months will not, I hope, obscure the very great contributions which you, Mr President, have made towards a definitive and just settlement of the long and troublesome Palestine question. The leadership which the American Government took under your inspiration made possible the establishment of a Jewish state, which I am convinced will contribute markedly towards a solution of the world Jewish problem, and which I am equally convinced is a necessary preliminary to the development of lasting peace among the peoples of the Near East.

So far as practical conditions in Palestine would permit, the Jewish people there have proceeded along the lines laid down in the United Nations Resolution of November 29, 1947. Tomorrow midnight, May 15, the British Mandate will be terminated, and the

Provisional Government of the Jewish state, embodying the best endeavours of the Jewish people and arising from the Resolution of the United Nations, will assume full responsibility for preserving law and order within the boundaries of the Jewish state, for defending that area against external aggression, and for discharging the obligations of the Jewish state to the other nations of the world in accordance with international law.

Considering all the difficulties, the chances for an equitable adjustment of Arab and Jewish relationships are not unfavourable. What is required now is an end to the seeking of new solutions which invariably have retarded rather than encouraged a final settlement.

It is for these reasons that I deeply hope that the United States, which under your leadership has done so much to find a just solution, will promptly recognise the Provisional Government of the new Jewish state. The world, I think, will regard it as especially appropriate that the greatest living democracy should be the first to welcome the newest into the family of nations.

Respectfully yours,

CHAIM WEIZMANN

The following day was the momentous 14 May 1948. In Tel Aviv, Ben-Gurion and the leaders of the *Yishuv*, the People's Council, were in constant session. As the world spun on its axis, by and by the United Nations General Assembly convened in New York, Weizmann was closeted with his entourage in his suite in the Waldorf Astoria and Truman was ensconced with his immediate advisers in the Oval Office.

Then a minor miracle for Truman: after lunch, Marshall called to say he would not make public his opposition to the president's policy. Truman had got his way: after all, the famous adage: "*The Buck Stops Here*" had been seen by every visitor, including Marshall, to the Oval Office of Harry S Truman since 1945.[272] The maxim was not only an acceptance of ultimate responsibility but also definitive as to where the power resided. Now, even the Greatest Living American had acknowledged it. The president had already decided to keep his word to Weizmann, so Marshall's capitulation was the icing on the cake.

"ISRAEL" IT SHALL BE

A formal request for recognition arrived at the White House from the office of the Jewish Agency in Washington. The name of the new country had yet to be inserted.

The previous day, on Rothschild Boulevard, the Tel Aviv Museum had been readied for a large meeting, yet the name of imminently emergent state was still a matter of debate. "Judea" and "Zion" were discussed and discarded. Ben-Gurion suggested "Israel" and it was accepted. Moshe Shertok prepared the first draft of the declaration of independence and Ben-Gurion both amended and finalised it overnight. *Shabbat* (the Sabbath) would start at 19:00 hours on Friday, so the declaration would have to be signed off well before then. A photograph of Herzl and two Zionist flags (the *Magen David*, the Star of David) were located and some parchment was found.

At noon in Tel Aviv on Friday, 14 May 1948, Ben-Gurion arrived at the Museum in a rented limousine, to lend him gravitas. Some 200 hundred Jewish Agency delegates and other

---

[272] The sign "*The Buck Stops Here*" that was on President Truman's desk ... was made in the Federal Reformatory at El Reno, Oklahoma. Fred A Canfil, then United States Marshal for the Western District of Missouri and a friend of Mr Truman, saw a similar sign while visiting the Reformatory and asked the Warden if a sign like it could be made for President Truman. The sign was made and mailed to the President on October 2, 1945: https://www.trumanlibrary.org/buckstop.htm

notables were already in place. The time and place of this providential event was a Jewish secret: the building was besieged by excited crowds. The press had been told to arrive at 15:30, but hours before that, there were few in Tel Aviv who had not sought to swell the multitude on Rothschild Boulevard.

The proceedings were in any event broadcast live on radio. The Declaration of Independence was proclaimed (in Hebrew, of course) and the People's Council members signed it. The provisional government's first decrees were also signed. Finally, the Israel Philharmonic Orchestra[273], conducted by Leonard Bernstein, led the assembly in "*HaTikvah*", which thereupon became the Israeli national anthem. The ceremony was over by 16:45.

THE FIRST RECOGNITION

Midnight in Tel Aviv (the moment at which British rule would end) is 17:00 hours in Washington DC. *"Eleven minutes later at the White House, Charlie Ross announced de facto recognition, by the United States, of Israel, as it was to be called".*[274]

The Jewish world erupted into unrestrained celebration. Within hours, the neighbouring Arab states, Egypt, Jordan (Transjordan) and Syria, together with Iraq, invaded the new-born state. This expanded greatly the war that the *Yishuv* had already been suffering for many months at the hands of the local Arabs, with the connivance of the British.

As Truman had resolved against all opposition from Marshall and the State Department, American recognition was the first. He had kept his word to Weizmann and plainly only Weizmann could have extracted that result. It should not, however, be

---

[273] Just then renamed from *Palestine Orchestra*, which had performed 140 times before Allied soldiers in WWII, including an 1942 performance for soldiers of the Jewish Brigade at El Alamein.

[274] *Truman*, David McCullough (ibid)

thought that Truman was so enamoured with the Zionist cause that his support was a foregone conclusion. Eddie Jacobson is reported to have noted anti-Semitic tendencies in Truman and had only just overcome them when he met the president in the Oval Office on 13 March 1948. Without Weizmann's magic there was a plain reversion to type within a year even on the seminal issue of the Negev (as described in panel 13).

13

TRUMAN WITHOUT WEIZMANN'S INFLUENCE

> On 29 May 1949 (after an armistice between Israel and Egypt three months earlier), Truman reportedly delivered an angry note to Israel demanding Israel withdraw from territories captured during the War of Independence. On 8 June, Israel rejected the American demand, on the basis that the Arab states had initiated the war in defiance of the 1947 UN partition resolution, and that "*the Arab attack... had created a new situation*". It seems that the matter was resolved between two Israel sympathisers. "*U.S. Ambassador to Israel, James G. McDonald ... later cabled White House aide Clark Clifford ... to inform him that Truman's note had 'embittered Israeli opinion' and that Premier David Ben-Gurion and foreign Minister Moshe Sharett might be forced "despite their will and better judgment to resist U.S. demands. ... The envoy suggested that 'Israeli concessions with refugees are possible if request for these are not again put in form of demand but under no circumstances except use of overwhelming force will Israel yield any part of Negev'"*.[275] No such force ever materialised and the Negev remains part (at 55%) of Israel to this day.

America's *de facto* recognition was followed quickly by (pre-Islamic revolutionary) Iran, Guatemala, Iceland, Nicaragua, Romania and Uruguay. Three days later, Soviet Russia accorded Israel *de jure* recognition, the USA granting it by the year's end. The British held back for a year before according *de facto*, and

---

[275] Source: The Jewish Telegraphic Agency: http://www.jta.org/1977/07/25/archive/documents-show-truman-demanded-israel-withdraw-from-areas-taken-during-the-war-of-independence

then a further year before granting *de jure*, recognition.

Accordingly, by total devotion to that which he had desired and striven for over half a century — within the time-frame willed by Theodor Herzl — by the magic of his personality and by his scientific successes, all of which had caused doors to be opened for him, to which none of his peers and colleagues had any access, Dr Chaim Weizmann finally achieved his goal — the foundation of the Jewish Homeland in *Eretz Yisrael*. The State of Israel took its place in the community of nations, as only the 57th state to become a member of the UN, on 11 May 1949.

In April 1956, the Parliament of the United Kingdom presented a gift to the Israeli parliament of the Knesset Menorah.[276] A new relationship was being forged. Sadly, Weizmann did not survive to see that, or the installation of the Menorah opposite the Knesset. He had died four years earlier.

CODA: *Dayenu*! It is sufficient for us.

As Jews traditionally sing from the *HaGaddah* on the eve of Passover, Weizmann's rendering of the State of Israel by his efforts in 1917 and a generation later, complete with the Negev and international recognition, would have sufficed the Israeli nation; but there was more. Weizmann understood, as should the man whose chemistry, in its twin manifestations, was the midwife of a nation state, that learning, study, science and technology would guarantee its future. It is to those attainments that we now turn.

---

[276] The bronze Knesset Menorah, which stands opposite the Knesset, is 4.30 metres tall, 3.5 meters wide and weighs 4 tons. It is said to be modelled after the golden candelabrum that stood in the Temple in Jerusalem. A series of bronze reliefs on the Menorah depict the struggles to survive of the Jewish people, depicting formative events, images and concepts from the Hebrew Bible and Jewish history. https://www.wikiwand.com/en/Knesset_Menorah

~~~
~~~

PART II

THE EDUCATIONAL ACHIEVEMENTS

18

EVERYTHING THE MIND OF MAN EMBRACES

At the opening session of The First Knesset on 14 February 1949, the First President of the State of Israel, Dr Chaim Weizmann, said he had dedicated his whole life:

> *"to making science and research the basis of our national undertaking. ... Let us focus our efforts first of all on increasing our creative ability by encouraging science and research in the State of Israel. Science and research are the basis of progress throughout the world. We must utilise all our achievements in science and research in the diaspora for building our country."*

RESTRICTIONS AND QUOTAS

In Europe, the Pale and Russia, Jews had customarily been severely restricted as to the professions they might enter. More often than not, engineering, technical or scientific training was out of the question for them. Yet, the Zionists appreciated that these were the very fields in which Jews would have to be schooled were a homeland for them ever to be built; and they resolved to overcome the problem. The concept of the *Teknikum* (later to become the Technion) in Haifa arose to deal with that. Weizmann's input to this project was limited but visionary and crucial.

Weizmann himself was keenly aware of the difficulties that Jewish youth had in seeking university places in Europe and, more especially, in Russia, where there was a quota system that restricted Jewish entry to 10.5% generally and 3% in St Petersburg and Moscow. Weizmann first saw an opportunity to rectify this in the context of the Democratic Faction. Almost two decades later, during the 1918 visit of the Zionist Commission to Palestine, he made good on his pledge to himself to bring about a Jewish university in Palestine. By his tenacity, and many other skills, he was central to the creation of the Hebrew University of Jerusalem. Tragedy was to throw up the third opportunity, which Weizmann grasped with both hands.

ISRAEL'S UNIVERSITIES AND THE WEIZMANN TRIO

There are today in Israel nine universities.[277] Chaim Weizmann played a part in the origins of three of them and, from them, we learn much about both the man and the powerhouse that is Israel today.

League tables showing the international standing of universities are rather like hotel classifications. Sometimes the justification for ascribing four stars rather than five, and vice versa, is hard to fathom. The reason may be that grading hotels and universities is an arcane art, understood by those in whose gift the ranking lies, rather than by those who might benefit from the results.

All that is an (unnecessary) apologia for the fact that the three Israeli universities considered here by virtue of their connection with Dr Chaim Weizmann, are way below the highest global rankings, the top places being dominated by those in the USA and the UK. Much depends on research facilities (where the Israeli examples are not lacking), the range of subjects taught (which in the case of one is consciously restricted to post-graduates) and numerous other factors. (Having said all that, panel 14 is informative about vital subjects affecting the Weizmann educational trio.)

14

THREE ISRAELI UNIVERSITIES MAKE WORLD'S TOP 100 LIST [278]

[277] Leaving aside the several private institutes of higher learning that also offer degree courses, one of which, the Interdisciplinary Centre (IDC) in Herzliya, which teaches in English will be a full university by the time you read this.

[278] From the Ynet News website 15 August 2021:- https://www.ynetnews.com/culture/article/r1aa2llgy

> The Hebrew University of Jerusalem ranks 90th for 2021 Academic Ranking of World Universities [ARWU] while Weizmann Institute of Science was placed 92nd and the Technion Institute of Technology claims 94th spot.
>
> Among 2,000 universities surveyed worldwide, three Israeli universities made the top 100 list, for the first time since 2013.
>
> Shanghai Ranking Consultancy, the independent body which publishes the yearly ARWU, bases its rankings on several key indicators, including the number of alumni and staff awarded Nobel Laureates and Fields Medalists, the number of highly-cited researchers and the number of articles published in the prestigious journals *Nature* and *Science*, among other criteria.

Irrespective of observer rankings, high or low, Israel is proud of her universities — and certainly of the Weizmann trio. Israeli tertiary educational institutions have brought about advances from which, not only the Israeli economy and her defence and security forces, but also the well-being of all mankind, has benefitted. This happy outcome can be attributed to two causes: war and Weizmann. We shall encounter them in that order.

ISRAEL DEFENCE ISSUES

Israel spends almost 5% percent of its gross domestic product ("GDP") on research and development (about double the OECD average), of which around 30% is military-oriented. In addition, some 5% of Israeli GDP is spent on its military budget (also way above the OECD average). These statistics were and are borne out of necessity. Survival always comes first and when as it was (for over a generation) a question of two or three million Jews holding out against hostile Arab nations with populations aggregating over 100 million, the need to level the playing- or rather the battle-field was a matter of urgent national importance. In this context, the universities played two rôles: to develop high-technology solutions, particularly those that would deliver exponentially greater fire-power or some other vital advantage in conflicts; and to turn out highly-educated young men and women who were capable of getting the best out of the equipment developed by or for them.

For many years after independence in 1948, the levels of expenditure mentioned were a burden that the country could neither afford to spend nor dare to reduce; for many years past now, they have matured into an investment that has paid vast dividends.

A great contributor to those dividends was and remains the close cooperation (based on the German model) between the universities and what was going on within their ivory towers, something that was established early on in the *Yishuv* years, well before 1948.

University partnerships with the military and with industry are not the only, nor the earliest, examples of this cooperation. It was the *kibbutzim* that first became used to developing their skills in tandem with one university or another. To take an early and familiar example, Israel is a world leader in many water-oriented techniques. The drip-system that conserves precious water as it succours the nation's agricultural products, was the result of years of co-experimentation between laboratory and field. Weizmann himself touched on water conservation techniques in 1947 when he persuaded US President Truman to restore the Negev to the Zionist part of the then soon-to-be-partitioned land.

The three greatest exponents of all of this have been the Haifa Technion (not to be confused with the quite separate University of Haifa), the Hebrew University of Jerusalem and the Weizmann Institute of Science at Rechovot. These then are the Weizmann Trio. From where did these three places of higher learning arise? In the latter two cases the answer is the Weizmann himself. In the first, the Haifa Technion[279], his contribution, though specific, was to be of defining importance.

---

[279] As it is now known but which started life as the *"Technikum"* or *"Teknikum"*.

Let us consider them in chronological order of establishment.

THE HAIFA TECHNION

In his 1902 novella, *Altneuland*[280], a visionary Theodor Herzl imagined Haifa as:

> *"a great park....with streets bordered with palms ... rows of trees served a double purpose. They gave shade by day, and at night shed light from electric lamps which hung from them like enormous glass fruits.... educated young men had become a great blessing for Palestine, for they had brought the latest methods of applied science into the country."*

Haifa, a city in which Jewish and Arab citizens have always mixed, living and working freely and peacefully together, with its large natural harbour, was then emerging as the industrial centre of Palestine and the obvious place to site an institution that was conceived to face towards industry.

In 1903, democratic elections were held in the *Yishuv* for a Jewish national assembly. Some 60,000 Jews voted and *"Zionist leader Dr. Menachem Ussishkin used the occasion to deliver a keynote address in which he expressed the urgency for an institution of higher education in Palestine. The convention supported a resolution for the establishment of a polytechnical institute in Palestine and the* [Haifa] *Technion — Israel Institute of Technology (at least on paper) was born."*[281]

On his death in 1904, tea magnate, Kalonimus Wolf Wissotzky, left a million Russian roubles to charity. The executor of his will was Achad Ha'am, who decided to apply 100,000 Wissotzky-legacy roubles to the establishment of the Technion. He and Shmarya Levin (both long-standing and loyal associates of

[280] Truly prophetic in so many respects, envisioning (for example) a Yishuv-wide wine industry, as Israel boasts today.

[281] http://pard.technion.ac.il/history/

Weizmann) would be influential in the creation of the new scientific-educational institution.

The land for the new university — it was originally to be called the *Teknikum* — was acquired from the Turks by Arthur Zimmerman[282], the German Under-Secretary for Foreign Affairs, in order to help spread German influence in Palestine. The building work was to be funded by donations, apart from the Wissotzky bequest, from German-American Jewish philanthropists, most notably Jacob Schiff, a New York investment banker of renown. From the outset the dominant influence was that of the *Hilfsverein* and it was decidedly German. That influence may also be seen in the choice in 1909 of the project's German architect, Alexander Baerwald.[283]

On 11 April 1912, the foundation stone was laid in downtown Haifa for the first academic institution to be established by the *Yishuv*; but behind the scenes of the construction work raged a battle between the Germans (the *Hilfsverein der Deutschen Jüden*, a global German-Jewish educational organisation) and the Zionists — the so-called War of the Languages. The battle lines were drawn between German (the pre-dominant language in science and engineering in the west) and Hebrew (which could claim no such pedigree, but which was fast becoming the local vernacular).

THE WAR OF THE LANGUAGES

In the Palestine of the twilight of the Ottoman Empire, the educational establishments, including the schools, were chips in a game played by the promoters of the languages of Hebrew (Ben-Yehuda's movement), German (the *Hilfsverein*) and

---

[282] Whose infamous eponymous telegram to Mexico would induce America's entry into the Great War in 1917.

[283] Who studied at the *Technische Hochschule Charlottenburg* between 1897 and 1901. He and Weizmann appear to have overlapped there by a year or two.

French (the *Alliance Israélite Universelle de Paris*, an association for universal assistance of Jews). Further German influence was to be seen in the organisation *Ezra* ("Help") which had long-term plans for the development of Haifa.

The battle for Hebrew as the language of the *Yishuv* was first waged by Ben-Yehuda in its schools and workplaces[284], and ended in victory for Hebrew, which formed part of the emerging national identity of the *Yishuv*. While within the confines of the German- and French-sponsored schools the children used the schools' respective official languages, once outside, in the schoolyard and beyond, thanks to Ben-Yehuda, they naturally conversed in Hebrew.

Weizmann, typically single-minded on this subject, worked through Levin to strike a decisive blow. He induced a strike of the teaching staff in the *Hilfsverein* schools (and, significantly, not in those of the *Alliance*) until the adoption of Hebrew as the language of the Technion was accepted. That determined the matter in favour of the bourgeoning national language. In February 1914, the Technion's Board of the Trustees resolved that the primary language of instruction in the Technion would be Hebrew. The *Hilfsverein*, piqued to say the least, terminated its sponsorship of the German-speaking schools of the *Yishuv*, all of which promptly fell into the lap of Ben-Yehuda, greatly hastening his work.[285]

It seems likely that without Weizmann's intervention German would have been the language of the Technion. By 1933 (and arguably much earlier), the words of the teaching staff and the student body would have stuck in their throats. Certainly, after Hitler's rise to power in Germany, no one in the Technion would

---

[284] See chapter 3.

[285] There are conflicting accounts of this episode in *Germany, Turkey, and Zionism 1897-1918*, Isaiah Friedman (Transaction Publishers, USA & UK, 1977), with a further account in *Fifty Years of Zionism*, Oskar K Rabinowicz (Robert Anscombe & Co Ltd, 1950), which is a critique of *Trial and Error*.

have wanted to conduct any of its affairs in German. By then, however, there would have been almost twenty years' accumulation of lectures, scientific reports and other papers, academic and administrative, in a language that would have sounded inherently inimical to the Technion. By being both long- and clear-sighted, and energetic, about it, Weizmann resolved the matter in favour of Hebrew early on in the life of the Technion. Thus, it may properly be said that Weizmann saved a vast amount of debilitating work, expense and anguish later by avoiding the necessary conversion of everything linguistic about the institution from German to Hebrew.

Upon the announcement of his elevation to the presidency of the new-born State of Israel in 1948, Weizmann received a cable at the Waldorf Astoria Hotel, New York:

THE CHAIM WEIZMANN DEPARTMENT OF CHEMICAL ENGINEERING OF THE TECHNION CONSIDERS GREAT HONOUR TO WHOLE PROFESSION FIRST PRESIDENT OF THE RESTORED STATE BEING AN OUTSTANDING CHEMIST AND A PIONEER CONQUERING DESERT BY SCIENCE AND TECHNOLOGY WISHES YOU MANY YEARS OF PRODUCTIVE WORK

HUGO HEIMANN, DEAN OF THE DEPARTMENT[286]

THE TECHNION TODAY

The Haifa Technion today is at the cutting edge of global scientific development in many fields. (For its range of disciplines, see panel 15). More than 100,000 degrees have been awarded, it has provided skills vital for the creation and protection of the State of Israel and it has been a principal driving force behind the growth of Israel's military and hi-tech industries. Its world-wide reputation for innovation is widely regarded as being on a par with MIT and Imperial College, London. While proficiency in English is required, for many

[286] Source - *Weizmann Archives: Technion/10-2840.TIF*

publications are in that language, Hebrew has been developed, with the required jargon, for all the activities of the Technion (but see the coda to this section).

15

THE TECHNION TODAY

The Technion today covers the following disciplines:

Aerospace engineering, architecture and town planning, biology, biomedical engineering, biotechnology and food engineering, chemical engineering, chemistry, civil and environmental engineering, computer science, education in technology and science, electrical engineering, energy research, humanities and arts, industrial engineering and management, materials science and engineering, mathematics, mechanical engineering, medicine, nanotechnology and science, physics and space research.

There are three Nobel Laureates in chemistry amongst the 565 faculty members, and the Technion is cited as one of the factors behind the growth of Israel's high-tech industry and innovation.

The Technion has been a main driving force for the establishment of the Israel's so-called Silicon Wadi, which refers to the high concentration of hi-tech industries (similar to Silicon Valley in California) throughout Israel, with especially high concentrations around Haifa, Caesarea, Petah Tikva, Tel Aviv, Ra'anana, and Herzliya Pituach.

CODA: There is today a new War of the Languages at the Technion. Its close association, indeed partnership, with Cornell University, New York City, and the 2015 establishment of the Guangdong Technion Israel Institute of Technology (Guangdong Technion) in China, has led to pressure to change the language of the Technion once again — to English. (Most academic papers are written in English in any event.) One suspects that Chaim Weizmann, who was single-minded about both science and Hebrew as essential elements of the Jewish state, would be, at least initially, ambivalent about it.

~~~

THE HEBREW UNIVERSITY OF JERUSALEM

EARLY ORIGINS

One of the many issues with which Weizmann concerned himself, and possibly the one by which he was most motivated, was the founding of a Jewish university in *Eretz Yisrael*. The idea was initially floated at the First Zionist Congress in 1897 by Professor Hermann Shapira, but he died the following year and no steps were taken for its realisation until Weizmann picked up the baton.

THE DEMOCRATIC FACTION

It was in 1900 that Weizmann, Buber, Feiwel and Motzkin formed the Democratic Faction[287] to promote culture and education in the ZO and practical development in the *Yishuv*. The ultimate expression would be the establishment of a Jewish university in Palestine.

At the Fifth Zionist Congress in 1901, Weizmann had the university proposal adopted as a formal aim of the ZO, and he followed that up with a pamphlet: *Eine Jüdische Hochschule* (A Jewish College), which he published with Buber and Feivel in 1902, describing and costing out the project. The paper stimulated enthusiastic support from all over Europe and Russia, from students, men of letters and scientists — and from Herzl. Contributions for the project were enthusiastically canvassed and granted. The next year, however, the Kishinev pogrom hit and, in the general trauma that followed, the university project had to take a back seat as the funds collected were diverted for the relief of the Kishinev community. The Jewish university proposal was neglected for a full decade.

Two events in 1912 may have catalysed Weizmann's revival of

[287] See chapter 4.
~~~

the idea of a Jewish University in Jerusalem: first, the Technion was being built in Haifa; and, secondly, that was the year in which Weizmann was disappointed at his failure to succeed to Perkin's chair in chemistry at Manchester University. Perhaps that stimulated a long-term plan in Weizmann's mind.

FORMAL ADOPTION

At the Eleventh Zionist Congress in Vienna in 1913, Weizmann, with the support of Dr Menachem Ussishkin (who had spoken in favour of the Technion in 1903), won the backing of the Congress for the establishment of the Hebrew University in Jerusalem. Weizmann declared, that the University would be *"more powerful than the fortunes of the millionaires"*[288] and that with it: *"we could achieve greater successes than other people with their armies and navies."*[289]

The proposal both won support and provoked opposition. This was, after all, the Zionist Congress and the auspices were those of the ZO. Even Achad Ha'am had his reservations. The War of the Languages was raging at the Technion, and the wealthy German Jews of New York would not be appreciative of the language for the new university in Jerusalem being Hebrew; but after 1914 (and the adoption of Hebrew at the Technion) there would have appeared, even to them, a certain inevitability about it.

The ZO president, David Wolffsohn, immediately made a substantial financial commitment *pour encourager les autres*, and others were indeed encouraged to do the same. Considerable funds were accumulated. Remembering Kishinev, Weizmann sought to secure the promise of the university this time around. He obtained the backing of Baron Edmond de Rothschild; but it was conditioned on Weizmann's winning over the formidable

---

[288] *Chaim Weizmann: A Biography By Several Hands* (ibid) by Sir Isaiah Berlin, see footnote 20.

[289] *Chaim Weizmann: A Biography*, Norman Rose (ibid)

professor and Nobel prize-winner, Dr Paul Ehrlich.[290] Weizmann travelled to Frankfurt-am-Main in Germany and swiftly charmed Ehrlich sufficiently for him to agree to head the steering committee of the nascent University. The first committee meeting was planned for 4 August 1914 in Paris. World War I broke out on 28 July and the proposal was, once again, shelved. This time, it would not take Weizmann a decade to revive it.

RENEWAL OF THE UNIVERSITY PROJECT

Three years into the Great War, the Balfour Declaration was won and the Zionist Commission to Palestine organised. Before leaving London for Palestine, Weizmann spoke to Balfour and obtained the Foreign Secretary's consent to laying the foundation stones of the Hebrew University on the plot of land acquired in 1916 by Ruppin on Mount Scopus. Of course, the consent of the British military would be required, as the war with the Turks had not yet been won.

After arriving in Palestine at the head of the Zionist Commission, Weizmann bided his time until he had won over Allenby. In May 1918, around the time of the general's weekend visit to Jerusalem[291], Weizmann put the matter to him. The general thought such a step was premature and pointed out that the war was still raging — guns were still being fired on the outskirts of Jerusalem, and Turkish troops were to be seen just beyond Jerusalem's hills. Weizmann, undaunted, replied:

> "*This will be a great act of faith — faith in the victory which is bound to come, and faith in the future of Palestine. I can think of no better symbol of faith than the founding of the Hebrew University, under your auspices, and in this*

---

[290] The world-famous scientist — who developed the first effective medicinal treatment for syphilis, thereby initiating (and also naming) the field of chemotherapy — had won the Nobel Prize in Physiology/Medicine in 1908.

[291] See Appendix 3.

hour."[292]

On the afternoon of 24 July 1918, on Mount Scopus, Weizmann laid twelve foundation stones of the Hebrew University — one for each of the ancient Tribes of Israel. Thousands attended the ceremony, including General Allenby himself, his staff and representatives of the Allied forces, together with Moslem, Christian and Jewish dignitaries from Jerusalem, and representatives of the *Yishuv*. As Weizmann recalls in *Trial and Error*:

> *"The physical setting of the ceremony was of unforgettable and sublime beauty. The declining sun flooded the hills of Judea and Moab with golden light, and it seemed to me, too, that the transfigured heights were watching, wondering, dimly aware perhaps that this was the beginning of the return of their own people after many days. Below us lay Jerusalem, gleaming like a jewel.*
>
> *We were practically within sound of the guns on the northern front, and I spoke briefly, contrasting the desolation which the war was bringing with the creative significance of the act on which we were engaged; recalling, too, that only a week before we had observed the Fast of the Ninth of Ab, the day on which the Temple was destroyed and Jewish national political existence extinguished — apparently for ever. We were there to plant the germ of a new Jewish life. ....*
>
> *The ceremony did not last longer than an hour. When it was over we sang Hatikvah and God Save the King. But no one seemed anxious to leave, and we stood silent, with bowed heads, round the little row of stones, while the twilight deepened into night."*

The first board of governors, then nominated, could hardly have been a more impressive conclave, including as it did Albert

---

[292] *Trial and Error* (ibid)

Einstein (who would accompany Weizmann on university fund-raising tours of America), Sigmund Freud, Martin Buber and Chaim Weizmann.

INAUGURATION

There was one ceremony, seven years later, out of the many that Weizmann attended in his events-crowded life, that meant the most to him: the official inauguration of the Hebrew University of Jerusalem, held on Wednesday, 1 April 1925. That day was the culmination of four days of celebrations and academic events. Jerusalem, which had never seen so many vehicles, was thronged with all who wished to be as close to the festivities as possible. Priority was, of course, given to those coming from abroad, most of them on their first visit to the Holy Land. Quite apart from the thousands from the *Yishuv*, and from beyond also, the headcount was truly impressive: dozens of political notables, over fifty delegates from universities and academic organisations, the leaders of the Jewish world, including Chief Rabbi Avraham Kook and Haim Nahman Bialik, and hundreds of public figures from all over the western world, including Field Marshall Viscount Allenby, Sir Herbert Samuel and the Earl of Balfour.

The crowds were organically accommodated by the topography, which provided a natural amphitheatre facing a wooden platform that was built for more than two hundred VIPs.

Having Lord Balfour present the main inaugural address was a political coup for Zionism. Along with the granting of the Mandate three years earlier (the year in which Arthur became Lord Balfour) it appeared to signify Britain's continuing interest in its Palestine project. Less than a decade had passed since Mark Sykes had pressed the Balfour Declaration into Chaim Weizmann's hand.

The official launch of the Hebrew University of Jerusalem was a personal triumph for Weizmann. He declared:

"The Hebrew University, while trying to maintain the highest scientific level, must at the same time be rendered accessible to all classes of the people. The Jewish workman and farm labourer must be enabled to find there a possibility of continuing and completing his education in his free hours. The doors of our libraries, lecture rooms and laboratories must be wide open to them all. Thus the University will exercise its beneficial influence on the nation as a whole and that its purpose was to teach everything that the mind of man embraces." [293]

Weizmann's long-cherished ambition, to afford to future generations of those living in Palestine and Israel the opportunities denied to past generations living in less enlightened circumstances, had finally been realised.

A walk today around the six campuses of the Hebrew U (as it is affectionately referred to) visually confirms that it is open to all: Israelis of all backgrounds, Jews (be they Ashkenazi or Sephardi), Arabs (be they Moslem or Christian, Bedouin or Druze), Circassians and many others, together with non-Israelis, all of whose various appearances give only a hint of the wide diversity of the student body originating from some 85 countries. Naturally, there is no crimping quota system in operation.

20

THE HEBREW UNIVERSITY TODAY

The Hebrew University in Numbers:	Innovation in Numbers:
23,500 students	Tens of millions of dollars in annual revenues
973 researchers	9,826 patents

[293] *Chaim Weizmann: A Biography*, Norman Rose (ibid)

7 faculties	2,753 inventions (150 per year)
6 campuses	600 commercial products
14 schools	880 licenses
Over 200 majors and programs	120 spin-off companies
Over 5,000 courses	
Prestigious Awards:	**Global Scope:**
1 Fields Medal in Mathematics	208 Student exchange programs with 95 academic institutions in 24 countries
1 Turing Award in Computer Science	220 Postdoctoral researchers from 26 countries
1 Gairdner International Award	320 Academic agreements with institutions in 44 countries
8 Nobel Prizes	2,000 Students from 90 countries attend the Rothberg International School each year
14 Wolf Prizes	
46 EMET Prizes	
100 Rothschild Prizes	
294 Israel Prizes	

THE WEIZMANN INSTITUTE

Rechovot was rarely far from Chaim Weizmann's consciousness. In *Trial and Error*, Weizmann recalls the Eisenberg family's *Aliyah* from Pinsk during his schooldays there (between 1885 and 1892). On his first visit to *Eretz Yisrael* in 1907, Weizmann met up with the Eisenbergs at Rechovot and decided that one day he would make his home there. He writes that *"forty years* [after the Eisenbergs' *Aliyah*] *I bought the land for our house in Rechovot"*[294] from the Eisenberg family. That

[294] *Trial and Error* (ibid)

would place his purchase around 1930. Joshua Reinharz[295] writes that Chankin bought the land in Rechovot[296] that would one day be the seat of the Weizmann Institute in 1890. The two plots today appear as one unit but, whatever the detailed story about the land deals, Rechovot clearly had deep roots in Weizmann's life. It was to develop a sturdy trunk, form large boughs, sprout many branches and deliver bounteous fruit, too.

THE AGRICULTURAL RESEARCH ORGANIZATION

The Palestine Office, inspired by Herzl, was established in Jaffa in 1908 as the operational branch of the ZO in Palestine. A decade later, in pursuance of the Balfour Declaration, Weizmann, as president of the ZF, led the Zionist Commission to Palestine. Once there, he merged the Palestine Office into the ZO. (It would become the Jewish Agency in 1929.)

Palestine Office departments were created for settlement, education, finance, immigration, statistics and agriculture. In 1921, the ZO set up the Agricultural Experiment Station (later the Agricultural Research Organization) in Ben Shemen, in the centre, close to today's Ben Gurion International airport.

Yitzhak Elazari-Volcani[297] was appointed head of the Station, and continued in that post until his retirement thirty years later. Under Volcani, the Station pursued many areas of research, including crop sciences, food technology and farm economics. In no small measure, the credit for the establishment of the Station was attributable to Weizmann. He was also instrumental

---

[295] *Chaim Weizmann: The Making of a Zionist Leader*, Jehuda Reinharz (ibid)

[296] Although elsewhere we have seen claims that Ruppin acquired it - possibly they did so together.

[297] Yitzhak Elazari-Wilkanski (1880-1955) from Vilna in the Pale, considered the founder of modern agriculture in Israel, wrote his doctoral thesis on his discovery of microorganisms in the Dead Sea, previously believed incapable of sustaining life.

in its move to Rechovot in 1932. When fate delivered the idea for a scientific institute, it was natural for him to suggest that it become the Agricultural Experiment Station's neighbour.

MARKS & SIEFF

Chaim Weizmann could charm strangers in a moment — and, in the next, convert them into life-long friends. Few personal friendships of his were as close, however, as those he enjoyed with Mancunians, Simon Marks and Israel Sieff. These two childhood friends, who became brothers-in-law, developed M&S into a legend in British business by the application of a few simple policies: buy British; give the customers excellent value; and treat the staff well (this last, not too obvious to most employers of the age, being something they shared, presumably unwittingly, with the Wissotzkys[298]).

Although Marks and Sieff were related by marriage to Sacher, despite their all living in Manchester, and notwithstanding that Sacher and Weizmann had met in 1905, it was not until 1913 that Sacher brought them all together. Once the light of that friendship had been kindled, it would burn bright for their joint lives. At the Weizmann Institute of Science at Rechovot, Israel, it shines still.

Simon Marks, Israel Sieff and Chaim Weizmann were to become increasingly involved with one another. The businessmen were optimists and:

> *"counter-balanced Weizmann, who was temperamental and often given to depression. In return, Weizmann can be said to have given them a Great Cause to work for in their lives. As Israel Sieff put it: 'Weizmann gave me, as he gave so many others, a vision and awareness, a sense of urgency and dedication, which made it seem in retrospect as though for*

[298] See Appendix 1.

me Zionism and Weizmann began in my life together.'"[299]

In 1916, Simon Marks was excused wartime duties to work in the Piccadilly offices of the ZF where he had a great deal of contact with Weizmann in the frenetic work that led to the Balfour Declaration the following year. Both Marks and Sieff were with Weizmann at the Paris Peace Conference in 1919, and at the San Remo Peace Conference in 1920. Even so, Weizmann saw much more of Sieff, for he served as secretary to Weizmann's 1918 Zionist Commission to Palestine, when they got to know one another very well indeed.

FROM PERSONAL LOSS TO NATIONAL GAIN

Weizmann had moved from Manchester to London in 1919. The Sieff and Marks families followed in 1926, when M&S relocated its headquarters to the capital. Israel and Rebecca Sieff had a son, Daniel, whose great interest was chemistry. Weizmann saw a fine future for young Sieff in chemistry, his own field, so took a personal interest in him.

In February 1933 (the month after Adolph Hitler came to power in Germany) Daniel Sieff died tragically young. The Sieffs turned to Weizmann for support and they would walk with him for hours, talking through their heartbreak:

> *"They discussed the boy and what he had hoped to become. He had been interested in science and had wanted to make it his career. With the vision and sensitivity that was Weizmann's enduring quality, he made a suggestion: The Nazi persecutions had already begun; persecutions that were to reach the climax of horror ten years later. Eminent Jewish scientists were being hounded out of their laboratories and Weizmann proposed that in Daniel Sieff's memory a science institute should be set up in Palestine. Weizmann saw, in such an institute, a sanctuary for many of*

[299] The Centre for Jewish Studies of Manchester University: http://www.manchesterjewishstudies.org/manchester-school/

the scientific refugees. But he also foresaw a research centre which would serve the needs of the country and at the same time form part of the world community of science. He had ideas, too, about the ways in which such an institute could help to break down the walls which fenced off one section of knowledge from another."[300]

In a little over a year, by the following April, with an initial generous endowment from the Sieff family and contributions from others, The Daniel Sieff Institute was opened at Rechovot. Weizmann was able to transfer his laboratory work there from London. He and Vera rented a small cottage nearby and participated fully in the collegial life and work of the Institute, which drew in some of the greatest scientists of the age, largely in the flight from the Nazis. Germany's loss was the *Yishuv*'s gain.

In November 1949, with the consent of the Sieff family, the name of The Daniel Sieff Institute was changed to that of the country's first president and, today, The Weizmann Institute of Science is widely recognised as one of the most impressive scientific research centres in the world.

Chaim and Vera Weizmann had their home built on the campus in 1936. After the three triumphs with President Truman in 1947 and 1948, and the installation of Chaim Weizmann as the first President of the State of Israel in 1949, that is where he and Vera lived out the rest of their lives together. First Israeli President, Dr Chaim Weizmann died at home in Rechovot on 9 November 1952, just short of his 78th birthday. Into those years, he had packed enough for several lifetimes of most other mortals.

The Institute today is a multidisciplinary research centre, with around 2,500 students for MSc and PhD qualifications and postdoctoral fellows — all scientists. As to the esteem with which its work is held, in 2015, the Centre for Science and

[300] *Chaim Weizmann: A Biography By Several Hands* (ibid) by Ritchie Calder.

Technology Studies at Leiden University in Holland ranked it tenth (behind nine US universities) in a review of publications from 750 research institutions around the world for the period of 2010-2013. Weizmann Institute researchers published 2,414 articles that were cited 27,859 times. Over 450 of the articles were in the top 10% of important articles published globally. (See also panel 16).

Chaim Weizmann both created the Institute and inspired its path to success, which has, in a direct line, fed into the success of the State of Israel.

16

FROM THE WEIZMANN INSTITUTE WEBSITE[301]

The Weizmann Institute of Science is one of the world's leading basic research institutions. It is comprised of 250 experimental and theoretical research groups across five faculties—Biology, Biochemistry, Chemistry, Mathematics and Computer Science, and Physics. Insights that emerge from its labs help provide a fundamental understanding of the human body and the universe, and lead to advances in medicine, technology, and the environment. This is science for the benefit of humanity at its best.

Weizmann Institute scientists are credited with inventing amniocentesis, blockbuster drugs for multiple sclerosis, nano-materials and compounds for industrial and medical uses, advanced computer technology, and breakthrough data-storage options. Scientists are investigating the intricacies of the immune system, breaking new ground in understanding rare genetic disorders, developing new breeds of plants, and elucidating physical properties of the universe.

Our cancer research has led to many discoveries, including the gene that encodes p53 — the tumor suppressor protein found to be dysfunctional in almost all cancers — and a protein that triggers chronic myelogenous leukemia, which provided the foundation for the development of Imatinib (known as Gleevec).

[301] https://www.weizmann.ac.il/pages/about-institute/research-and-discovery

> Our investigations led to the basis for the drug Erbitux to treat colorectal cancer and head and neck cancer, and many other insights in breast and ovarian cancer, prostate cancer, and more.
>
> Our neuroscientists have revealed how the brain and nervous system develop and function in health and disease, with insights on neurodegenerative diseases such as Alzheimer's and Parkinson's and mental illnesses and conditions such as autism, depression, and schizophrenia. One of the Institute's strengths is its development of basic research tools, such as nuclear-magnetic resonance for the study of biological and non-biological materials.
>
> Professor Ada Yonath of the Department of Structural Biology received the Nobel Prize in Chemistry in 2009 for deciphering the structure of the ribosome, which has implications for the development of new antibiotics and better understanding resistance to antibiotics. In addition, she has elucidated the modes of action of many antibiotics that target the ribosome and revealed mechanisms of drug resistance, paving the way for structure-based drug design.
>
> The Weizmann Institute has historically led the way in computer science research; in the 1970s, the algorithm that allows for safe and secure computer transactions, RSA, was co-invented by our scientists and provided the foundations for start-up companies that fuel Israel's booming telecommunications industry. Three of our computer scientists have won the Turing Award, considered the "Nobel of mathematics".

With four major diplomatic and three significant educational triumphs to his credit, surely Weizmann's reputation, as the indispensable Zionist was secure forever. Alas, no.

~~~
~~~

19

REPUTATIONS IN CONFLICT

NO SUBSTITUTE AVAILABLE

Despite all that has been said about Weizmann and the loyalty to him he would arouse in others, he was never given carte-blanche in or by the ZO. Indeed, as the British became, during the 1930s and the 1940s, increasingly destructive of the interests of the *Yishuv*, Weizmann's efforts to maintain a working relationship with them were deeply distrusted and resented within the ZO. His compatriots then more easily associated him with the "enemy" than with themselves.

At the 22nd Zionist Congress in 1946, Weizmann lost a key vote on his proposal that he attend the London Conference on Palestine. Weizmann regarded the ballot's negative outcome (assiduously worked for by Ben-Gurion) as amounting to a vote of no confidence, and he resigned the ZO presidency; yet he was plainly irreplaceable, for the position lay vacant for the next decade. Then, the year after he was discarded, came the need to seek the first of the great concessions required of President Truman.[302] The Zionists at the UN in New York realised that they had no other statesman or diplomat in Weizmann's league — one might say, not even the chairman of the Jewish Agency from 1935, David Ben-Gurion.

A GENERATION-LONG CONFLICT

While, by 1948, it was preordained that Chaim Weizmann would be the first president of the State of Israel, its first prime minister was, similarly, destined to be David Ben-Gurion, Weizmann's nemesis. They knew each other of old, the feud between them dating back as far as 1918. Ben-Gurion was to win the final battle — that of the reputations — as he rose to become (as the first prime minister of the State of Israel) the undisputed political leader of the Israeli nation, replacing Weizmann, who

[302] See chapters 16 and 17.

had held the position of leading Zionist for the previous 30 years.

As President, Weizmann was in decline. Along with his eyesight and his general health, so too were fading — or being reduced by others — his celebrity and distinction, which were all but buried with him in 1952. Today, Weizmann's reputation as one of the essential nation-builders of Israel is almost invisible, even amongst scholars and academics in the field of Zionism, in Israel and beyond. In no small measure, and perhaps overwhelmingly, this results from the mutual enmity of the two great men. When and how did it arise?

SIMILARITIES AND CONTRASTS

The backgrounds of Weizmann and Ben-Gurion (born *Grün* and commonly referred to as "BG") were not dissimilar: both came from the Pale of Settlement (though Weizmann was Russian and BG Polish) and each was exposed to *Hovevei Zion* at a young age. Weizmann always championed Practical Zionism; BG was undoubtedly a practical Zionist. On the other hand, while Weizmann's father was a non-professional manual worker and businessman, and Ben-Gurion's father was a lawyer (of sorts), Weizmann aspired to the professional class, BG becoming essentially associated with the ordinary Jewish, and especially *Yishuv*, working man.

It was as a student at the University of Warsaw in 1905 (just before his *Aliyah*) that BG joined *Po'alei Zion* ("Workers of Zion", the Social-Democratic Jewish Workers' Party). Later, in 1918 America, BG started an action committee within the American *Po'alei Zion* ("APZ") to agitate its establishment with pro-active, strongly workers-oriented, policies. As a student, Weizmann too had been a Zionist activist, for he had initiated the ginger group, the Democratic Faction in 1901, to shake up Herzl and the ZO.

BG'S ALIYAH

In 1906, twenty year old David Ben-Gurion became part of the Second Aliyah and, within weeks after his arrival in the *Yishuv*, was elected to the central committee of the newly-formed Jaffa branch of *Po'alei Zion*. Typically, committee members were Marxists and BG's political sympathies were with them. BG, however, wanted something more for the workers of the *Yishuv*, so he introduced a strongly nationalist (ie Zionist) programme for them to pursue. Ben-Gurion was then content, alongside his political activism, to pick oranges, at first in Petah Tikva and, one year on, in the Galilee. Once there, he joined a local group of armed watchmen guarding isolated Jewish agricultural communities.

In November 1911, Ben-Gurion changed direction and went to study law in Turkish Salonika (Thessaloniki to the Greeks) and later Constantinople.[303] It was there that his friendship with Ben-Zvi was cemented, and BG changed his name from Grün to Ben-Gurion. As yet, he envisaged no future for Palestine outside the Ottoman Empire.

The outbreak of World War I in 1914 found Ben-Gurion and Ben-Zvi back in Jerusalem. Keen to assist the authorities (and, as later became clear, showing poor judgment[304]) they formed a Jewish militia and recruited over 40 Jews to fight with the Ottoman Army. For their pains, the two compatriots were deported by the Turks to Egypt, most young men born outside Palestine being susceptible to such deportation.

Ben-Gurion and Ben-Zvi, their enthusiasm for the Turkish cause

---

303 It is interesting to note that, while most of the laws of Israel are based on the English Common Law, or are new codes passed by the Knesset, Israeli land law to this day is Turkish.

304 Despite the Turks' plain antipathy to the Yishuv, as described in some detail in *The Aaronsohn Saga*, Shmuel Katz (Gefen Publishing House, Jerusalem and New York, 2000).

undiminished, moved to the (then neutral) USA and, over the following three years, toured 35 American cities seeking to raise a pioneer (*Hechalutz*) army 10,000 strong to fight for the Turks. In 1917, Chaim Weizmann's rather different loyalties and activities were to induce another change of direction in the life of David Ben-Gurion.

THE BALFOUR DECLARATION

The Balfour Declaration had an impact on the Jewish world at least as electrifying as had Herzl's *Der Jüdenstaat* two decades earlier and possibly more so. Just as every Jew soon heard of the pamphlet, and the celebrity of its Viennese author, so the fame of the Declaration and its facilitator also become a global Jewish phenomenon; and just as Weizmann realised in 1896 that a new day had dawned for Zionism, BG came to a similar realisation in 1917. Indeed, it had a keen, personal effect on him — a volte face. BG at last saw that the future of the *Yishuv* was unlikely to be dictated by the Turks and he realised that his loyalties must lie with the British, a decision reinforced by Allenby's almost contemporaneous capture of Jerusalem.

Led by Ben-Gurion and Ben-Zvi, APZ began to recruit volunteers for Jabotinsky's Jewish Legion; and the two compatriots themselves, both into their thirties, enlisted in April 1918. After a period of training in Canada, they were sent to Egypt, where they became part of the British Army, and underwent further training — until and beyond the end of the war. All the while, BG was yearning to return to Palestine, the more so once he heard about Weizmann's Zionist Commission to Palestine in the spring of 1918.

THE CONFLICT'S STARTING POINT

BG dearly wished to be in on the ground floor of the Palestine Commission. First, he sought to join by reason of his association with APZ, which had been offered seats on the Commission for two representatives. While Ben-Zvi and Ben-Gurion were the obvious nominees (being in Egypt, on Palestine's doorstep), the

APZ Central Committee preferred to relinquish one place and send only one delegate, Isaac Zar (possibly in retribution for BG's action committee that had harried the APZ establishment). According to Shabtai Tevet (a biographer of Ben-Gurion), BG remonstrated:

> *"'This was a sad, a very sad chapter,'... 'one of political filth of the ugliest American kind ...'"* [305]

Next, from his British army camp in Egypt, Ben-Gurion approached David Eder, acting chairman (whenever Weizmann was absent from Palestine) of the Palestine Commission, for help with applications for leaves of absence, but:

> "[b]*lind to the potential of the workers' movement and to its strength, he* [Eder] *did not think that unification of the workers' parties was a cause worthy of intervention with the military high command to obtain long leaves for Ben-Gurion, especially since he* [Eder] *believed,* ***with Weizmann****, that Palestinian Jews were petty, vociferous, and bordered on the hysterical. Ben-Gurion's request was denied.*"[306] [Emphasis added.]

According to Teveth:

> *"Eder and Weizmann considered Ben-Gurion a 'political agitator unworthy of their notice.'*[307] *... Ben-Gurion accused*

---

[305] *Ben-Gurion: The Burning Ground 1886-1948*, Shabtai Teveth, (Houghton Mifflin Company, 1987).

[306] *Ben-Gurion: The Burning Ground 1886-1948*, Shabtai Teveth (ibid)

[307] While there are five hundred references to Weizmann in Teveth's book, Weizmann, in *Trial and Error* (ibid), makes only a handful of references to BG, all to do with the last days before the Declaration of Independence and covered here in chapter 17. Jehuda Reinharz, in *Chaim Weizmann: The Making of a Zionist Leader (ibid),* makes no reference to BG. Of the Weizmann biographies the author has considered, only *Chaim Weizmann: A Biography* (ibid) by Norman Rose, makes a substantial number of references to BG (142) but there is little cross-referencing to the matters dealt with by Teveth.

> *Eder and Weizmann of hostile intentions."*[308]

Ben-Gurion's confrontation with Eder, over what Eder considered to be Ben-Gurion's improper attempts to join the Commission, which Eder rebuffed, must have been wounding for Ben-Gurion. BG may have suspected Weizmann's hand in his exclusion by Eder[309] — and he may well have been right.

This episode was, according to Tevet: "*the starting point of Ben-Gurion's conflict with Weizmann*"; and thus the scene was set for a simmering feud between two great Zionist leaders that was to last through the Mandate years and into the life of the State of Israel — with repercussions beyond that of Weizmann.

THE RIVALRY

Back in 1918, it did not take long for Ben-Gurion to appreciate that his political ambitions and Weizmann's prominence would make them natural rivals as future contenders for the leadership of the Zionist movement. Weizmann, however, at the pinnacle of his Zionist endeavours, or still ascending to even greater heights, was unlikely to have been aware of the challenge that would be coming from outside the Zionist élite, or from beneath (as he might have perceived it).

For the time being, Weizmann, was the leader of the Zionist world and Ben-Gurion was seeking to catch up. Even Ben-Gurion conceded that:

> *"The Zionist Organization has in Weizmann a dedicated, diligent, and multitalented leader. I do not agree with his politics. In my view he has not risen to the challenge. There is, however, no denying that he has done wonders. He has not demanded all that he should have, nor done all that he*

[308] *Ben-Gurion: The Burning Ground 1886-1948,* Shabtai Teveth (ibid).

[309] BG was even to threaten to sue for defamation of character but was dissuaded: *Ben-Gurion: The Burning Ground 1886-1948,* Shabtai Teveth (ibid)

> *could have, but what he has done is enough to make his name immortal,"*[310]

but BG's implication was that Weizmann had achieved not only much but also enough, and should now stand aside for a younger, aspiring generation.

Their paths first crossed in late 1918 at a reception for Weizmann and his Zionist Commission, organised by the *Yishuv's* Provisional Council to celebrate his achievement with the British the previous November. After Weizmann's address, there was the usual question and answer session and:

> *"Ben-Gurion ... asked why Weizmann had not 'simply* [demanded] *a Jewish state in Palestine'; whether 'a National Home and a Jewish state are one and the same thing'; and what rights would 'be granted to the Arab population.' In fact he asked nine questions, many more than anyone else, giving Weizmann sufficient opportunity to distinguish him from the crowd and probably to remember his face."*[311]

Of course, the questions betray a certain youthful naivety (or disingenuousness), but Weizmann answered patiently, explaining to the younger man about the conflicting demands of ambition and practicality.[312]

Ben-Gurion was demobilised from the British Army in April 1920, and immediately got down to his political work in the *Yishuv*.

---

[310] *Ben-Gurion: The Burning Ground 1886-1948,* Shabtai Teveth (ibid)

[311] *Ben-Gurion: The Burning Ground 1886-1948,* Shabtai Teveth (ibid)

[312] Weizmann might have said (as quoted of him from time to time) *"Politics is the sense of smell, to predict what can – and what cannot – be achieved. One should demand only that which can be achieved".*

WHEN GREEK MEETS GREEK

Ben-Gurion realised that he needed to meet Weizmann.

How might that go? There had been a time when Weizmann had been in Ben-Gurion's position: as the instigator of the Democratic Faction, Weizmann had sought a meeting with Zionist leader, Theodor Herzl.

Herzl and Weizmann had been from different worlds; so too, despite their common Pale of Settlement origins, were Weizmann and Ben-Gurion. In 1901, one was the celebrated author of *Der Jüdenstaat* from Vienna, the other a raw émigré scientist from the Russian Pale. By 1918, the former aspirant had become the President of the ZF, leader of the Zionist Commission, into middle age and patrician in his disposition. He had achieved international acclaim as a scientist and was the *de facto* world leader of the Jews. Financially secure and British in his sympathies and bearing, Weizmann was every inch the Jewish aristocrat.

Ben-Gurion was only twelve years younger than Weizmann, but still nowhere near his middle years. He had first arrived in Palestine with the Second *Aliyah* and was a proud, self-proclaimed member of the Jewish working class. His platform was that a Jewish state would be borne only from *"a socialist association of the working class, which would set up a socialist society, would be able to fulfil Zionism and build Palestine"*[313] and he cut a less impressive figure than Weizmann, both aesthetically and linguistically — not that he would have allowed that to bother or impede him.

Perhaps Weizmann has set the scene for us (without naming names) in a letter to Eder dated 8 June 1920, complaining about the *Yishuv*:

> *"The telegrams and also the letters which have been coming*

[313] *Ben-Gurion: The Burning Ground 1886-1948*, Shabtai Teveth (ibid)

from Jerusalem lately are most perturbing, and it is difficult to imagine that people have lost their heads to such an extent. It becomes almost impossible to work systematically and prepare all. ... There is apparently a spirit of bitterness and vindictiveness abroad which will make it very difficult for [Herbert] *Samuel or for that matter, for anybody else to carry on, and it will be the duty of the Zionists and of all those who really care for work in Palestine to take stern measures and to bring about a radical change. .... I think an end must be put to the hysterical state into which part of the Palestinian population has apparently worked itself.*

One could have expected that there would be more patience, and more self-control at a time like this but apparently personal ambitions and petty vanity are taking the upper hand. They seem to excel in a game of showing cheap heroism and fictitious martyrdom, and candidly I am beginning to sympathise with the British Administration more now than I ever did before. If when Mr Samuel arrives they are going to besiege him with all their "demands, protestations and requests", Mr Samuel will be utterly disgusted and will turn his back on the Jewish community just as the others did, and our best chance will have gone."[314]

One might easily guess that, with that background, the stage was set for a bitter confrontation.

Ben-Gurion had his first audience with Weizmann in London, just before the July 1920 World Zionist Conference[315] convened in the celebratory mood created by the Balfour Declaration. Perhaps Weizmann remembered his first audience with Herzl, when the great man had taken the wind out of the young

[314] Extracted from the full letter at *Weizmann Archives: Feisal/12-580.TIF*

[315] Not to be confused with the ZO's Twelfth Congress held the following year in Carlsbad (Karlovy Vary), Czechoslovakia.

activist's sails by defusing his possible hostility with indulgence. In any event, when Weizmann and BG met face-to-face for the first time, while Weizmann:

> *"could have treated Ben-Gurion like a poor relation, ... instead* [he] *extended a hearty welcome and spoke with him as an equal, in his best folksy manner."*[316]

Weizmann appeared to take BG into his confidence, informing him comprehensively about both his past achievements and future plans for the *Yishuv*. BG was swayed, and communicated his approval to his comrades back in Palestine. They, however, were not over-impressed and, when they joined BG in London for the conference, they formed the view, together with BG, that Weizmann had exaggerated some of the information imparted to Ben-Gurion. They decided Weizmann should be confronted publicly.

THE 1920 WORLD ZIONIST CONFERENCE

Weizmann's speech opening the conference was compelling and inspiring. The delegates hung onto every word of his:

> *"'brief sketch' of the situation in Palestine,* [which] *afforded Weizmann the opportunity to shine and win over his audience, body and soul."*[317]

Weizmann then, arguably, went too far, reflecting his 8 June letter to Eder, but now publicly, blaming:

> *"the Yishuv for all the mishaps and troubles that had occurred. 'The Eretz-Israelis', he said, 'were excitable, impulsive, and took themselves far too seriously; the parties in Palestine were unruly,'* and *'the Jews there suffer from hypertrophy.' By contrast, the British administration was*

---

[316] *Ben-Gurion: The Burning Ground 1886-1948,* Shabtai Teveth (ibid)

[317] *Ben-Gurion: The Burning Ground 1886-1948,* Shabtai Teveth (ibid)

stable and practical."[318]

Ben-Gurion responded with a furious attack on Weizmann. He lamented that the Commission had:

> "*set up an iron wall between them and denied Eretz-Israelis access to the administration*" ... charging that Weizmann had ... "*repaid the British by assuming a moderate line and making concessions. The result — here Ben-Gurion reached the gravest offense of all — was that the administration's sympathy had turned into an ever-growing hostility that served only to incite the Arabs to raids on Jewish settlements and pogroms in Jerusalem. Ben-Gurion placed the responsibility for the spilled Jewish blood neither on the Arabs nor on the British, but on Weizmann.*"[319]

Now it was BG who had overreached himself. Teveth concedes at this juncture that:

> "*There can be no doubt that personal considerations and covert ambitions drove Ben-Gurion*" and that "*Ben-Gurion's wild exaggeration ensured a resounding defeat.*"[320]

Weizmann, concluding, was dismissive of Ben-Gurion's impertinence and mocked him mercilessly, whereupon:

> "*The delegates rose to their feet as one and gave Weizmann a seemingly endless ovation.*"[321]

Ben-Gurion no doubt nursed his wounds and awaited a rematch. There were to be several.

A full decade passed and in 1931 Ben-Gurion felt strong enough

---

[318] *Ben-Gurion: The Burning Ground 1886-1948,* Shabtai Teveth (ibid)

[319] *Ben-Gurion: The Burning Ground 1886-1948,* Shabtai Teveth (ibid)

[320] *Ben-Gurion: The Burning Ground 1886-1948,* Shabtai Teveth (ibid)

[321] *Ben-Gurion: The Burning Ground 1886-1948,* Shabtai Teveth (ibid)

to determine to render Weizmann, whether or not holding the office of the ZO president, subordinate to the Executive:

> *"Sharett put it plainly: Ben-Gurion wanted 'a coalition without Weizmann yet in contact with him'* warning against *'the illusion that it is possible to leave Weizmann out and at the same time keep him working for the Zionist movement.' But that was exactly what Ben-Gurion was determined to do."*[322]

(In 1947/8, that was effectively what came about: Weizmann was to work his last three great diplomatic coups, those with Truman, despite being out of office.)

The conflict rumbled on throughout the 1930s and the 1940s, and, as the years went by, Weizmann's problems became threefold for, unlike BG, he was seen as an appeaser of the British; he had no political base; and his health was deteriorating. Further, while he was not completely opposed to violence for Jewish defence, he would make no concession to terrorism. Others were less squeamish.[323]

No attempt is made here to chronicle further the many clashes between Ben-Gurion and Weizmann in the 1930s and the 1940s, for this work is about Weizmann's major achievements. (The less weighty successes, and his defeats, have been dealt with by other writers — and they do not detract from Weizmann's diplomatic successes without which there might never have been

---

[322] *Ben-Gurion: The Burning Ground 1886-1948*, Shabtai Teveth (ibid)

[323] In November 1944 in Cairo, Lord (Walter Guinness) Moyne was assassinated by *Lehi*, a self-declared Jewish terrorist group, sending shock waves through the Western world and the *Yishuv*. Moyne remains a controversial character for the Jews. A S Yehuda of the New School for Social Research, a private research university in New York, accuses Moyne of having encouraged Arab racism against Jews, while Jewish historian Bernard Wasserstein, rejects those views. Weizmann was dismayed and unforgiving, not least because Moyne was close friend of Winston Churchill.

a State of Israel in which BG could become its prime minister.) Specifically here, the proposition is that Weizmann's reputation was diminished as a consequence of his feud with BG. A significant witness is now called to establish this point.

THE RIFT

Meyer Weisgal, another product of the *heim*, with a formidable intellect, was from 1921 until 1930 the first head of the Zionist Organization of America. In 1940, he was appointed Weizmann's personal assistant and they remained closely associated until Weizmann's death[324], Weisgal going on to be President of the Weizmann Institute of Science from 1966 to 1969. The reader might think of him, while plainly a disciple of Weizmann, as sufficiently of good faith as to give an honest account of events, not least because of the quality of the evidence he cites.

In his autobiography[325], Weisgal consciously seeks to put the record straight on the "rift", as he calls it, between Weizmann and BG, and illuminates BG's animosity towards Weizmann as the 1940s opened.

Weisgal first suggests that there was no fundamental dissimilarity of views between the two great titans of Zionism. Accordingly, he argues, if the rift was not political, it could only have been personal. Weisgal explains:

> *"Ben-Gurion wanted to be in command or — to put it more elegantly, he was impatient for the crown of Zionist leadership. As a result he had to find fault with Weizmann, impute to him political shortcomings, and invent political differences. This he did with bravura and utter disregard for*

---

[324] Referred to as a *"devoted friend of Weizmann in all his Zionist struggles"*: *Chaim Weizmann: A Biography By Several Hands* (ibid) by Ritchie Calder, and co-edited by Weisgal.

[325] *Meyer Weisgal ... So Far*, Meyer Weisgal (ibid)

fact."[326]

THE BILTMORE CONFERENCE

By the 1940s, the USA had achieved the global pre-eminence that the UK had enjoyed a generation earlier. The shock of Pearl Harbor revivified the American economy on a scale and at a pace unequalled in history. It was plain that after World War II America would be the world's most influential power in every field, including furthering Zionist ambitions.

As a result of the 1939 British White Paper, which imposed a halt on Jewish immigration to Palestine — just as the Jews who would become Hitler's victims most needed sanctuary there — Weizmann, contrary to his reputation for invariably appeasing the British, conceived the idea of a conference in America to oppose British policy. Weizmann was still working diplomatically and politically on Britain's policy, but he knew he needed to unify the disparate Zionist organisations in America as a counterbalance to the British, still firmly entrenched in Palestine.

Weizmann demanded the creation of a Jewish Commonwealth in Palestine, and he carried that demand into a conference to be held at the Biltmore Hotel in New York. Weisgal was tasked by Weizmann with arranging a great convention of all American Zionist groups for May 1942, at what became known as the Biltmore Conference. Since Weisgal organised the conference for Weizmann, agreed the agenda in detail with Weizmann and opened the proceedings, it was obvious, he argues, that Weizmann had inspired the assembly.

BG's attendance at the 1942 conference was inevitable and to be expected, for he had become the leader of the centre-left political party, *Mapai*, in 1930 and, from 1935, he was also chairman of the executive committee of the *Sochnut* (the Jewish Agency).

[326] *Meyer Weisgal ... So Far,* Meyer Weisgal (ibid)

His political powerbase in the *Yishuv* was thus substantial. (Weizmann, despite being the ZO president from 1935 had no such political or grass-roots underpinning.)

Weisgal reports:

> *"During the sessions of the Emergency Council preceding the Conference, Ben-Gurion's behavior put a terrific strain on everyone. He was tempestuous, convulsive and threatening. He berated people and was intolerant of any point of view that seemed at variance with his own. He acted as if he alone were conscious of the war and the danger to Palestine."*[327]

The conference proceeded, notwithstanding the extraordinary behaviour Weisgal describes, and there was at the end the agreement for US-wide cooperation that Weizmann had sought, to be known as The Biltmore Program.[328] Following approval by the Zionist General Council in Palestine, it was adopted as the platform of the ZO.

The histrionics were not over, however:

> *"After the Conference ... Ben-Gurion began his attack on Weizmann. He wrote him a letter which for downright discourtesy was unique in Zionist affairs: either Weizmann was to subordinate himself completely to the directives of Ben-Gurion or Ben-Gurion would demand his resignation. It was, in view of Weizmann's commanding position in the world Zionist movement, a piece of nonsense."*[329]

A meeting of all the leading American Zionists was called. Ben-Gurion addressed them for two hours, alleging that:

---

[327] *Meyer Weisgal ... So Far,* Meyer Weisgal (ibid)

[328] For the full text see: http://www.jewishvirtuallibrary.org/the-biltmore-conference-1942

[329] *Meyer Weisgal ... So Far,* Meyer Weisgal (ibid)

> *"Weizmann was playing a lone hand, that he was making the most serious political mistakes, and that if there was as yet no Jewish army, Weizmann alone was to blame. Either Weizmann was to change completely his course of action or submit his resignation.*
>
> *His statement, inferentially, bordered on a charge of treason. (Incidentally, the night before I had visited BG at his hotel on Lexington Avenue to warn him of his folly and to try and convince him that he would find no support for his accusations against Weizmann — not even among his Labor Zionist colleagues.)*
>
> ...
>
> *Weizmann's reply to Ben-Gurion was brief and devastating. To that kind of accusation there could be no reasoned reply. He told Ben-Gurion that he was having hallucinations and that the entire procedure was nothing but an attempt at political assassination."*[330]

Finally, so far as this episode is concerned, Weisgal describes how BG, in his memoirs published in the 1960s, sought comprehensively to ascribe to himself the credit for the Biltmore Conference. (This was consistent with BG's criticism of Weizmann as being in the pocket of the British: how else to overcome the inconvenient truth that Weizmann had organised the Biltmore Conference specifically to overcome the hostility of the British to the *Yishuv*?)

Taking together those few episodes, one can see that BG was tempestuous, intolerant, overwhelmingly ambitious and continuingly pugnacious, not least at Weizmann's expense. This is not the sort of opponent that one would choose for one's twilight years.

The worst was yet to come.

---

[330] *Meyer Weisgal ... So Far*, Meyer Weisgal (ibid)

THE DECLARATION OF INDEPENDENCE

In May 1948, as the independence of the State of Israel was declared in Tel Aviv by David Ben-Gurion, a telegram was despatched to Weizmann in New York from the Provisional Government of the State of Israel, as follows:

> "ON THE OCCASION OF THE ESTABLISHMENT OF THE JEWISH STATE WE SEND OUR GREETINGS TO YOU, WHO HAVE DONE MORE THAN ANY OTHER LIVING MAN TOWARD ITS CREATION. YOUR STAND AND HELP HAVE STRENGTHENED ALL OF US, WE LOOK FORWARD TO THE DAY WHEN WE SHALL SEE YOU AT THE HEAD OF THE STATE ESTABLISHED IN PEACE."

Ben-Gurion was a signatory and, sure enough, Chaim Weizmann was elected President two days later. Was this sufficient reward for all that Weizmann had wrought?

Weizmann could not be in two places at once. Having been officially invited (rather, beseeched) by the Zionist's UN representatives' cable to travel from London in January 1948 to see President Truman, he had been required by the president to remain there until after despatch of the USA's first telegram of recognition of the Jewish state, on 14 May. Weizmann was then free to go (and went to Switzerland via London), but a further four months would elapse before the provisional government would be ready for its first president to set foot on Israeli soil. Ben-Gurion made it clear to Weizmann that suitable arrangements would be made for his reception *"round the middle of September."*[331]

The Declaration of Independence was, of course, signed in Tel Aviv. One must ask: had Weizmann been there and not in New York, could he have been excluded from participation at the ceremony declaring Israeli independence — and from being a

---

[331] Letter from Ben Gurion to Weizmann (in Vevey, Switzerland) dated 15 August 1948, in reply to that of Weizmann to Ben Gurion of 26 July 1948. Source - *Weizmann Archives: 1948/22-2854.TIF*

signatory to the Declaration itself? Decidedly not. Yet no space was left for Weizmann's *ex post facto* signature upon the Declaration.

Ben-Gurion's biographer, Shabtai Teveth, covers the subject in a short paragraph:

> *"When the state was established, Ben-Gurion, rejecting a nearly unanimous demand, refused to allow Weizmann to add his signature to the Declaration of Independence ... insisting on the technical argument that Weizmann was abroad when it was signed."*[332]

Weisgal puts into perspective, at greater length and with authoritative detail, the question of the signatories, asserting that twelve spaces for signatures were left for those detained elsewhere:

> *"Ten of them were in Jerusalem* [then under Arab siege]. *Two of them were as far abroad as Weizmann — in New York. Yet place was left for their signatures. Could not the same consideration have been extended to Weizmann: 'You who have done more than any other living man toward its creation?' Apparently not. So the question remains: was there design? I have an opinion but not an answer. There was a long-range view of history behind this technical omission*
>
> ....
>
> *the Declaration of Independence of the State of Israel was not a technical document, rushed through in the heat of battle. Every name affixed to it was an everlasting honor for the generations to come. Its text and signatories would be reproduced thousands of times over in history books and first-grade primers."*[333]

---

[332] *Ben-Gurion: The Burning Ground 1886-1948*, Shabtai Teveth (ibid)

[333] *Meyer Weisgal ... So Far*, Meyer Weisgal (ibid). So finally, the mundane: the history books by which generations of Israelis, *Sabras* and *Olim*, were

Teveth puts the question of motive beyond doubt with these chilling words:

> *"With Weizmann out of the way, Ben-Gurion, as the sole leader of Mapai, remained alone at the Zionist summit."*[334]

It seems reasonable to conclude that the suppressing of Weizmann's reputation upon and after the formation of the State came from the most powerful man in the country, the prime minister, given the animus that he had always shown to Weizmann. That is not to say that Weizmann was lily-white (for example, his tendency to aloofness and his arrogance towards the *Yishuv* in the 1920s) or always well-advised (for instance, in remaining aloof from party politics), but, for meanness of spirit and crude spitefulness, the omission of Weizmann from the crowning glory of his life's work, the Israeli Declaration of Independence, appears as a blot on the reputation of the State of Israel to whose birth he was clearly essential.

CODA: Revealingly, Weisgal asserts that at the funeral in 1966 of Vera Weizmann, "[t]*he only eminent figure in the State of Israel to absent himself from the funeral, and to express no condolences either publicly or privately, was David Ben-Gurion.*"[335]

~~~

educated about the heroes of the creation of the State of Israel, by omission, confirm Weisgal's fears.

[334] *Ben-Gurion: The Burning Ground 1886-1948*, Shabtai Teveth (ibid)

[335] *Meyer Weisgal ... So Far*, Meyer Weisgal (ibid)
~~~

20

WHAT MANNER OF MAN?

"Miracles sometimes occur, but one has to work terribly hard for them."

Dr Chaim Weizmann

THE MIRACLE WORKER

Weizmann's circle included the legendary Jewish physicist, Albert Einstein. The two toured the United States in the 1920s, to raise money for the Hebrew University project and became great friends, although Weizmann was never able to recruit Einstein for Zionism.

Einstein was, of course, a much more widely-celebrated scientist than Weizmann, but flawed in many ways, and certainly unable to boast the breadth of talents with which Weizmann had been endowed. Having studied the mysteries of the universe, Einstein is reported to have said: *"being an atheist was presumptuous"*[336]; so, if Albert Einstein was prepared to concede the possibility of a Deity, perhaps it is not fanciful to regard Weizmann's triumphs as miraculous — indeed, as a series of miracles — because of the fortuitous confluence of factors which he was able to exploit. Let us conduct a short review with three questions:

- What were the chances that at the very time the British were led by politicians with Zionist sympathies, and on the cusp of their making Britain's long-signalled move to take control of Palestine, Weizmann would be on hand, a leading-light in the very branch of science required for British wartime salvation ?

- Given all that, what were the chances that Weizmann would be able not only to provide that salvation but also, through his networking, to attain advantages that would lead to the

---

336 *Einstein's Greatest Mistake: The Life of a Flawed Genius,* David Bodanis (Little Brown, 2016)

realisation of his life's dream?

□ Finally, what were the chances that he alone would be able to work his magic with a political leader of a later generation on another continent for three further advantages essential to that dream?

If all that had not taken Divine intervention, something else must have been at work.

GENIUS AND THE WORLD'S FIRST 21ST CENTURY MAN

Whether or not the miracle thesis commends itself, it should be acknowledged that Weizmann was a genius, by reason of his extraordinary accomplishments in science and in Zionism, both outcomes having been sought in parallel.

The political accomplishments that Weizmann made — that were demonstrably available to him alone — have been considered in detail and, apart from reminding ourselves of them:

> □ the 1917 Balfour Declaration □ Truman's replacing the Negev into the Jewish sector of the Partition map just before the November 1947 UN vote on Partition □ Truman's January 1948 agreement to block the State Department's attempt to revert to Trusteeship and □ Truman's April 1948 agreement that the USA should be first to recognise the State of Israel upon its Declaration of Independence the following month

they need no further reiteration here.

As to Weizmann's triumphs through his laboratory work, most scientists are satisfied with a handful of patents, but Weizmann was as prolific with his patent registrations as with so much else.

Some of the Weizmann patents were earned while he was working his way up the faculty ladder at Manchester University and busy motivating the Manchester School to produce Zionist literature (and making his own literary contributions). Even as he was developing acetone production as from 1915, he was canvassing a broad range of British politicians over Palestine (despite their being preoccupied with a gargantuan struggle with Germany that they were not yet winning), while he worked on Justice Brandeis and others in the USA with his "barrage of telegrams" when all seemed lost. Still, throughout 1916 and 1917, he kept at his patent applications. He did not tire of this throughout his life.

Altogether in the 20th century, Weizmann registered 235 patents: 20 in the first decade, 34 in the second, 44 in 1920s, 57 in the 1930s and 78 in the ten years ended, in 1949, with his 75th year[337] — and all this while otherwise fully occupied.

As to the Weizmann Process, it has been said that its rapid wartime expansion from laboratory to industrial scale: *"was not only unique among microbiological processes used in industry, but was also the forerunner of the rapid expansion of penicillin production during World War II, as well as of the breadth of operations of many of today's biotechnological processes"*.[338] Indeed, it is regarded, even today after the passage of a century, as commercially valuable, with many applications.

On the *Weizmann Organism*, the bacterium, *Clostridium acetobutylicum*, the Wikipedia entry (its accuracy approved for this work by a British professor of biochemistry) repeats, but succinctly, what we have considered so far[339]; and then, to bring

---

[337] And two more in 1950 aggregating 235. Source: the Weizmann Archives, Rechovot.

[338] http://www.chemistryexplained.com/Va-Z/Weizmann-Chaim.html#ixzz4n7FG9rQf

[339] https://www.wikiwand.com/en/Clostridium_acetobutylicum:

Clostridium acetobutylicum, ATCC 824, is a commercially valuable bacterium sometimes called the "**Weizmann Organism**", after Jewish-Russian-born Chaim Weizmann. A senior lecturer at the University of Manchester, England, he used them in 1916 as a bio-chemical tool to matters completely up-to-date, lending force to the assertion that Weizmann was the world's first 21st century man, it refers to the field of genetic engineering, the direct manipulation of an organism's genome using biotechnology. Although it took root in the last quarter of the 20th century, genetic engineering is very much 21st century technology. The Wikipedia entry continues:

IN GENETIC ENGINEERING

> In 2008, a strain of Escherichia coli was genetically engineered to synthesize butanol; the genes were derived from *Clostridium acetobutylicum*. In 2013, the first microbial production of short-chain alkanes was reported — which is a considerable step toward the production of gasoline. One of the crucial enzymes — a fatty acyl-CoA reductase — came from *Clostridium acetobutylicum* [ie The Weizmann Organism].

Thus we see Weizmann's work from over one hundred years ago having application throughout the 20th century and directly contributing to today's cutting-edge science. Together with his instinctive, prodigious and massively-fruitful networking, Weizmann truly points the way for all those who hope to excel

---

produce at the same time, jointly, acetone, ethanol, and butanol from starch. The method has been described since as the ABE process, (Acetone Butanol Ethanol fermentation process), yielding 3 parts of acetone, 6 of butanol, and 1 of ethanol. Acetone was used in the important wartime task of casting cordite. The alcohols were used to produce vehicle fuels and synthetic rubber.

Unlike yeast, which can digest sugar only into alcohol and carbon dioxide, *C. acetobutylicum* and other Clostridia can digest whey, sugar, starch, cellulose and perhaps certain types of lignin, yielding butanol, propionic acid, ether, and glycerin.

In Genetic Engineering

In 2008, a strain of Escherichia coli was genetically engineered to synthesize butanol; the genes were derived from *Clostridium acetobutylicum*.[1][2] In 2013, the first microbial production of short-chain alkanes was reported[3] - which is a considerable step toward the production of gasoline. One of the crucial enzymes - a fatty acyl-CoA reductase - came from *Clostridium acetobutylicum*.

in our time: science and technology — and networking.

WHAT MANNER OF MAN?

So, possibly a conduit of miracles, truly a genius and the world's first 21st century man, Weizmann was all of these; but what of the man himself, his character and personality?

As early as 1887 in Pinsk, at the time of his Barmitzvah, young Chaim was described by his contemporaries as:

> *"combining luminous intelligence and uncommon capacity for thorough and continuous work, with a strength of character, vitality, gaiety and a biting wit which gave him an easy ascendancy over his milieu".*[340]

and we know that the adult Weizmann had seductive charm and abundant charisma from the outcomes of his associations with a wide range of people from the most illustrious British and American politicians, through the Rothschilds, the philosopher, Achad Ha'am, assorted scientists, soldiers and others. There are further insights, too.

Professor E B Fred of the University of Wisconsin, who worked with Chaim Weizmann during 1920-1921, wrote:

> *"He was a fine specimen, ... and a very able speaker. ... he kept all of us busy trying to protect him from the endless number of people ... who all wanted to see him and have him give a lecture."*[341]

Weizmann had *"found Truman an encouraging listener at their first meeting on 4 December 1945"*[342] so Truman, in return,

---

340 *Chaim Weizmann: A Biography By Several Hands* (ibid)

341 Professor Selman Waksman, Professor Emeritus (Microbiology) at Rutgers State University, in New Brunswick, N.J., USA, Nobel Laureate in Physiology and Medicine (1952. writing in *Chaim Weizmann: A Biography By Several Hands* (ibid).

342 *Chaim Weizmann: A Biography By Several Hands* (ibid) by Abba Eban.

presumably found him fascinating, as did so many others; and plainly Weizmann must have captivated President Truman to have wrought three major concessions — one might even describe them as gifts — from him within the space of a few months. This seems to fit with Truman's assessment:

> *"He was a wonderful man, one of the wisest people I think I ever met ... a leader, one of the kind you read about."*[343]

US judge, Samuel I Rosenman[344], is said to have coined the historic term "*New Deal*" for FDR, for whom he had written nearly every speech. He may be assumed to have been a considerable personality in his own right for he was one of Truman's closest political advisers and wrote many of his speeches, too. Yet Rosenman was described as *"a willing victim of Weizmann's personal spell"*.[345]

According to Norman Rose:

> *"Naturally, he* [Weizmann] *was concerned with maintaining the highest standards. Pedantic in his personal and scientific habits, he would not countenance slovenliness in others. His attitude did not always win him friends, but it earned him respect."*[346]

Before the publication of his biography of Weizmann[347], historian Joshua Reinharz wrote about Weizmann: *"He referred to himself as 'ein anstaendiger Mitteleuropaeer'* [a decent

---

[343] *Truman, David McCullough (ibid)*

[344] also Democratic Party activist and presidential speechwriter, he was the first to hold the position of White House Counsel.

[345] *Chaim Weizmann: A Biography By Several Hands* (ibid) by Abba Eban.

[346] *Chaim Weizmann: A Biography*, Norman Rose (ibid)

[347] *Chaim Weizmann: The Making of a Zionist Leader*, Jehuda Reinharz (ibid)

middle-European] and continues: *"Richard Lichtheim*[348] *described Weizmann's acculturation thus:*

> *'My first clear recollections of Weizmann stem from the Ninth Congress in Hamburg in 1909. There he was, still one of the young delegates with little influence. Nevertheless, I remember him at this Congress as a unique phenomenon worthy of note. .... very erect and yet somewhat languid. Once in a while he looked down at the other delegates with a faint mocking smile. Judging by his yellow-white facial complexion, his goatee and his slightly wide cheek-bones, he appeared to be of the 'Russians'. But in his well-tailored dark suit, in his upright posture which had an air of listlessness, in his self-possession and control over his actions he was already an 'Englishman' ... He knew — and never forgot — that he hailed from Motol near Pinsk. He knew the Jews of Eastern Europe and understood them. But during his many years in Germany and Switzerland he outgrew the narrow boundaries of the shtetl and became a European.'"*[349]

Israel Sieff knew Weizmann better than most. One of the Manchester School, Sieff was Weizmann's secretary on the Zionist Commission to Palestine in 1918, and accompanied him to the Paris and subsequent post-World War I conferences. There had to be a first meeting, of course, and Sieff, a luminary of the British business scene, recalls it (in 1913) in great detail in his memoirs:

> *"I was struck by his personality almost before I had taken in the details of his appearance. It was magical, overwhelming, irrevocable. He was not above middle height, had a dark,*

[348] From 1913 to 1917, Lichtheim was the representative of the Zionist world organisation in the then Ottoman capital, Constantinople. In 1921, Weizmann recruited Lichtheim into the Zionist Organisation.

[349] *Chaim Weizmann: The Shaping of a Zionist Leader before the First World War*: Jehuda Reinharz (Journal of Contemporary History, Vol. 18, No. 2, April, 1983)

small pointed beard, and a rather unusually youthful pinkish face for one who was clearly a Central European Jew. His eyes were full of life, but they were sombre. As he rose to greet us his mien was that of a man who knew he carried a burden, yet it was vigorous and utterly unpretentious. ... The introductions were made: Dr Chaim Weizmann, lecturer in chemistry at Manchester University; his wife Vera. I had been a Zionist for seven years. At the age of seventeen I had joined the Manchester Zionist Organisation, a branch of the Zionist Organisation of England. I had known a good deal, therefore, about Dr Weizmann, before I met him. But the moment I met him he became my master.

The expressions on his face changed quickly and easily, as his discourse moved along, like illustrations of his theme. His voice had light and shade, but never lost intensity. He talked quickly and confidently with a heavy accent, which somehow one hardly noticed while he was speaking. He was an intellectual; yet he was pre-eminently what the Jewish people call folks-mensch, a man of the people, of the masses not of the elite, a leader in whose breast beat the common heart of man. I listened to him rapt.

He spoke first of his own particular conception of the way to establish a Jewish national home in Palestine and swept me off my feet. It was not just because his notion of what Zionism should be was in perfect form and depth what I in cruder terms believed: he made it sound as practical as it was poetical."[350]

Israel Sieff's son, Marcus, who would succeed him as CEO of M&S (and be invited by Ben-Gurion to 1948 war-torn Israel to lend his British World War II logistics expertise to the fight for survival), confirmed his father's views in his own memoirs:

"As a youth I was perhaps more conscious of being a Zionist than a Jew; I was an early disciple of Weizmann. Though

[350] *Memoirs*, Israel Sieff (ibid)

Simon [Marks] *followed with enthusiasm and commitment, it was father who in 1913 led the two families into Weizmann's camp. Weizmann, then a lecturer in chemistry at Manchester University and president of the English Zionist Federation, was virtually, though not officially, the leader of world Zionism. Father had become a Zionist seven years before he set eyes on Weizmann; he had joined the Zionist Organization at the age of seventeen but, as he recorded, 'The moment I met him he became my master. I listened to him rapt.' The following week Father introduced Simon to him. He said, 'Simon too immediately fell under his spell.'"*[351]

Another Weizmann devotee, Meyer Weisgal, writes:

"Without question, the life of modern Israel is the real expression of Dr Weizmann's astonishing gift for creation. Perhaps more than any other statesman of our time, he succeeded in effecting an organic fusion between the abstractions of the mind and the practical activities demanded by man's physical existence. This fusion is reflected in the very core of life in Israel today. It is part of the flavour of Israel's politics, part of the cacophony of its unflagging discussions, of its intellectual posture, of its argumentativeness, of its addiction to theoretical formulae and its adoration of dedication. In all these, one recognizes easily two major and familiar chords the spiritual turbulence of pre-revolutionary Russia and, perfectly parallel with it, the basic values of Anglo-Saxon democracy.

Just as these were the twin paths along which Weizmann's political concept developed, with no disharmony or clash ever interrupting their growth so Israel itself is an organic

351 *Don't Ask the Price*, Marcus Sieff (Fontana Press, 1987)

coalescence of both types of social organization."[352]

It may seem fitting, or perverse, to give Israel's first prime minister, David Ben-Gurion, who opposed and harried Weizmann at every opportunity for three decades, the opportunity to comment on Weizmann's personality; yet BG was nothing if not complex. Writing the preface to *"Chaim Weizmann: A Biography By Several Hands"*[353], Ben-Gurion explained that it was only when appearing before the Zionists that Weizmann appeared as *"a man of moderation, a man of compromise"*. When he spoke to the non-Jewish world, BG explained: *"I was ... astounded by the inner forcefulness, sometimes even aggressiveness, of his manner* ... [and that only then did he display] ... *the full force of Jewish anguish, the historic humiliation of our people ... the profound truth of both our miseries and our hopes sprang from his throat."*

Reproduced at Appendix 5 are a lengthy extract from the preface to *"Chaim Weizmann: A Biography By Several Hands"* and a most complimentary letter to Weizmann in 1937, both from Ben-Gurion's pen, including these words:

> *"There is no other man or circle of men in the Jewish people that can compare with you .... you are the champion of the Jewish people, not because you have been elected (to this post) by a majority, but because you were born for it; the 'Shechinah'* [divine presence] *of the Jewish People rests upon you."*

Ben-Gurion concluded his letter with the words: *"I love you with all my heart and with all my soul"*.[354]

---

[352] From *Chaim Weizmann: A Biography By Several Hands* (ibid) by Meyer Weisgal.

[353] Often used as a source in this work and co-edited by Meyer Weisgal.

[354] This, and what we see in Appendix 5, appears irreconcilable with what was examined in chapter 19. The answer to the conundrum must be that Ben Gurion believed in what he wrote to and about Weizmann, but his

Of course, Weizmann could be aloof, depressive and tetchy in equal measure, and was dismissive, not to say caustically critical, of the disposition and attitudes of the *Yishuv* in the 1920s; but there is no evidence of his being as destructive of others or their reputations as BG was with him. Weizmann was, to the contrary, generous, warm and accessible; charismatic, bewitching and seductive, a recruiter of the unsuspecting; to many the deliverer of miracles; and to many more a genius.

Weizmann was no politician, but above all was a true statesman. According to British Labour politician, Richard Crossman[355]: *"He was the only truly great statesman I have ever known."*

The last word goes, fittingly, to another great British academic and product of the *heim*, the philosopher Sir Isaiah Berlin[356]:

> *"Dr Chaim Weizmann was the first totally free Jew of the modern world and the state of Israel was constructed, whether or not it knows it, in his image."*

With every new success, through the achievement of each new miracle of Israel's science and technology, its innovation and its stature in the modern world, that becomes increasingly clear. Israel at seventy-five years of age truly reflects the image of Dr Chaim Weizmann.

~~~

supreme ambition to be remembered as the most important contributor to the birth of the Jewish State overrode all his other considerations.

355 Richard (Dick) Crossman OBE, was a pro-Zionist British Labour Party MP and a good friend of Dr Weizmann in his later years.

356 Writing in 1957. As to Sir Isaiah Berlin, see footnote 20.
~~~

EPILOGUE

Is history driven by events or by people — or by the chance interaction of the two? Often, an individual is placed within the swirl of events and is able to react and project him/herself (cometh the hour, cometh the man) so as to achieve outcomes for a cause greater than his or her own financial or cultural enrichment. Just occasionally, such a person needs to identify not only from where events have come but, more importantly, to where they may be headed, or steered. Then the ability to appreciate how to him or her alone has been given not only the required talents but also the ability to deploy them to achieve, in a scintilla of time over the course of human history, what is instantly required — that takes a very special person.

It is true that Weizmann had a formidable supporting team in the Manchester School and the ZF, each with their connections to — some very much a part of — the British establishment and political class; but it was he who entranced them all, not least the politicians, and made them willing workers for his goal.

True it was, furthermore, that those politicians had as aims, at the back of their collective minds (and perhaps not so far back), that the British Empire and the route to India might be well served by the establishment of a Jewish home at the eastern extremity of the Mediterranean. Nevertheless, as a story of the right man, enjoying the right chemistry and connections with the right facilitators, being in the right place and at the right time, while it may have an equal in some region of the world other than Eurasia, at some historical point that has been lost to our consciousness, as part of the story of Zionism and the establishment of the State of Israel, it has no obvious or apparent competitor.

Had Herzl not observed the Dreyfus trial, perhaps some other writer would have put out an electrifying pamphlet like *Der Jüdenstaat* by the start of the 20th century; had Ben-Gurion fallen by the wayside, perhaps Moshe Shertok would have succeeded him and achieved the same results for the *Yishuv*; had fate dealt some cruel blow to Abba Eban, who worked so hard at the UN in 1947 and 1948, there might have been another to take his place — but, as for achieving what Weizmann did in extracting the Balfour Declaration from the British in 1917, there could have been, and there was, no substitute. There was no substitute either for the presidency of the ZO for the decade following his departure from that office in 1946; nor could any other person be found to score the three Truman coups in 1947/8.

Then one must take into account the educational investments which Weizmann made in Haifa, Jerusalem and Rechovot. They set the scene for the special place that Israel has carved out in the hi-tech world in which we all live. That he was a scientist, that he leveraged his science to stimulate the Balfour Declaration, that he infused Israeli life with an appreciation of the central importance of education, and especially scientific education, are not coincidental to Israel's progress in the world but rather the direct result of his drive and focus.

For all these reasons, whatever the contribution of others, Weizmann was the *sine qua non*: not only did Weizmann have, amongst all the Zionists, no equal, but also every role he played was truly monumental. The beneficiaries of this extraordinary contribution to Israel, as its seventy-fifth year approaches, are the Israeli people.

He could have wished for no better reward.

~~~
~~~

APPENDIX 1

PRE-HERZLIAN ZIONISM

For those, like Theodore Herzl, not steeped in the history of Zionism, some consideration of the proto-Zionists and the pre-Herzlian Zionists might be helpful.

First, we may marvel at some rabbinical proto-Zionists. Rabbi Menachem Mendel of Vitebsk (c1730-1788), with Rabbi Abraham Kalisker and their 300 disciples, undertook Aliyah to Safed (Zfat) in *Eretz Yisrael* as early 1777. A little later, the great sage, Elijah ben Solomon Zalman, the Vilna Gaon (1720-1797), inspired over 500 of his disciples to undertake Aliyah with their families between 1808 and 1812.

Another rabbinical luminary, Rabbi Zvi Hirsch Kalischer (1795-1874), in his 1862 *"Drishat Tzion"* (Sermon on Zion), set out what would today be called a roadmap to Zion. He advocated what he saw as self-help immigration, by collecting funds from Jews to finance *Aliyah*, the purchase and cultivation of land in *Eretz Yisrael* and the establishment there of an agricultural college and a Jewish military guard for security. (Rabbi Kalischer, noticing the emergence of politically-influential Jews such as Isaac Moïse Crémieux, Sir Moses Montefiore and Albert Cohn, thought the time for propounding his ideas propitious.)

Finally, Rabbi Judah Alkalai (1798-1878), who had studied in Jerusalem, by his 1857 work *"Goral la-Adonai"* (Destiny of the Lord), advocated the return of the Jews to the Holy Land and the renewed glory of Jerusalem.

Then there were the secular Jewish proto-Zionists. The Jewish-French philosopher, socialist and a founder of Labour Zionism, Moses Hess (1812-1875), an associate of Karl Marx and Frederich Engels, advocated, in *"Rome and Jerusalem, The Last National Question"* (1862), the resolution of the Jewish Question through the creation of a socialist state in *Eretz Yisrael*.

A more activist, if quixotic, approach was taken in the New World by Mordecai Manuel Noah, a Jewish-American journalist, playwright, philanthropist and utopian. In 1813, while Consul to the Kingdom of Tunis, he rescued American citizens enslaved by Moroccans. Yet, in 1815, he was removed from his post[357] on the basis that his religion was "an obstacle to the exercise of [his] Consular function." As a pre-cursor (though a less successful one) to Herzl, this story probably has no equal, for, in reaction to his demotion, he single-handedly tried, in 1825, to establish a refuge for Jews of all nations. On an island in the Niagara River that marks part of the border between Canada and the USA, he established his sanctuary, naming it "Ararat" (the biblical resting place of Noah's Ark). The project failed immediately through lack of support, and even opposition and ridicule, from Jews in both America and Europe. Undeterred, Noah proclaimed his beliefs in his 1844 book, *"Discourse on the Restoration of the Jews"*, that the Jews would return and rebuild their ancient homeland, calling on America to assist them.

Now we turn to the Christian proto-Zionists. Lord Shaftesbury, an English politician, philanthropist and social reformer, with his 1841 *"Memorandum to Protestant Monarchs of Europe for the restoration of the Jews to Palestine"*, was instrumental in the establishment, in 1838, of a British consulate in Jerusalem, the first diplomatic mission in the city; and Viscount Melbourne (the mentor of the teenage Queen Victoria) headed a Whig (Liberal) British government which was reported in *The Times* in August 1840 to be considering the question of a Jewish return to the Holy Land.

In 1841/2, Charles Henry Churchill, the British consul in Damascus, conducted correspondence with Sir Moses Montefiore, about the first formal political plan to create a Jewish state in the Holy Land. Churchill wrote: *"I cannot*

[357] By US Secretary of State James Monroe. The incident caused widespread outrage.

conceal from you my most anxious desire to see your countrymen endeavour once more to resume their existence as a people".

George Eliot, the pen name of Mary Anne Evans (1819-1880), poet, journalist, translator and one of the most beloved of Victorian era authors, published in 1876 *"Daniel Deronda"*, the last of her seven novels, a fusion of social satire and moral quest, with overtones of deep empathy for Zionist and Kabbalistic ideas. (See also panel 1.)

Benjamin Disraeli (another favourite prime minister of Queen Victoria[358]) was baptised as an infant and raised in the Protestant faith; but was recognised, especially by his detractors, as Jewish (or Jew-ish). Disraeli wrote an 1877 article, *"The Jewish Question is the Oriental Quest"*, conjecturing that within fifty years a nation of one million Jews would reside in Palestine under British supervision.[359]

(This English Protestant tradition of goodwill to Zionism would achieve its zenith shortly after Chaim Weizmann became a British citizen in 1910 and made a vital contribution to the welfare of the people to whose ideals he thereby pledged himself.)

While plainly Britain led proto-Zionist thinking and activity, there was some, also mainly Protestant, contribution too from the New World. For example, in 1842, Joseph Smith, founder of the Latter Day Saints movement (the Mormons), sent Orson

[358] The Queen is said to have told her eldest daughter: *"The present man will do well. ... He is very peculiar, thoroughly Jewish looking ... but very clever and sensible ... He is full of poetry, romance and chivalry. When he knelt down to kiss my hand, he said 'In loving loyalty and faith'".*

[359] Only found at: https://www.wikiwand.com/en/History_of_Zionism. In 1927 British Mandated Palestine, there were 185,000 Jews. It was some time during the year of the establishment of the State of Israel, 1948, that the Jewish population reached the one million mark.

Hyde as an emissary to the Holy Land to dedicate it in anticipation of the return of the Jews and in 1844, George Bush (1796-1859), professor of Hebrew and Oriental literature at New York University from 1832 to 1846, published *"Valley of Vision; or, The Dry Bones of Israel Revived: An Attempted Proof of the Restoration and Conversion of the Jews"* [advocating] *"the literal return of the Jews to the land of their fathers."*[360]

Protestant theologian, William Eugene Blackstone, submitted a petition, in 1891, supported by a Memorial[361] to the US president calling for the return of Palestine to the Jews, although nothing

---

[360] Shalom Goldman, Asian Studies Department, Dartmouth College, writes in *American Jewish Personalities*:-

Despite his high praise for the study of the language preserved by the Jews, Bush, in the tradition of the European humanist scholars, did not have much regard for the Jews as a people. Though his biblical studies eventually led him to advocate the return of the Jews to Ottoman-ruled Palestine, he cannot be considered a philo-Semite [as evidenced by this passage]: *And this, he said, is not to be effected by miraculous means. Nothing more is implied than that it will be so ordered in Providence that motives will be furnished for such a return, appealing it may be to the worldly and selfish principles of the Jewish mind. It is by no means improbable that the affairs of the nations, or the progress of civilisation, may take such a turn as to offer to the Jews the same carnal inducements to remove to Syria, as now promote them to emigrate to this country. Indeed when we consider the force of national predilections naturally operating with that people, and drawing them with a mighty attraction to their paternal soil, we can scarcely doubt, that a much less degree of worldly inducement will suffice to turn their faces and their footsteps thither than to any other region of the earth.*

http://americanjewisharchives.org/publications/journal/PDF/1991_43_01_00_goldman.pdf

[361] Signed by 413 prominent Christian and a few Jewish leaders in the United States, including John D. Rockefeller and J.P. Morgan, senators, congressmen, religious leaders of all denominations, newspaper editors, the Chief Justice of the U.S. Supreme Court and other notables, the "Memorial" to President Harrison called for American support for the return of the Jews to Palestine.

came of it. (The document foreshadowed Theodor Herzl's 1896 pamphlet, *Der Jüdenstaat.*) In 1916, Judge Louis Brandeis asked Blackstone to send a copy of the Memorial to President Woodrow Wilson, and it is thought partly to have induced Wilson's support for the Balfour Declaration.)

There is no definitive point in history at which a seer should be categorised a Zionist rather than a proto-Zionist, and the choice made here is quite arbitrary. It is argued, however, that proximity in time to Herzl, coupled with activism, identifies Leon Pinsker to head the list of those on the verge of the Herzl era. Here we see much interaction between Jew and Gentile, such that it would be artificial to separate them.

Judah Leib Pinsker (1821-1891) anonymously published a pamphlet, *"Auto-Emancipation"* in 1882, in which he argued that, given European attitudes, the Jews could not be truly free unless established in their own land. Responsible for the establishment of the *Chovevei Zion*, he established in 1890 the *"Society for the Support of Jewish Farmers and Artisans in Syria and Palestine"*, which, renamed the Odessa Committee (the sometime secretary of which was Achad Ha'am), by 1897 boasted 4,000 members. Yet, its membership peaked at only 5,000 in a Russia of more than 5 million Jews.

Peretz Smolenskin (1842-1885), a Russian Jewish novelist, writing in Hebrew, was a leader in the revolt of young Jews against pre-Enlightenment conservatism. His Hebrew periodical, *HaShahar* (The Dawn), was highly influential in promoting Jewish nationalism. Around 1880, he became deeply interested in schemes for the colonisation of Palestine and became associated with South African-born British author, traveller, Christian mystic, sometime British member of parliament and diplomat, Laurence Oliphant.

The story of Laurence Oliphant (1829-1888) is a fascinating one, with an unlikely connection to the Israeli national anthem, HaTikvah (The Hope), and, without too much of a stretch, to

Achad Ha'am. Oliphant spent his early childhood in Colombo, Sri Lanka (then called Ceylon). He and his father are credited with bringing 30 tea plants from China to Ceylon and establishing its tea industry.

In 1879, Oliphant settled in Palestine, where he hoped to promote Jewish agricultural settlement, to alleviate Jewish suffering in Eastern Europe. He visited Constantinople, the seat of the Ottoman Empire, which controlled the Holy Land, seeking a lease on the northern half, where he intended to settle large numbers of Jews (and this prior to the first wave of Jewish settlement by Zionists, the First Aliyah, in 1882). Oliphant did not regard his task as insurmountable, given there were large numbers of Christians in England and the United States who supported this plan. With financial support from the Christadelphians[362] and others in Britain, Oliphant amassed sufficient funding to purchase land and settle Jewish refugees in the Galilee — yet was unable to acquire from the Turks the territory he sought. Oliphant and his wife, Alice, divided their time between the German Colony in Haifa and the Druze village of Daliyat al-Karmel on the eastern slopes of Mount Carmel. He employed as his secretary Naftali Imber.

Naftali Herz Imber (1856-1909), a Jew and a Hebrew-language poet, moved to *Eretz Yisrael* in 1882 to become secretary to Laurence Oliphant, and moved with the Oliphants between their two homes. In 1886, he published a first book of poems, *Barkai* (Morning Star) in Jerusalem, which included *Tikvateinu* (Our Hope), first written in 1877 in Romania. His were the words that became the libretto of the Zionist anthem and, on 14 May 1948, the Israeli national anthem, *HaTikvah*[363].

[362] The Christadelphians: those who believe that God is the creator of all things and the father of true believers, that he is a separate being from his son, Jesus Christ, and that the Holy Spirit is the power of God used in creation and for salvation.

[363] First chosen as the anthem of the First Zionist Congress in 1897.

Kalonimus Wolf Wissotzky, in another intriguing connection, founded the Wissotzky Tea Company in 1849 Moscow. From the early 1900s through 1917, Wissotzkys was the largest tea company in the world. Following the 1917 Bolshevik Revolution, all private businesses in Soviet Russia were sequestered; yet, mainly due to the company's complex employees' benefits scheme, it took fully two years for the Soviets to complete their takeover of Wissotzkys.

A decade earlier, Wissotzkys had established in London their Anglo-Asiatic company. They employed as their London manager Achad Ha'am, upon his resignation as editor of Zionist journal, *Ha-Shiloach* (which Wissotzky had partially funded). Further, Wissotzkys acquired tea plantations in both India and Ceylon. (It is tempting to believe that Wissotzkys acquired their Ceylon plantations from Laurence Oliphant, and that his move to *Eretz Yisrael* inspired that of Wissotzkys in 1936.) Weizmann's and Achad Ha'am's paths, which had diverged when the former left Berlin in 1897, were now in close orbits, for Weizmann was by then well-entrenched in Manchester. London was from there a train journey of a few hours, so the two were able to pick up where they had left off — except that now the scientist and the philosopher were peers and became close friends.

Achad Ha'am became the executor of the will of Wissotzky on his death in 1904, which was to give Weizmann his first opportunity to influence education and science in Palestine.

In 1883, while a student of 19, Nathan Birnbaum founded *Kadimah* ("Forward"), the first Zionist student group in Vienna. It was Birnbaum who coined the terms "Zionism", in 1890, and "political Zionism", in 1892 — just in time, one might think, in view of what would follow only five years later: Herzlian Zionism and the First Zionist Congress.

[If the reader wishes to resume to the narrative, he/she should return to page 33.]

~~~
~~~

APPENDIX 2

MINUTES OF A MEETING OF THE WAR CABINET HELD AT 10, DOWNING STREET, SW[364]

WEDNESDAY, OCTOBER 31, 1917, AT NOON

The Prime Minister [David Lloyd George]

The Right Hon the Earl Curzon of Kedleston, KG, GCSI, GCIE

The Right Hon the Viscount Milner, GCB, GCMG

The Right Hon G. N. Barnes, MP

The Right Hon A. Bonar Law, MP

Lieutenant-General the Right: Hon J C Smuts, KC

The Right Hon Sir E. Carson, KC,

The following were also present [for resolution 12]:—

The Right Hon A J Balfour, CM, MP

Lieutenant-Colonel Sir M P A Hankey, KCB, *Secretary.*

Fleet Paymaster P H Row, RN, *Assistant Secretary.*

Captain the Hon W Ormsby-Gore, MP, *Assistant Secretary.*

12. With reference to War Cabinet 245, Minute 18, the War Cabinet had before them a note by the Secretary (Paper G.-164) and also a memorandum by Lord Curzon (Paper GT-2406) on the subject of the Zionist movement. The Secretary of State for Foreign Affairs stated that he gathered that everyone was now agreed that, from a purely diplomatic and political point of view, it was desirable that some declaration favourable to the aspirations of the Jewish nationalists should now be made. The vast majority of Jews in Russia and America, as, indeed, all over the world, now appeared to be favourable to Zionism. If we could make a declaration favourable to such an ideal, we. should be able to carry on extremely useful propaganda both in Russia and America. He gathered that the main arguments still put forward against Zionism were twofold:—

(a.) That Palestine was inadequate to form a home for either the Jewish or any other people.

(b.) The difficulty felt with regard to the future position of Jews in

364 See: http://filestore.nationalarchives.gov.uk/pdfs/large/cab-23-4.pdf

Western countries.

With regard to the first, he understood that there were considerable differences of opinion among experts regarding the possibility of the settlement of any large population in Palestine, but he was informed that, if Palestine were scientifically developed, a very much larger population could be sustained than had existed during the period of Turkish misrule. As to the meaning of the words "national home," to which the Zionists attach so much importance, he understood it to mean some form of British, American, or other protectorate, under which full facilities would be given to the Jews to work out their own salvation and to build up, by means of education, agriculture, and industry, a real centre of national culture and focus of national life. It did not necessarily involve the early establishment of an independent Jewish state, which was a matter for gradual development in accordance with the ordinary laws of political evolution. With regard to the second point, he felt that, so far from Zionism hindering the process of assimilation in Western countries, the truer parallel was to be found in the position of an Englishman who leaves his country to establish a permanent home in the United States. In the latter case there was no difficulty in the Englishman or his children becoming full nationals of the United States, whereas, in the present position of Jewry, the assimilation was often felt to be incomplete, and any danger of a double allegiance or non-national outlook would be eliminated Lord Curzon stated that he admitted the force of the diplomatic arguments in favour of expressing sympathy, and agreed that the bulk of the Jews held Zionist rather than anti-Zionist opinions. He added that he did not agree with the attitude taken up by Mr Montagu. On the other hand, he could not share the optimistic views held regarding the future of Palestine. These views were not merely the result of his own personal experiences of travel in that country, but of careful investigations from persons who had lived for many years in the country. He feared that by the suggested declaration we should be raising false expectations which could never be realised. He attached great importance to the necessity of retaining the Christian and Moslem Holy Places in Jerusalem and Bethlehem, and, if this were to be effectively done, he did not see how the Jewish people could have a political capital in Palestine. However, he recognised that some expression of sympathy with Jewish aspirations would be a valuable adjunct to our propaganda, though he thought that we should be guarded in the language used in giving expression to such sympathy.

The War Cabinet authorised:—

The Secretary of State for Foreign Affairs to take a suitable opportunity of making the following declaration of sympathy with the Zionist aspirations:—

> *"His Majesty's Government views with favour the establishment in Palestine of a national home for the Jewish people, and will use its best endeavours to facilitate the achievement of this object, it being clearly understood that nothing shall be done which may prejudice the civil and religious rights of existing non-Jewish communities in Palestine, or the rights and political status enjoyed by Jews in any other country."*

2, *Whitehall Gardens, S.W., October 31, 1917.*

~~~
~~~

APPENDIX 3

CHAIM WEIZMANN'S LETTER TO VERA WEIZMANN

To Vera Weizmann, London. *Tel Aviv-Jaffa, 26 May 1918*

My darling Child,

I'm writing a few words as I want to tell you about two interesting things. I told you in my last letter that relations between us and the administration left much to be desired. There was insufficient understanding and insufficient appreciation of the whole significance both of the movement and ·of the Declaration, and therefore — with the agreement of my colleagues and of Gore, and in order to clear up everything completely, I decided to take a bold step-namely to have an interview with the Commander-in-Chief and to discuss everything with him, frankly and seriously. I did this and it proved to be quite the best measure. I talked to Allenby for about 2 hours and told him clearly that if they continue to confuse us with the Arabs the whole time and apply the principle of numerical justice to us, it will be ridiculous to talk about a National Home, because it· will be an Arab N[ational] *H*[ome], *not a Jewish one, and I pointed out all the consequences of such a regime. I found him to be an understanding, friendly and sympathetic man, and am very happy that I took this step, which was a very risky one. Things could not have ended better than they did.*

Afterwards we invited A[llenby] *to be the guest of the Jerusalem Jewish community and he came the day before yesterday. We received him in a private house (now empty) situated in the Boukharan Jewish quarter. He came with his retinue and drove in the first carriage with the Governor of Jerusalem, ·Storrs, and myself, with the others following behind. The streets were lined with children who showered him with flowers. The order was exemplary and the crowd of many thousands behaved admirably. There were no policemen and order was maintained by the Maccabi, that is the Jewish athletic association. He was greeted with Hebrew songs. Then, under the open sky, the two senior rabbis welcomed him on behalf of the city and I on behalf of the Commission, and I presented him with a tiny Torah. He was touched and was actually moved to tears and he replied with a very friendly speech; afterwards there was a tea with music and everything went like clockwork. Everybody went away delighted. It was a magnificent Jerusalem display.*

The second thing is that tomorrow I'm going with Gore to Hedjaz, that is to Aqaba, from there to Amman, to the Arab army headquarters for an interview with Feisal, the son of the Sherif of Mecca. This is a difficult journey, which will take altogether (there and back) about 2 weeks. Afterwards I shall go to Egypt for 2-3 days' rest and then, in the middle of June, shall return and get back to work again. There's still very, very much to do. De facto the work has now just begun. I can't understand why all the others are still delaying so.

Your letters, my darling, arrive rarely, very rarely! But I'm not worrying any more, for everybody is suffering from this calamity. Communications are impossible. Telegrams sometimes take two weeks to arrive and the thread gets completely lost. At headquarters they have regard for us now just as much as they used to in London, and it was essential that this should be so, otherwise we would have been paralyzed.

I can't understand how Sokolow allowed himself to go in for such foolish things as dinners in his own honour. This all seems so dreadfully petty compared to the difficult, but at the same time sublime reality here.

I've bought various things for you, Verusya, dear. I hope very much that you'll like them. I think they're your taste. I shall try to choose some more!

I'm sending Benichka some interesting stamps! I kiss and hug you and the children.

Kindest regards to Nurse.

With all my love,
For ever your
Chaimchik

[In Translation]

Source: *Weizmann Archives - Feisal/16-427.TIF*

~~~
~~~

APPENDIX 4

DEPRIVATION OF PALESTINIAN STATEHOOD

A PERSONAL VIEW FROM THE AUTHOR

When the Zionist Commission, led by Chaim Weizmann, arrived in Palestine in 1918, all that the bulk of local Arabs wanted was to be left alone to tend their goats on the land of who-knew-whom in far-away Constantinople or Damascus. As the great Arab scholar, Bernard Lewis, teaches: *when an Arab looks towards the horizon, it is not to discern where a distant frontier may lie. Arab lands to him are as a vast ocean.* He and his ancestors of countless generations had been content to reside quietly in an Ottoman backwater, content also that Filastin, or Palestine, was merely a southern Syrian province. Not for the Palestinians the equivalent of a Herzl to meet the German Kaiser Wilhelm II at the *Mikveh Yisrael* agricultural college, east of Jaffa, in 1898, to sell to him the idea of an independent Palestinian (rather than a Jewish) or Arab state (as in Herzl's 1896 epoch-making pamphlet, *Der Jüdenstaat*), or with Sultan Abdul Hamid II, ruler of the Ottoman Empire in Constantinople, in 1901 to issue the same plea.

In fact, the Palestinian Arabs had some 450 years in which to seek to persuade their Ottoman rulers that they should be granted a their own homeland in Southern Syria. It just did not occur to them. It was not until the Jews began to make the land produce enough to sustain them and those who came from surrounding Arab lands equally as from the Pale of Settlement, that there were the first stirrings of a nationalist urge.

The arrival of the British — Weizmann's Zionist Commission in the spring of 1918, hot on the heels of Allenby's British Army in Jerusalem the previous December — awoke a dormant Arab consciousness about their own position in Palestine. It seems that it was one thing to be neglected and ignored by Constantinople for almost half a millennium but quite another when the same disregard, or worse, closer scrutiny, began to emanate from London.

The local Arab elite then found its political identity but, other than awakening a violent objection to increasing numbers of Jews which expressed itself in the form of pogroms and the marauding of Jewish settlements, they created nothing more, and certainly no significant institutions with which they would be able to carve out a Palestinian movement for independence in Palestine.

Weizmann, immediately alive to the predicament of the Palestinians, undertook, in June 1918, an arduous journey to the desert north of Aqaba, where he met with Emir Feisal, the would-be king of the independent Syria he expected would emerge from WWI, as a reward for leading the Arab Revolt against the Turks. Early in 1919, Weizmann signed an agreement with Feisal in London whereby Arab and Jew would work and live in peace and harmony in Palestine. Feisal added a manuscript rider to the agreement to the effect that if he did not get his Syrian state, all bets were off.

Early in January 1919, WWI over, a series of peace conferences were held in and around Paris. The Syrian representative (Feisal's man) at the Paris Peace Conference, Chekri Ganem, spoke generously:

> *Palestine is incontestably the Southern portion of our country. The Zionists claim it. We have suffered too much from sufferings resembling theirs, not to throw open wide to them the doors of Palestine. All those among them who are oppressed in certain retrograde countries are welcome. Let them settle in Palestine, but in an autonomous Palestine, connected with Syria by the sole bond of federation. Will not a Palestine enjoying wide internal autonomy be for them a sufficient guarantee?*
>
> *If they form the majority there, they will be the rulers. If they are in the minority, they will be represented in the*

government in proportion to their numbers.

Pursuant to the secretly-forged Sykes-Picot agreement, the Middle East was carved up between Great Britain and France. The latter got Damascus and held onto it, dashing any hopes that Feisal had about being the ruler of Syria. With his hopes went the Weizmann-Feisal pact and any prospect of cooperation between the *Yishuv* and their neighbouring Arabs.

A Jewish homeland was an aim of the international community who enshrined the Balfour Declaration in the Mandate Document pursuant to the Treaty of San Remo in 1922. (This was the first of two such international endorsements, the second being the outcome of the UN general assembly vote of November 1947.)

So far, then, we have seen the Palestinians deprived of a state by the Turks for 450 years, and then by the French in 1922. Even more significantly, there was no suggestion of autonomy in southern Syria for the Palestinians being granted by Feisal (had he not been sent packing by the French). Apparently, nobody recognised the Palestinians as a body of people, discrete from the Syrians. They would have been Syrians, not Palestinians, living in Southern Syria alongside an autonomous Jewish entity. They were to be offered an opportunity in the following decade.

The British Peel Commission was formed in 1936 to see how the increasingly mutually-hostile Arab and Jewish entities could be, instead, mutually accommodated in Palestine. Peel offered a Two State Solution — called Partition. At last there was something upon which the Jews and Arabs could agree: each agreed that it was unacceptable and rejected the idea out-of-hand. One man saw the flicker of the light of redemption in the Partition proposal, and that man was Chaim Weizmann.

Weizmann carried the concept of Partition in his mind (and doubtless his heart) for a further decade — through World War II and the Holocaust, through his ejection as President of the World Zionist Commission in 1946 (for being too closely identified with the British) and into the crucial year of 1947. His opportunity was provided by the UN.

The British, exhausted fiscally and otherwise, extricating themselves from the desolation of World War II, bereft of the desire to continue with the Mandate a day longer than necessary, tossed the hot coals of the warring Arabs and Jews of Palestine into the hands of the newly-formed United Nations (successor to the League of Nations). The UN proposed Partition — a Two State Solution. The representatives of the *Yishuv* at the UN, spurred on by Weizmann, lobbied furiously for it. The Arabs again rejected it.

Then, thanks to the magic worked by Weizmann on two separate occasions with President Truman, a tiny state was declared by Ben-Gurion just before Shabbat on May 14, 1948. It comprised the Galilee, Hadera to Gadera, including the wasp's waist of twelve kms in the Sharon region, and — due entirely to Weizmann and his influence on Truman — the Negev. Utterly indefensible borders were transformed by the war thrust on Israel by five invading Arab armies, into just-about-defensible borders. The West Bank was held by Jordan. No one living there thought to call it Palestine. No one calling himself a Palestinian protested.

So, responsibility for starving the Palestinians of their own state is not down only to the British, with their Balfour Declaration. It lies also with Emir Feisal who, in signing with Weizmann a pact that would have given the Jews their homeland, omitted to identify another for the Palestinians; the French, who deprived Emir Feisal of his Syrian state; the League of Nations, who conferred the Mandate on Britain; the Arabs at the UN who rejected Partition (the Two State Solution) in 1947; the Jordanians who took Judaea and Samaria in 1948 but made no move to create there the State of Palestine; and the indigenous people of Southern Syria who were not motivated to seek a state for themselves until they saw the permanence of the Jewish State after the Six Day War of June 1967.

The Palestinians did not see themselves in national, or nationalistic, terms until the PLO/PLA materialised in 1964. Yasser Arafat neglected to demand the West Bank from the Jordanians for a Palestinian state; nor did he embark on his terrorist activities to fight Jordan for control of those areas. He undertook terrorism with the intention of destroying Israel, the Six Day War conferring on the PLO/PLA the mantle of freedom fighters for the West Bank. Later, with his terrorism, Arafat drove away all save the most left-wing Israelis from the promise held out by the Oslo Accords with his Second Intifada.

It is a long tale of disappointment (and possibly not an exhaustive one), but what runs through the whole story of Palestinian state-starvation has been their own culture. At first bucolically simple; later, it sought to change but not constructively. When they should have been mimicking the *Yishuv* (which spent the Mandate years creating a state-in-waiting, with many institutions fully operational, ready for 15 May 1948), the Palestinian leadership adopted revanchism, nihilism, pogroms, terrorism, anti-Jewish racism, the BDS movement and implacable hostility to compromise, twice rejecting Partition (the now supposedly-craved Two State Solution).

Pity the poor Palestinians. Whether in pre-1948 Palestine, the West Bank or refugee camps in Lebanon, their leadership has preferred to brutalise them for further struggle with the Jews, whom Arabs traditionally regard as inferior, as *dhimmis*[365], in preference to seeking to improve their lot by compromise with those who have patently taken great strides since 1917, to the

[365] For a fine exposition of the *dhimmi* issue, see the works of Bat Ye'or, (the pseudonym of Gisèle Littman), author of the history of religious minorities in the Muslim world and of modern European politics. See for example: *Europe, Globalization and the Coming Universal Caliphate*, Bat Ye'or, Fairleigh Dickinson University Press, Madison Teaneck 2011.

benefit of Arab and Jew alike within Israel's borders. (When mercurial Israeli MK, Avigdor Lieberman proposed in 2006 that 130,000 Israeli Arabs become citizens of a Palestinian state without leaving their homes, by way of land swaps, the most vocal opposition came from those — Israeli Arabs — who did not wish their political status to be altered.)

Day by day, Israeli Arabs and Israeli Jews live in peace and harmony alongside each other. Israeli Jews get on just fine side-by-side with Israeli Arabs on the road; on the sidewalks; in the shops, supermarkets and shopping malls, as both consumers and sales staff; on the promenades and on the beaches; in hi-tech companies; and most especially in the health service, as major consumers and equally major providers. The Israeli Arabs' disposition of calm dedication and courtesy is appreciated and reciprocated by the Jewish Israelis.

They know they are different from one another; but so are the Scots from the English, and the English from the Welsh. They all need to rub along together and they do. Israelis all need to rub along together and we do. Israelis think that Palestinian Arabs are like those divided from the Israeli variety (gentle, polite and indulgent) by lines on maps. Israelis do not blame Palestinian Arabs as a whole when things go horribly wrong. They blame their leadership. So should they. Were that leadership to adopt a more constructive approach, and abandon their traditional and failed policies that they continue to espouse and teach their children, Israel would confer on them a cornucopia of beneficence.

The Abraham Accords point to a different solution. A warm peace, burgeoning trade — anticipated to be worth $1 trillion to Israel over the next ten years — between Israel and the Gulf Arabs, show an alternative path, a route to shared riches for generations just and yet to be born.

One can but hope and pray.

APPENDIX 5

BEN-GURION ON CHAIM WEIZMANN

Extracted from *Chaim Weizmann: A Biography By Several Hands*, edited by Meyer W Weisgal and Joel Carmichael (Weidenfeld and Nicolson, 1962)

Weizmann, wrote Ben-Gurion, was:

> *"the seer and man of action; he had to grapple with all the hindrances that confront the man of action.* but *foresight was not enough for him: he bent all his immense abilities toward the realization of the vision. His greatness as a Zionist lay in the fact that he strove, and built, and laid foundations. There are no bounds to the lofty spirit of those who live in a world peopled by fancies, nor any limit to their loquaciousness; Weizmann was a man of action ... Weizmann was the only practical man among all the Zionist leaders, and the only one among them who left the Diaspora not through external persecution or edict, or catastrophic upheaval. He had a proud and assured position in England such as was given to few Jews in the world, but he belonged to a family of outstanding pioneers and men of action. He identified himself personally with the undertaking in Eretz Israel and settled in this land.*
>
> ....
>
> *"Dr Weizmann's testimony before* [the Peel Commission of 1936] *was, perhaps, the most profound and penetrating analysis ever given of the plight of the Jewish people and their position in the non-Jewish world, coupled with the strongest and most vigorous claim ever put forward for the immediate creation of the Jewish state as the only deliverance from the danger threatening the Jewish masses. I do not think there is in the whole of Zionist literature anything as profound, as awe-inspiring, as penetrating, or as true.... Weizmann ... dwelt only on the six million Jews in Europe, devoid of hope and facing imminent danger. He expressed this theme of direct and urgent danger with deep Jewish emotion and the prescience of a prophet of doom; his statement made a tremendous impression upon his listeners. For the first time we then heard fall from the lips of statesmen in whose hands lay the fate of Palestine the explicit term, the Jewish state."*

> *"With his intuitive perception Weizmann had felt that these six million were the mainstay of the Zionist cause at this period. He wanted to save them for their own sake, for the sake of their people, and for the sake of the future Jewish state."*

BG then referred to:

> *"the crowning disaster in Weizmann's political career, because he cherished a deep faith in the British people. Indeed, his entire political creed was built upon Jewish-British cooperation. But his Zionist and Jewish convictions triumphed even over this blow, though not immediately or easily; from the White Paper of 1939 until the UN decision in 1947 Dr Weizmann was beset by a gnawing inner confusion and stress, and I believe that he failed to find his way."*
>
> *"But even in these years we witnessed his human greatness. He performed his Zionist tasks with complete dedication,.... he always towered head and shoulders above the people, serving the movement loyally"*

Finally, BG introduced his own letter (below) as "*testimony to the feelings I and millions of other Jews always had toward him*", which had been written after the Zionist Congress in 1937, where BG had been fighting Weizmann as vigorously as he could:

> *'Dear and venerated Chaim:*
>
> *I am very, very sorry, much more than I can express in words, for having caused you yesterday, before the close of the Agency (session), distress and suffering. I have loved you all my life; all Jews have loved you since those great days of the Balfour Declaration. But you were sevenfold dearer to me when I saw you after the ninth Zionist Congress (1931). In your distress and humiliation a new Weizmann revealed himself to me then not Weizmann the leader, the magician and charmer, but Weizmann the man, full of pain, wounded, writhing in his anguish and conquering, with supreme moral heroism, his personal ambition, putting himself as an ordinary, devoted soldier at the service of the Movement that had wounded him.*
>
> *Your exile lasted four years; during those four years I and many of my comrades had a bitter feeling; as if we were partners in the cruel stratagem used against you. Your return to the leadership of*

the Movement seemed to me not only a political need but, first and foremost, a moral necessity. The Zionist Movement was not flourishing; it was burdened by the sin of having 'stabbed its teacher'. From the political point of view you remained the leader even when not elected to the official Presidium, but we felt that we must give back to the Zionist Organization its honesty towards itself. Therefore it was a must that the eighth Zionist Congress should re-elect you.

And after I had the privilege of working closely with you, I saw you in a new light. I never was a blind follower of yours, and I never will be. I did not always agree with you; whenever I felt that I had to oppose you, I did so; if in the future I again see a need to oppose you, I shall do so again.

But even in the fury of battle my feelings of love and veneration for you were not diminished by one iota. I know that you are the champion of the Jewish people, not because you have been elected (to this post) by a majority, but because you were born for it; the 'Shechinah' of the Jewish People rests upon you. And, during the last few months, when the great hope of establishing a Jewish state began to glimmer, I saw this 'Shechinah' shining over you with a great and new light, and a new power of youthfulness, revealed itself in you, with grace and charm to an extent invisible to my eyes before. And, although even in those months, I have sometimes disagreed with you about one detail or another, I know that this time you are bearing upon your shoulders a historic burden not borne by any other Jew for the last two thousand years. I also know that every one of us now, more than ever before, stands by you with all his heart and with all his might so that you may succeed in carrying out the stupendous task imposed on you by the historic destiny of our people the renewal of the Kingdom of Israel.

The task imposed on you now, is in my view, greater and more difficult than the burden of the Balfour Declaration. The hindrances and pitfalls on your road are now more manifold than ever. There are more objective hindrances and there are also more enemies, not only from the outside, but also from the inside. Our enemies have been joined by the cowards and the blind. But if the number of our opponents has grown, so has our strength our strength in the country, our strength in the Jewish people, and our strength in the world. And you are the personal focus of this strength. There is no other man or circle of men in the Jewish people that can compare with you. I do not believe the superficial theory that history is made by personalities. But I do believe that unique personalities are the emissaries of the collective energies of nations and of classes in history. The Zionist enterprise and Zionist vision have beamed all their light on their supreme emissary, and this light is growing apace. . . .

There are in Eretz Israel one hundred thousand Jewish workers, and I am one of them and no more than that. As one of them, you are dear to me as the Chosen One of the people; as one of them, I know that I must stand by you, and as one of them I pray for your success.

I am sorry that I caused you grief. When I saw you yesterday in your anguish I was unbearably sorry because I love you with all my heart and with all my soul. I want you to know that I had not intended to grieve you. Let us hope that we shall soon have a more satisfactory state of affairs.

With love and confidence, D. Ben-Gurion

BIBLIOGRAPHY

After The Victorians: The World Our Parents Knew, A N Wilson (Random House, 2006)

American Jewish Personalities, Shalom Goldman, Asian Studies Department, Dartmouth College

Anti-Judaism: The Western Tradition, David Nirenberg (Norton Press, 2013)

Balfour and Weizmann: The Zionist, the Zealot and the Emergence of Israel, Geoffrey Lewis (Continuum UK, 2009)

Ben-Gurion: The Burning Ground 1886-1948, Shabtai Teveth, (Houghton Mifflin Company, 1987)

Britain and the Arab Middle East: World War I and its Aftermath, Robert H. Lieshout (I B Tauris & Co Limited, London & New York, 2016)

Chaim Weizmann: A Biography By Several Hands, edited by Meyer W Weisgal and Joel Carmichael (Weidenfeld and Nicolson, 1962)

Chaim Weizmann: A Biography, Norman Rose (Weidenfeld and Nicolson, 1987)

Chaim Weizmann: The Shaping of a Zionist Leader before the First World War: Jehuda Reinharz (Journal of Contemporary History, Vol. 18, No. 2, April 1983)

Churchill and the Jews, Martin Gilbert (Simon & Schuster UK Limited, 2007)

Development of Emerging World Youth, Yedla C Simhadri (Mittal Publications, 1989)

Don't Ask the Price, Marcus Sieff (Fontana Press, 1987)

Einstein's Greatest Mistake: The Life of a Flawed Genius, David Bodanis (Little Brown, 2016)

Europe, Globalization and the Coming Universal Caliphate, Bat Ye'or (Fairleigh Dickinson University Press, Madison, Teaneck, 2011)

Fifty Years of Zionism, Oskar K Rabinowicz (Robert Anscombe & Co Ltd, 1950)

Germany, Turkey, and Zionism 1897-1918, Isaiah Friedman (Transaction Publishers, USA & UK, 1977)

Harry S. Truman: A Life, Robert H Ferrell (University of Missouri Press, 1994)

Memoirs, Israel Sieff (Weidenfeld and Nicholson, 1970)

Meyer Weisgal ... So Far, Meyer Weisgal (Weidenfeld and Nicolson, 1971)

Palestine, Land of Promise, Walter Clay Lowdermilk (Harper New York, 1944)

T. E. Lawrence and Zionism - Jewish Historical Studies, Cecil Bloom (Jewish Historical Society of England, Vol. 38, 2002)

The Aaronsohn Saga, Shmuel Katz (Gefen Publishing House, Jerusalem and New York, 2000)

The Course of Modern Jewish History, H M Sachar (Vintage Books, 1990)

The History of Zionism, Nahum Sokolow (Longmans, 1919)

The Zionist Commission and the Jewish Communities of Greater Syria in 1919, Andrew J. Patrick, Assistant Professor of History, Tennessee State University (Jerusalem Quarterly 56, 2014)

The Innocents Abroad, or the New Pilgrims' Progress: Being Some Account of the Steamship Quaker City's Pleasure Excursion to Europe and the Holy Land, Mark Twain (Published by Reader's Digest Association, 1990)

Theodor Herzl: Founder of Political Zionism, Israel Cohen (Thomas Yoseloff, London, 1959)

Trial and Error: The Autobiography of Chaim Weizmann (Schocken Books, 1966)

Truman, David McCullough (Simon & Schuster, 1992)

Warrant For Genocide, Norman Cohn (Penguin Books, 1970)

Winston Churchill: The Wilderness Years, Martin Gilbert (Pimlico Press, 2004)

Woodrow Wilson and the Balfour Declaration, Richard Ned Lebow (The Journal of Modern History Vol. 40, No. 4, The University of Chicago Press, 1968)

INDEX

Aaronsohn
Aaron, 112, 139
acetone, 100, 101, 102, 103, 107, 115, 167, 169, 171, 173, 252, 253
Achad Ha'am, 18, 28, 29, 40, 50, 52, 56, 63, 83, 85, 93, 111, 112, 213, 219, 254, 268, 269, 270
AGRICULTURAL EXPERIMENT STATION, 225
Aliyah, 8, 19, 29, 30, 38, 39, 40, 50, 63, 74, 83, 86, 224, 232, 233, 238, 264, 269
Allenby
General, 128, 129, 140, 221
General Edmund, 131
America
United States, 2, 108
ammunition, 98, 100
anti-Semitism, 19, 22, 34, 43, 44, 46
Anti-Semitism, 13
Aqaba, 142, 143, 161, 162, 186, 276
Arab Revolt, 110, 161, 164
Asquith, 94, 99, 101, 129
assimilationists, 23, 46, 55, 90, 117, 122, 126
Balfour, 4, 63, 67, 75, 76, 92, 94, 95, 104, 106, 107, 109, 112, 113, 114, 115, 118, 119, 120, 121, 122, 123, 124, 125, 126, 127, 132, 133, 135, 137, 145, 147, 153, 154, 157, 159, 181, 187, 189, 199, 220, 222, 225, 227, 234, 239, 251, 263, 268, 284, 285, 287, 288
Balfour Declaration, 4, 63, 67, 92, 106, 107, 109, 112, 113, 115, 120, 121, 122, 123, 124, 126, 127, 132, 133, 135, 137, 145, 147, 153, 154, 159, 181, 189, 199, 220, 225, 227, 234, 239, 263, 268, 284, 285, 288
barmitzvah, 15, 19, 20, 37
Baron, 39, 40, 41, 47, 48, 50, 83, 92, 113, 136, 219
Baron Edmond
Rothschild, 39, 40, 41, 48, 50, 83, 92, 136, 219
Belarus, 9, 12, 13
Belorussia, 12, 37
Ben-Gurion
David, 18, 52, 231, 233, 234, 247, 249, 259
Ben-Yehuda, 37, 38, 48, 87, 214, 215
Ben-Zvi
Yitzchak, 233
Berlin, 20, 21, 24, 25, 26, 28, 29, 30, 31, 32, 41, 42, 43, 50, 52, 53, 55, 57, 76, 85, 89, 97, 129, 177, 260
Bismarck, 24, 47, 97
Brandeis
Justice Louis D, 115
British, 8, 13, 20, 23, 35, 37, 39, 48, 59, 62, 63, 67, 71, 74, 75, 76, 78, 83, 87, 90, 91, 92, 93, 95, 96, 97, 99, 100, 101, 102, 103, 104, 107, 108, 109, 110, 111, 112, 113, 114, 115, 118, 119, 126, 128, 129, 130, 131, 132, 133, 135, 136, 137, 138, 139, 140, 141, 143, 146, 147, 148, 151, 153, 154, 155, 158, 159, 161, 162, 163, 164, 165, 166, 168, 170, 171, 172, 173, 174, 181, 182, 183, 184, 187, 189, 191, 194, 196, 197, 199, 201, 204, 205, 220, 226, 234, 235, 237, 238, 239, 240, 241, 242, 244, 250, 252, 254, 256, 260, 262, 263, 265, 266, 268, 273, 284
Buber, 55, 59, 60, 218, 222
Cabinet
War, 99, 108, 109, 120, 121, 122, 123, 124, 126, 127, 128, 129, 138, 199, 272, 274
Chankin
Joshua, 82
Charles Dreyfus, 65, 71
chemistry, 17, 20, 22, 31, 53, 57, 65, 72, 73, 87, 88, 89, 107, 206, 217, 219, 227, 257, 258, 262
Chovevei Zion, 8, 15, 19, 28, 30, 40, 48, 50, 52, 268
Churchill, 35, 74, 75, 92, 102, 104,

109, 126, 138, 155, 157, 158, 162, 165, 170, 173, 177, 242, 265, 287, 288
Winston Spencer, 74
Clostridium acetobutylicum, 89, 252, 253
Commission
Palestine, 133, 135, 136, 137, 140, 141, 142, 143, 164, 209, 220, 225, 227, 234, 235, 236, 237, 238, 241, 256, 275, 288
Congress, 51, 52, 53, 59, 60, 61, 63, 65, 69, 71, 73, 74, 79, 87, 88, 129, 158, 176, 177, 196, 218, 219, 231, 239, 256, 269, 284
Constantinople, 56, 59, 160, 233, 256, 269
cordite, 100, 101, 102, 115, 253
Curzon
Lord, 124, 272, 273
Darmstadt, 22, 23, 26, 41, 57, 76
Declaration of Independence, 33, 191, 204, 235, 247, 248, 249
Democratic Faction, 59, 60, 61, 67, 85, 209, 218, 232, 238
Der Jüdenstaat, 48, 49, 50, 52, 69, 234, 238, 262, 268
diplomatic coups, 158, 242
Disraeli, 91, 130, 266
Dreyfus, 43, 44, 46, 65, 71, 72, 73, 75, 77, 78, 262
Captain Alfred, 44
Egypt, 96, 129, 130, 131, 137, 138, 146, 161, 173, 188, 204, 233, 234, 235, 276
Einstein
Albert, 222, 250
Elazari-Volcani
Yitzhak, 225
England, 2, 4, 8, 21, 36, 45, 47, 64, 66, 68, 74, 77, 78, 84, 86, 91, 92, 105, 106, 162, 252, 257, 269, 283, 288
Enlightenment, 8, 15, 16, 24, 25, 33, 35, 37, 41, 268
Eretz Yisrael, 6, 8, 9, 15, 21, 28, 29, 36, 37, 39, 40, 50, 52, 53, 61, 73, 74, 79, 80, 82, 84, 85, 87, 148, 187, 206, 218, 224, 264, 269, 270
Europe, 12, 14, 15, 17, 24, 26, 34, 55, 65, 66, 68, 71, 80, 85, 92, 97, 99, 100, 134, 136, 140, 163, 164, 165, 167, 173, 177, 180, 182, 183, 184, 188, 191, 209, 218, 256, 265, 269, 283
explosives, 57, 98, 101
FDR, 169, 170, 171, 174, 175, 176, 199, 255
Feisal
Emir, 142, 143, 145, 161, 162, 186
Feisal-Weizmann Pact, 145, 146, 147, 154
Feivel, 18, 55, 157, 218
fin-de-siècle, 25, 47
Foreign Office, 63, 109, 119, 121, 146, 179
France, 12, 15, 24, 34, 43, 44, 45, 47, 92, 96, 97, 98, 99, 100, 101, 109, 113, 114, 131, 134, 136, 138, 152, 170, 176, 178
Fribourg, 52, 53
Ganem
Chekri, 148
Gaster
Dr Moses, 18, 52, 64, 65, 66, 68, 87, 111, 113
Gentiles, 15, 23, 26, 108
German, 9, 22, 23, 24, 25, 26, 33, 37, 38, 41, 42, 43, 56, 57, 58, 66, 78, 81, 97, 118, 122, 123, 135, 136, 138, 167, 170, 173, 212, 214, 215, 219, 269
Germans, 22, 41, 43, 46, 86, 118, 120, 122, 126, 133, 135, 138, 165, 167, 168, 177
Germany, 15, 20, 22, 23, 24, 31, 42, 47, 53, 56, 57, 76, 78, 92, 97, 98, 99, 100, 118, 131, 134, 167, 168, 173, 177, 180, 182, 215, 220, 228, 256, 287
Great Britain, 8, 9, 74, 96, 97, 99, 100, 104, 108, 109, 130, 136, 146, 153
Great War, 90, 96, 98, 100, 104, 136, 154, 167, 214
Haifa, 38, 72, 83, 110, 118, 182, 184,

209, 212, 213, 215, 216, 217, 219, 269
Haskalah, 16, 19, 26
Hebrew, 9, 16, 17, 26, 37, 38, 39, 51, 57, 58, 71, 78, 82, 87, 138, 139, 160, 204, 209, 212, 214, 215, 216, 217, 218, 219, 220, 221, 222, 223, 250, 267, 268, 269, 275
Herzl, 16, 33, 41, 42, 43, 44, 46, 47, 48, 50, 51, 52, 53, 56, 59, 60, 61, 62, 63, 68, 69, 73, 74, 91, 118, 203, 206, 213, 218, 225, 232, 234, 238, 239, 262, 265, 268, 288
Holocaust, 152, 168, 179, 182, 183
Holy Land, 8, 16, 35, 36, 37, 40, 63, 79, 80, 82, 86, 96, 154, 172, 182, 222, 264, 265, 267, 269
House
  Colonel, 120, 124, 167
Israeli, 37, 145, 186, 188, 191, 204, 206, 210, 211, 233, 247, 249, 268, 269
Jacobson
  Eddie, 18, 27, 157, 177, 178, 179, 192, 194, 198
Jaffa, 35, 56, 81, 82, 83, 131, 142, 225, 233, 275
Jerusalem, 36, 42, 59, 65, 67, 69, 72, 75, 82, 83, 95, 106, 107, 118, 127, 131, 132, 133, 136, 138, 142, 143, 152, 154, 160, 164, 184, 209, 212, 218, 219, 220, 221, 222, 233, 234, 239, 241, 248, 264, 265, 269, 273, 275, 288
Jewish Homeland, 73, 108, 117, 161, 206
Jewish lobby, 180, 192, 194, 199
Jewish National Home, 150, 151
Jewish Question, 41, 42, 46, 47, 48, 93, 96, 104, 117, 264, 266
Jewish State, 48, 50, 51, 52, 95, 147, 187, 188, 192, 195, 197, 199, 201, 202, 217, 247, 265, 273, 283, 284, 285
Judaism, 23, 34, 58, 78, 83, 287
Kaiser, 56, 97
Kishinev, 62, 63, 67, 218, 219
Laski
  Nathan, 75, 78
Lawrence
  of Arabia, 110, 161
  T E, 110, 143, 144, 157, 161, 162, 288
Levin, 18, 27
Lilienblum, 16
Lloyd George, 63, 91, 94, 95, 99, 101, 104, 106, 120, 122, 126, 131, 135, 148, 159
Lord Balfour, 222
Manchester, 4, 65, 66, 67, 69, 71, 73, 74, 75, 76, 77, 78, 86, 87, 89, 90, 91, 93, 94, 96, 101, 105, 107, 108, 111, 114, 117, 122, 126, 147, 219, 226, 227, 251, 252, 256, 257, 258, 262
Manchester Guardian, 87, 91
Mandate, 39, 153, 154, 155, 158, 159, 164, 181, 182, 197, 199, 200, 201, 222, 236
Marks
  Simon, 73, 90, 93, 111, 226, 227
Marshall, 157, 174, 177, 192, 193, 195, 196, 200, 202, 203, 222
  General George, 173, 176
Maskilim, 9, 16, 26
Massel, 71
Mendelssohn, 24, 25, 26
Montagu, 48, 121, 122, 199, 273
  Edwin, 120
Montefiore, 20, 35, 36, 40, 264, 265
moshavim, 40, 160
Motol, 12, 13, 14, 16, 17, 18, 19, 20, 23, 26, 30, 256
Motzkin, 18, 27, 28, 53, 58, 59, 67, 218
National Home for the Jewish people, 128, 274
Nazi. *See* Nazis: Nazism
Negev, 175, 185, 186, 187, 188, 195, 206, 212, 251
Nili, 112, 138
Oizer, 13, 15, 16
Ormsby-Gore
  William, 109
Ottoman Empire, 13, 36, 56, 99, 129, 131, 137, 153, 159, 161, 214, 233, 269
Pale, 8, 9, 12, 13, 14, 16, 34, 55, 58,

64, 74, 83, 85, 93, 133, 209, 232, 238
Pale of Settlement, 8, 9, 12, 14, 74, 133, 232
Palestine, 8, 13, 14, 16, 19, 21, 29, 35, 39, 50, 51, 52, 56, 59, 64, 65, 75, 76, 78, 79, 80, 81, 82, 84, 85, 89, 93, 94, 95, 99, 106, 108, 110, 112, 113, 114, 115, 117, 118, 119, 120, 121, 122, 123, 124, 126, 127, 129, 130, 131, 134, 136, 137, 138, 139, 140, 141, 143, 144, 145, 146, 149, 150, 151, 153, 154, 155, 157, 158, 159, 160, 161, 162, 163, 164, 171, 172, 177, 179, 180, 181, 182, 183, 184, 186, 191, 192, 194, 196, 197, 199, 201, 204, 209, 213, 214, 218, 220, 222, 225, 227, 231, 233, 234, 235, 237, 238, 239, 240, 244, 245, 250, 252, 256, 257, 265, 266, 267, 268, 269, 272, 273, 274, 283, 288
Paris Peace Conference, 148, 149, 150, 151, 152, 153, 227
Partition, 52, 164, 165, 180, 182, 183, 184, 185, 188, 189, 191, 195, 197, 251
patent, 73, 101, 103, 251, 252
patents, 31, 52, 57, 72, 73, 77, 87, 103, 157, 223, 251, 252
Peel Commission, 164, 165, 183, 283
Perkin, 65, 66, 71, 73, 87, 89, 101, 219
Pinsk, 17, 18, 19, 20, 23, 25, 26, 28, 30, 31, 47, 52, 57, 76, 83, 224, 254, 256
Pinsker, 15, 16, 18, 47, 50, 268
pogrom, 62, 63, 85, 218
pogroms, 19, 22, 30, 42, 61, 62, 67, 74, 154, 241
Political Zionism, 79
Practical Zionism, 79
President of the State of Israel, 228
Protestant, 36, 37, 62, 91, 159, 182, 265, 266, 267
Proto-Zionists, 35, 36, 37, 91, 264, 265
Rechovot, 73, 76, 83, 187, 189, 192, 224, 226, 228, 252
recognition, 30, 33, 148, 154, 195, 200, 203, 204, 206, 247
Roosevelt
  Franklin Delano, 169, 175
Rothschild, 35, 39, 47, 48, 50, 92, 106, 107, 111, 112, 113, 117, 118, 121, 136, 203, 204, 219, 223
Royal Navy, 97, 99, 100
rubber crisis, 169, 170, 171, 172
Ruppin
  Dr Arthur, 82
Russia, 8, 12, 13, 14, 15, 19, 20, 23, 26, 34, 50, 74, 85, 97, 109, 110, 126, 133, 134, 137, 141, 167, 177, 205, 209, 218, 258, 268, 270, 272
Sacher
  Harry, 72, 73, 87, 90, 93, 111, 112, 113, 226
Samuel
  Herbert, 18, 94, 95, 99, 111, 112, 113, 120, 159, 162, 222
San Remo Peace Conference, 227
Scott
  Charles Prestwich, 91
Sharett
  Moshe, 242
shells, 98, 99, 100, 101, 103, 115
Shertok
  Moshe, 200, 203
Sieff
  Israel, 58, 73, 79, 89, 90, 93, 112, 136, 137, 147, 226, 256, 257, 288
Smolenskin, 18, 37, 268
Sokolov
  Nahum, 150
Sophia, 53, 58
Soviet, 12, 126, 133, 135, 177, 180, 189, 191, 205, 270
Soviets, 177, 180, 270
State Department, 179, 180, 186, 192, 195, 200, 251
State of Israel, 6, 39, 69, 70, 86, 146, 177, 206, 209, 216, 229, 231, 247, 248, 249, 251, 266
Suez Canal, 96, 107, 129, 130, 173, 186

Sykes
Sir Mark, 108, 113, 131, 136, 139, 159
synthetic rubber, 88, 165, 169, 170, 172, 173, 253
Syria, 50, 110, 113, 115, 130, 131, 143, 144, 145, 146, 148, 149, 150, 152, 153, 160, 162, 204, 267, 268, 288
Technion
Haifa, 38, 212, 213, 215, 216, 217, 219
Tel Aviv, 82, 136, 163, 192, 200, 202, 203, 204, 217, 247, 275
the Politicals, 70, 78, 79, 85
the Practicals, 70, 78, 85
Transjordan, 143, 153, 155, 162, 188, 204
Truman
Harry, 10, 158, 171, 172, 174, 175, 176, 177, 178, 179, 180, 181, 183, 187, 188, 189, 191, 192, 193, 194, 195, 196, 197, 198, 199, 200, 201, 202, 203, 204, 212, 228, 231, 242, 247, 251, 254, 255, 263, 280, 288
Trusteeship, 180, 181, 191, 192, 196, 199, 200, 251
Turkey, 78, 99, 118, 129, 134, 160, 177, 215, 287
Uganda, 62, 63, 64, 69, 73, 75, 91, 96
UN, 180, 183, 184, 188, 189, 191, 192, 194, 195, 196, 199, 200, 206, 231, 247, 251, 284
United Nations, 52, 180, 181, 184, 199, 201, 202
UNSCOP, 183, 184, 188
Vera, 58, 65, 74, 76, 77, 84, 86, 89, 92, 93, 142, 157, 228, 249, 257, 275
Khatzman, 58
Vienna, 41, 42, 46, 47, 48, 68, 138, 219, 238, 270
Wallace, 173, 174, 175, 176, 177
Henry A, 171
Vice President, 175
Weisgal
Meyer, 18, 192, 200, 243, 244, 245, 246, 248, 249, 258, 259, 288
Weizmann Institute of Science, 212, 226, 228, 229, 243
Weizmann Organism, 89, 252
Weizmann Process, 88, 89, 101, 102, 103, 107, 115, 169, 172
White Paper, 165, 169, 244, 284
Wilhelm
II, 56, 97, 118, 136
Wilson
President Woodrow, 120
Wissotzky, 85, 213, 214, 270
Wissotzkys, 270
World War I, 90, 118, 131, 143, 157, 176, 181, 220, 233, 256, 287
World War II, 96, 109, 165, 168, 177, 179, 180, 181, 191
Yishuv, 8, 9, 35, 36, 38, 39, 40, 41, 48, 50, 53, 59, 136, 137, 138, 139, 140, 141, 144, 158, 159, 160, 163, 164, 165, 173, 182, 191, 192, 199, 200, 202, 204, 212, 213, 214, 215, 218, 221, 222, 228, 231, 232, 233, 234, 237, 238, 240, 242, 245, 249, 260, 263
Zangwill, 48, 62, 64, 69, 74
Zion, 8, 9, 16, 19, 30, 50, 62, 63, 78, 83, 105, 117, 137, 140, 141, 203, 232, 233, 264
Zionism, 6, 9, 16, 19, 28, 29, 30, 31, 33, 34, 36, 37, 42, 46, 47, 48, 49, 50, 51, 52, 53, 54, 56, 58, 61, 63, 67, 68, 69, 71, 73, 75, 76, 78, 79, 83, 85, 86, 87, 90, 92, 96, 99, 105, 107, 111, 112, 115, 118, 120, 122, 137, 143, 147, 154, 157, 159, 162, 165, 178,179, 215, 222, 227, 232, 234, 238, 243, 250, 251, 257, 258, 262, 264, 266, 270, 272, 273, 287, 288
Zionist, 4, 9, 14, 15, 16, 17, 19, 20, 25, 26, 27, 28, 29, 30, 31, 32, 33, 34, 35, 36, 39, 40, 46, 47, 50, 51, 52, 53, 54, 55, 56, 58, 59, 60, 61, 62, 63, 65, 67, 68, 69, 71, 73, 74, 76, 77, 78, 79, 82, 83, 84, 85, 87,

89, 90, 93, 104, 105, 108, 109, 111, 112, 113, 114, 117, 118, 119, 120, 121, 123, 124, 126, 127, 133, 135, 137, 138, 143, 144, 145, 147, 151, 152, 158, 159, 161, 164, 170, 177, 179, 183, 184, 189, 192, 203, 209, 212, 213, 218, 219, 220, 225, 227, 230, 231, 232, 233, 234, 235, 236, 237, 238, 239, 240, 242, 243, 244, 245, 246, 247, 250, 251, 255, 256, 257, 266, 268, 269, 270, 272, 273, 274, 283, 284, 285, 286, 287, 288

Zionist Commission, 136

Zionist Congress, 51, 68, 73, 183, 285

Zionists, 25, 53, 59, 63, 65, 78, 90, 93, 110, 111, 113, 115, 117, 121, 122, 123, 128, 135, 143, 144, 147, 149, 150, 151, 152, 154, 157, 159, 160, 180, 182, 183, 184, 189, 192, 199, 209, 214, 231, 239, 245, 259, 264, 269, 273

ZO, 9, 51, 53, 56, 59, 61, 67, 77, 78, 81, 82, 126, 148, 158, 186, 218, 219, 225, 231, 232, 245

Printed in Great Britain
by Amazon

14119557R00173